MW01169727

RAINBOW WARRIOR:

HEALING on the RED ROAD

RAINBOW WARRIOR:

HEALING on the RED ROAD

*Serpentbird's journey of Awakening,
Illuminating the Priestess Path
with Medicine Wheel Ceremonies*

by

Lori Michelle Abel

Rainbow Warrior: Healing on the Red Road
©2024 Lori Michelle Abel

Edited by Diane Sova, Global Spirit Editing
Cover photo of Serpentbird by Illup Gravengaard
All poetry by Lori Michelle Abel

Serpentbird Media
serpentbirdtribe@gmail.com
www.serpentbird.com

Contact the author at loriabel@gmail.com

ISBN: 979-8-9920330-0-7
Library of Congress #2024924588

Foreword

There is a saying "Not only do we hear with our ears, we also hear with our eyes, we hear with our heart, and we hear in the silence, for in the silence you will hear the most profound lessons in life."

As we go through our journey in life, one of the things I have noticed while assisting others on their journey is that most people have disconnected with themselves. Have you ever had the experience of going through the day, then all of a sudden you realize it's 9:00 pm? You know you were doing things during the day but can't seem to remember. Why is that? My belief is you forgot to include yourself in the process.

One of the most challenging things we face in our journey is to remember to include ourselves. We can be so busy thinking about all the things that we have or need to do that we forget to be in the moment. The "to do" list takes over and we do not allow ourselves to be with what we are doing. For instance, what did you have for breakfast today? Most people cannot answer me, or they need to take a few moments to think about it. Why is that? Because they most likely weren't there.

If we believe that life is a journey, shouldn't we include ourselves? When we take the time to allow ourselves to be present, our mind quiets down. It begins to listen to the silence. Next time you have your morning ritual, allow yourself to experience it - truly. Don't take it for granted. If you drink coffee or tea in the morning, be with the coffee or tea. Allow yourself to experience it for the first time. How hot is it, how much cream, how much sugar or honey? You'll begin to realize that it is now this cup, not yesterday's cup. It is when you allow yourself this experience, you set the pace for the rest of the day. You now know what it feels like to be present. When the day get lost or chaotic, take a moment and reconnect.

We don't remember much of days that we just went through or ran through, but we do remember the moments that came alive. These are the moments that become memories and lessons. May your journey be filled with wonder, great lessons, and a deep connection to self and to Mother Earth. Aho.

Abe Daniels, Windwalker
2024

Introduction

Serpentbird's Journey Walking the Medicine Wheel

This Memoir is sectioned into 5 parts.

You will travel with me around the MEDICINE WHEEL as you would in one of my ceremonies. You can get a feel of how I use this ancient tool, which I call "ancient technology," to advance quickly on the spiritual path.

PART ONE: The Hawk's Beginnings
Imagine your feet walking to the East gate and follow me to the BIRTH stage of life. Hawk is a messenger and *visionary* that sits in the Eastern quadrant and flies above the land to see the whole landscape.

PART TWO: The Wolf Seeks the Serpent
Walk to the South quadrant and understand the Wolf is the teacher. At this point of my journey, I was finding out "who I was" as an individual by howling and finding my "*voice.*"

PART THREE: The Serpentbird Healer
Next you arrive in the West to experience my individuation as a healer. The Snake lives in the West and represents transmutation and transformation. Here I practice my "*intuitive healing arts.*"

PART FOUR: Bear-ing the Inside
In the North quadrant, feel the intense qualities I had as a "*warrior and my journeys for power.*"

PART FIVE: The Center
Arrive at your destination in the center of the wheel. You will experience your God-Self and join the Serpentbird Rainbow Warrior Tribe!

Table of Contents

PART ONE: THE HAWK'S BEGINNINGS

"Behold, I send you forth as sheep in the midst of wolves:
be ye therefore wise as serpents, and harmless as doves." Matthew 10:16

My name is Lori Michelle Abel and this is the story of Serpentbird. I believe that I was asked by God to come back to Earth to assist humanity in choosing a path of peace during the Ascension. The ceremonial name Serpentbird implies an experience of death and transformation, going beyond the limits of physical perception to expand human consciousness. I often use the avatar name of Serpentbird to assist in my expansion. In this process, I encourage humans to transcend mundane reality in a materially driven world and ask them to enter a magical world instead, a world of limitless human potential and the supernatural experience of co-creating with God and the forces of nature.

I have used the name Serpentbird since 2006. In that timespan, an energetic 'lighthouse' program has permeated the United States and throughout my travels, I have offered prayers of gratitude on the land from sea to shining sea. I use the Serpentbird energy as 'spirit animal' energy to create ceremonial spaces like the Medicine Wheels. Serpentbird, with my former incarnations in Egypt, including one as Queen Hatshepsut, is working to build a healing bridge that will complete eons of slavery and sexual trauma of women and men on Earth.

It is extremely difficult to believe that I have chosen to incarnate on Earth now. However, it is my calling in life to be a spiritual healer and teacher, bringing tools of healing to help people reawaken to their true nature, which is GOD, which is love.

Writing this memoir has been a powerful way for me to process my lessons and pain. It became a way of solidifying my shamanic path. Journeying alone to sacred sites within the United States awakened and transformed my soul to a higher dimension. Traveling through the west provoked me to shake, dance, and move like a kundalini serpent. I developed a deeper trust in myself and healed my self-esteem issues.

Many friends and clients don't understand what it means to do this type of 'work' alone, but my spirit requires much solitude and the freedom to move in any direction at any time. The growth I experienced during this phase of my life would not have occurred with the speed and depth necessary for rapid transformation had I traveled with a partner.

At this critical turning point in the history, we are growing through the weeds and concrete paths of dark cities filled with fear. We are even experiencing the dismantling (and hopefully re-building) of the United States. The rebirth of the United States is predicted in the stars as currently the country is experiencing a Pluto return and the completion of a major cycle. We are awakening to new challenges and seeing division between the races. We also see division or ostracism in spiritual communities or families where we previously felt included. We are seeing skin color as a deterrent for peace. We are seeing our belief systems in black and white, standing in stark contrast to transform our consciousness at a rapid pace. I do believe decolonization is needed for the deep healing of our land. It is clear to me that land is not a commodity, it is sacred land still occupied by our ancestors.

Ultimately, a rebellion from patriarchy to matriarchy will occur, as that is what is needed to balance and harmonize the energy of Mother Earth. In 2021, I asked Mother Earth directly, "What will it take to save the environment?" She replied immediately that she wants women to spill their menstrual blood on the land and "take it back" to "save our planet." Ultimately, I believe that the way to rebalance our world and save our earth is to implement rematriation and indigenous knowledge systems. In my mind rematriation is the return to a way of life that lives in reverence for nature. Of course, other practical solutions will include returning stolen lands and sacred sites to Indigenous people, caretaking the seeds for our foods, and returning seeds to their place of origin.

When I first created www.serpentbird.com in 2008, my vision was to create a website that combined art with environmental issues. I only had a surface level "innerstanding" compared to what I know now. I am still evolving and working toward the highest level of what it means to "return the sacred" and assist humanity in "returning to the Divine Feminine."

From the Iroquois Confederacy Constitution – Article 44:

"The lineal descent of the people of the Five Nations shall run in the female line. Women shall be considered the progenitors of the Nation. They shall own the land and the soil. Men and women shall follow the status of the Mother."

I carry medicine from many lifetimes on Earth. In this present incarnation, Serpentbird walks the earth as WOMAN. In many previous lives as a medicine man or stone keeper, I am now here in the flesh on planet Earth, walking the Priestess path. Souls who incarnate in many lifetimes accumulate knowledge and therefore wisdom from all lifetimes.

During my quest from 2007 to 2014 on the Red Road, I sought enlightenment. It was difficult to access my past lives, so I used different methods of meditation to discover details about lives that I lived as an Indigenous person here in what is now the United States. I went as deep as I could go in meditation, searching with a burning desire to heal myself.

This story relates a series of journeys I took to help me remember the past lives I have lived. The journeys were pilgrimages to power places or sacred sites where I lived during other lifetimes. The themes that unfolded are much like the seeking of a holy grail. Each sacred site is a piece in a puzzle for completion of my soul's cycle of Truth. As you read this memoir, you will experience my search, revealing a flow pattern of transmigration of my soul from life to life mostly through Arizona, New Mexico, and Colorado.

I had no idea how many missions it would take until I finally reached a pinnacle in realization of my own Truth. In the holy-grail vessel, I returned to the Magic of my own self! It was something I recovered, after paying a price by playing 'small.' My own suffering helped me realize how much freedom I truly have in this life and that I will not be persecuted for it in this incarnation, especially as a female.

As I walked upon the paths of Mother Earth in the United States, I used common sense and my own eyes to see the old America, the way it was during Indigenous times. My eyes lit up when I encountered roads and signs indicating Arapaho or Hopi presence. I was excited seeing indications of the vast habitation of the beings that lived in harmony with the Earth. This contrast became more vivid and clear where the land was wrecked and harnessed by the white man.

The Pleiadian beings shared with me that my soul is RED. I know it sounds crazy, but my consciousness sees everything this way. Imagine what it is like to have native people see my white skin and dismiss the true nature of my soul's experience.

When I began my quest to learn from wisdom keepers like Grandfather Martin in Hopi and native teacher Firedancer, I believed I needed their Indigenous knowledge and help. In reality, it is the Indigenous tribes of this country that need us, the Rainbow Warriors. They need our youth, our optimism, and our positive energy to help protect their land, water resources, and culture.

Sharing this memoir through public talks will be a substantial key for me to awaken my personal power, because my voice is the activation. I refer to it as "the key to Chiron." Chiron is the asteroid that helps you find your soul wounds in this lifetime and teaches how to heal them. From my Chiron healing, I am asked to just "be myself."

Recent generations have been persuaded that following the status quo is safer. In this incarnation, my lesson is to have a strong self-identity. That identity, however, eluded me because as a young woman growing up my freedom and confidence was highly damaged by my family. The identity as a warrior could only be unearthed by traveling and spiritual seeking with passion.

The stories in this book are Medicine Stories. They are stories of ceremony and the mystical experiences of awakening to my multidimensional self. While holding the medicine for awakening, there are some activities I can partake in and some I cannot. This is to protect and uphold the purity within my vessel. I must honor the DNA and gifts I hold. The same goes for the Yoni, which is a sacred container.

While reading these pages, I ask you to deeply connect and open your heart to the energy in the stories and poems, preserving the sacred vibration in them. Throughout the process of recalling the memories, I prayed with Tobacco and meditated with Masters including Jesus and the Pleiadians, to co-create each line in this book. Therefore, you are holding in your hands a book of holy wisdom, infused with Divine Poetic Light. I encourage you to refrain from putting this book on the floor or on the ground, in respect for the nature of the material.

I follow Spirit on a never-ending quest for the Self. I am Serpentbird, the one who flies into the flame of God's light. I merge and allow old shadow parts to be transmuted. You could say that dispelling darkness is my daily pastime. My food is the dead skin of the past, and like the Condor Eagle

I circle above the environment, cleaning the land of Indian wars of the past. It is obvious that the experience of death and rebirth cycles happen frequently for me, because it strengthens my ability to adapt and gain wisdom in diverse, strange, and even miserable environments and circumstances.

Sedona, Arizona was a critical mentor in my Ascension, because it is a living, breathing, feminine holy place. Sedona is not the original name, but for the sake of familiarity I mention the colonial name. It is important to note that Sedona is known by many different indigenous names. One I will mention here is Palatkwapi, the "Red House." Hopi legend states that it was once a great temple city of wisdom built by the Star People - the Kachinas.

In 2020, I was called back to Sedona to assist a group of souls at a particular massage spa who shared an Egyptian timeline in the third dynasty. This soul group held a lot of traumas, especially around sexual abuse of women. I was sent there because I had to repay much harm I had done within that timeline as well.

In the chapters that follow, you will understand in more detail why Sedona was essential to my awakening. For clarity in understanding this material, I will add that Sedona showed me an energetic picture about a tool for ascension used for reflection. It is a Medicine Wheel. It is important to know that I had to write this memoir, because this life is a 'completion' lifetime for me. The practice of writing out my realizations in black and white has helped me digest my lessons and heal them once and for all.

From 2007-2024, I journeyed this vast land of America in five different cars, I think people will most likely wonder, "Why didn't she have a van?" "Exactly," I say. The bicycle I rode was a GIANT road bike I called Black Beauty. The vehicles I drove were Hyundai one, the Reggae Love Machine; Hyundai two, the Vision Quest; a 1994 Subaru, The White Unicorn; a VW Golf, My Sister's Car; and my Kia Soul, The Red Dragonfly.

These travels showed me what America 'could be.' As I drove through the busy highways of LA or small villages on the Hopi Reservation, I saw how much 'togetherness' we are missing. We need solutions to work together to exist outside of the Patriarchy. We need to remember what a community actually is and does! This is Serpentbird medicine. You can relearn what community really is through my Medicine Wheel Ceremonies and the Rainbow Warrior Tribe, who I have trained to use the teachings.

It is my belief that "states" are not states and "countries" are not countries. Map boundaries could be represented by marks of Mother Earth's veins. The maps I see in my vision of America is her true lifeblood. Her veins are the rivers and waterfalls that pour into her seas. What America *could be* is of our own design, separate from the current controllers of the masses. In my opinion, we must value ourselves and nature and resources much more than we do now.

There are people who believe there is no need for the physical body to make pilgrimages to obtain samadhi and enlightenment. However, my mission and purpose are tied in with making healing 'land payments' to the many power sites in this country. Land payments help balance the weather on Earth. The mission I had in Santa Fe, New Mexico, as you will see toward the end of this memoir, could not have been experienced with the depth and potency of history without physically being one with the land and nature there.

The Goddess Sedona in Arizona made it possible for me to learn that I needed an Earth-based practice of ritual as my personal medicine, so that I could safely recover my lost soul parts in this lifetime. In learning the ceremonial method of the Medicine Wheel, I have been able to help others with this practice by leading group ceremonies.

On one of my pilgrimages to Santa Fe, I discovered through necessity something that surprised me. Our ancestors once offered colored stones, prayers, or food as land payments in a natural part of keeping life in balance. I offered my pain and sorrow back to the land, to return the memory of life trauma not fully processed during one of my past lives. Once my body's DNA or cellular memory had been cleared of the past trauma, the wheel turned once more. I could see and feel that the land and animals were happier! As a result, I was given profound joy and ecstasy from the spirits and the land.

While seeing the immense beauty of the United States, I believe my mission is to be a guardian of water through sacred activism. I feel called to be a voice for the land, especially her rivers. In modern Indigenous campaigns like "Land Back" and "Water Back," there is a need to restore the governance of people over the water on their own lands. Perhaps that is one reason why time and time again, I have made pilgrimages close to rivers. I used my artistic talents of drawing, painting, writing poetry, and making movies, to show just how sacred our land 'could and should' be. As for now, there are many humans who do not see the holy value our land has unless it can be used as a commodity.

What we need are solutions so that we can work together in small communities and groups that can exist outside of the Patriarchy. In my mind, I don't even think of state lines or countries, because my DNA remembers an entirely different paradigm. The gift that Serpentbird brings is the ability to combine practical everyday actions to save our planet, with prayer rituals that support the unseen spiritual dimensions.

I made two loops around the country between 2008 to 2019. Both loops, or what could be seen energetically as infinity signs, were made as I traveled through Sedona as the Omega point, or eye of the needle. Sedona was a critical mentor in my Ascension because she is a living breathing feminine holy place.

Through Rainbow Warrior Healing on the Red Road, I am sharing the experience of 'phase one' of my ascension. You could say that during this phase, I spent my journey learning to become a healer, which was really a subtractive process. The purpose was to find a healing modality that could unwind my DNA, releasing traumatic memories of past lives from my cells. While I was on solo journeys in nature, I took magic mushrooms in a Shamanic way. Usually, I did this on a mountain or alone in a forest, holding the actual plant in my hand, saying prayers over it, and giving thanks before 'journeying.' However, the more conscious I became and adept in meditation of the Akashic Records, I found I could not swallow them anymore. I advocate for anyone on the path of 'Wayshower' to partake in plant medicine only as needed.

The purpose of phase one was to realize my intrinsic self-worth and clarify my soul purpose, which has four components. Number one is my Voice, number two is as Storyteller, number three is Intuitive, and number four is Journeys for Power. These help bring me into the fool's journey of zero point. At times I need to wipe the slate clean and reinvent myself. The way I use and express these gifts is up to me, to combine in whatever way to affect our human consciousness. I am excited to continue blending different talents such as art, writing, films, healing, meditation, hatha yoga, dance, and teaching to uplift humanity.

Phase two, though unwritten, is where most of my karmic debts were dealt with and 'The Work' began. The buzz word for this is embodiment. I intend to take all I learned on my travels and teach others what I know about healing one's own body, mind, and spirit.

Phase three will be revolutionizing the world by HEALING humanity through the crystallization of my knowledge of healing and art modalities with videos, books, and ceremonies. While visualizing my future, it is imperative that I fulfill my dharma and listen to the guidance from the ancestors. The hand of God is on me, and I am at a point where the guidance I receive from the ancestors is so prevalent in my dreams that I can only follow what they show me is my next assignment.

I perform the Medicine Wheel crystal healing ceremonies both as a solo ceremonialist or when leading groups. The Medicine Wheel is a foundation for my teachings, and I will continue to hold large group ceremonies and priestess initiations to accelerate planetary healing.

I often perform solo ceremonies along the portals within the Dragon Line that consists of Hogbacks or long narrow ridges. This Dragon Line runs north and south through Colorado. In 2023, I spent time in Golden and Morrison Colorado, singing to the ancient rocks for up to two hours and discovering how to activate the rain cycles. At times, I design small circle grid works to harmonize and stabilize the Ley lines on the planet. Grid work is needed to prevent natural disasters and harmonize the rain cycles, because humans don't often bless the land and send love to the land.

The Medicine Wheel is a vessel, a safe zone for healing. It is a place that is a representation of the Quantum Field, which holds a zero-point vibration beyond all time and space, therefore giving greater access for healing at the speed of light. The Medicine Wheel is also an access point into the Akashic Records. This zone allows us to free the body from the captivity of the stories we carry from lifetime to lifetime in our DNA. It is an experience of freedom that even our governments don't want us to have. They do not want us to be naturally healthy and human free-spirit souls. Most of all, they don't want us gathering in circles where power is shared and everyone has a voice.

To be in the center of the wheel is to experience God. From the energetic center point, it gives a freedom from pain, and even birth and death can be sensed through prayer in oneness with the Divine presence. The crystal wheel is defined in diagrams that have helped me measure my growth and development. Many times, my experiences in the medicine wheel brought emotions and memories to the surface. I would then find it essential to process deep "samskaras" with a qualified regression therapist.

The Rainbow Warrior Healing on the Red Road is my chosen title for the journey between 2008-2024, because my soul craved to know more about my Indigenous past lives. The Rainbow Warrior prophecy was told from indigenous tribes such as the Hopi, Cree, Zuni, and Cherokee. It is the prophecy that humanity would one day need to reunite all four races to restore Mother Earth. When I saw this prophecy on a variety of websites, I broke out in tears. When I was around eleven years old, while sitting next to a river, I could hear this 'call.' I knew that one day I would be asked by God to stand up for the preservation of our land and water. I knew it would take the mindset of Unity Consciousness and a bringing of all races together to accomplish this task.

Typing these words invokes deep sorrow and pain, because as COVID brought trauma to 2020, it became clear to me how much peace we need. I understand that the teachings of peace within the Medicine Wheel need to be preserved by me. While seeking the lost teachings among Native American elders, I experienced sadness, because I know even they are struggling to keep this lost knowledge alive in the hearts of their people. The symbol of the rainbow is also, of course, a great ally and teacher when presenting the importance of water on the planet. Many healers use the rainbow as a metaphor for visualization in body healing. The rainbow is also a sign given by the holy ones of divine protection.

The rainbow is revered by children, as you may know, because of its purity and colors, holding hope, excitement, and optimism. My Native American teacher Firedancer gave us a visualization of the rainbow in her ceremonies, as a way to clear unwanted energies that are not of God. I saw a story on the internet describing the prophecy of Warriors of the Rainbow. It made me cry instantly, but with tears of pain, not joy. I had yet to understand that my white skin was actually red in many past lives. My tears were for the loss of my Tribe, our ceremonies, and our land. Even now, my soul has not fully recovered from these losses.

As for the Rainbow Warriors on the planet right now, I feel it is also part of my soul mission to gather them into a cohesive community to help restore the beauty and peace on Earth. As my travels continue, I see that my gift lies more in the harmonization of connection through ceremony, rather than getting my hands in the dirt and building physical gardens. The Age of Aquarius has dawned, yet as Kaypacha says, "This generation is only beginning to plant seeds for the new paradigm of unity consciousness."

My material essence as a Rainbow Warrior consists of a native 'red' soul walking around in a European 'white' body. I feel a concern presenting this material, being a Jewish, white-skinned woman of European descent. In a time where people are quick to scream appropriation, I do not always freely speak about my soul essence. Shouldn't a peaceful warrior be able to wear a feather or two in her hair? Can't she wear a turquoise necklace? I often wonder how to present myself, either as Lori or as Serpentbird, without experiencing criticism. I find it sad that even in 2024, I have to tiptoe around social norms.

It is my belief that as a collective, we have not yet grown to understand the nature of the soul. The soul is colorless, but full of energy transmigrating from body to body. We attempt to complete what can never be completed because the soul is eternal! My role is to help others learn about their woundedness with a variety of healing tools like the Medicine Wheel and accessing the Akashic Records. By putting these tools in practice, we can access lost parts of the soul and bring them into oneness.

I am aware that I alone do not have all the solutions needed to bring the planet into harmony and balance. I know that I am a healer and spiritualist, who doesn't always know how to solve problems on a material level. I am aware that most likely the world will go through a de-dollarization process in 2024. Many land-grabs by other countries will be coming in to exploit our sacred lands and resources further. I always wish I could solve more of our problems on a tangible level; however, I offer the gifts that come naturally to me. Perhaps these and other solutions will be offered by you!

Medicine Wheel Poem

Scream to escape, Scream the beginning
to exit the matrix modern life has constructed.
Scream to exit, Scream to enter
and create a portal to rebuild the Sacred Circle.
Scream to enter
Scream to exit
Scream to be birthed
Scream to die.

With intensity invite the Sky
Invoke the elemental beings
Invoke the Magic Initiate into Love
Create the Spokes, Turn the Wheel.
Begin again with foolish zeal.
See through illusion
The East door awaits.
To kill duality, I pursue
pulling the Seven Sisters
through my crown's gate.
Let the Pleiades pour Star knowledge
and purify my mind to wide light
The medicine wheel is only the beginning
as you see the end begins again,
because the circle doesn't break.

The sacred hoop creates, creates,
Mothers Web won't destroy
your biggest dream it only employs
Dance the fool Dance, as many times as you need,
Mother Earth's beauty and bounty feed.

She assists the soul, as my foot - skin, drinks
Journey to Journey creation blinks
NOW is the only moment,
Yet we destroy her, while she forgives
Through storms and fire, let us restore

While we remember Who we were,
My ancient blood remembers
I was each race of the four directions
Within my soul every medicine is represented here.
The ancients were reborn into crystal seeds.

With the Sacred Chanupa born within, Come with me
And begin to unite the Rainbow Warrior Tribes
Who are making the Earth green again.

Pisces, Wounded Healer

Water remembers the stories of our collective history within its structure. I will explain what I know so far in my awakening as a healer and teacher. We know that Indigo children have come to this earth to heal the collective. My experiences have proven that I can heal collective traumas through my waters, the cells of my own body. Water inspires energetic flow without structure, which is also the type of spiritual path I prefer, one without structure! I want to inspire an evolution of the consciousness of humanity from religion to spirituality.

WATER MOVES! I am always changing and learning new things. It is between my will and that of "God." I never allow my life to become stagnant. People tend to see my gypsy life as a fault. I feel they judge me by labeling me as "nomadic." The TRUTH is that I have an extraordinary mission to help humanity remember the sacredness of water.

Water is Life. Change is the only thing in life that is constant. My strength is to go with the flow, but to have adventures, and find "home" within myself in this lifetime. As a healer, I hold an understanding of the depth of emotion within the human experience. My natal chart clearly shows a Pisces Sun sign, but I am much more than that. I have a grand water trine from Pisces to Scorpio and Cancer. This gives me great ability to know all kinds of waters - and emotions.

Pisces is the ocean, the vastness from which all waters arise and to which all waters eventually return. It's the tides and currents that fill the land all around the Earth. Scorpio is deep water, water without a seabed. It is the mystery and uncertainty of emotions. Yet that is my life challenge: to master my emotional depth.

My Scorpio North Node is a powerhouse for knowing how to be the ultimate transformer, and alchemist. Cancer is the summer rains and the waters of springs and brooks. It is the water of childhood in the form that nurtures. Strong currents of these waters can be extremely uplifting, or depressing. The only way for me to cultivate a more consistent vibration is to do yoga and breath work. I have more or less succeeded in controlling my emotions by how much practice I incorporate in my life.

Pisces and Indigo children have the gift of Empathy. Empathy is much like water; it often flows into containers without boundaries. I am surprised when my clients ask me, "What is an empath?" That's difficult to put into words, when this power comes naturally!

AN EMPATH IS ONE WHO FEELS YOUR PAIN. A client asked, "But how do you feel my pain?" I froze while trying to find the words to answer her question. Empaths relate to you through a sixth sense. It isn't something you can understand with your mind. That is why I say it is a blessing and a curse. My empathy can be so heightened that I feel the emotional pain of a client before I even meet them in the treatment room. I see energy blocks through my third eye and read emotions that are attached to organ systems or chakras.

My vibration and energy level can drop dramatically, much like the pressure you feel as the weather changes. When I feel someone else's highly charged energy field, I feel charged. If a person's energy field is draining, my energy drops as well, even before attempting to do bodywork. This whole experience has made it extremely challenging to carry out "hands-on-the-body" types of healing modalities. However, it has also made me fine-tune my perceptions and discernment of subtle energy. The bottom line here is the need to have very strong personal boundaries.

I can tell you that it is healthier to operate through compassion rather than empathy. I looked at my empathic skills as a "superpower" for years. However, since my abilities are operating all the time, I must consciously prepare myself before working at a spa or healing center. My empathic feelers tap into someone's field before they even arrive for a massage or energy work session. This automatic "superpower" can be invasive and draining for me at times. If I can have compassion for someone and turn off the 'empath switch,' it is a safer way for me to hold space for their healing.

As a Pisces healer, I am the one chosen in my family line to heal my own body, mind, and soul – as well as those of my unwell ancestors. I learned that I was the 'one' from a psychic in Los Angeles. Therefore, healing my family and thus the planet became the by-product of my body healing.

My mother and sister are unaware that I have been carrying out the work of healing my family's ancestral line. Our belief systems are so strikingly different that in 2020, I chose not to communicate with either of them again. This separation from them causes me immense suffering when I see other families that seem to have a healthy means of relating. However, one of the women healers I received counsel from informed me that if their beliefs or jealousies had not come off in this way, I would not have delved as deep into my own internal healing.

These days you hear lightworkers speaking of creating a "safe container." I can create that safe container for my client's healing, however for much of my life with my family, there was no safety. I had to learn by exploring many methods of healing to remove depression and insecurity. As a watery empath, I later discovered where I would draw the boundary lines between you and me, us and them. If one feels the whole of humanity, its sorrow and pain, how can one know separateness?

I need to mention that I never took ANY medication for my mental well-being at any point on my journey. My inner wisdom knows that prescription drugs from "Big Pharma" are not a solution for the root cause of emotional and mental health. Did I suffer from schizophrenia? At times, yes. Did I suffer from depression, trauma, and PTSD? Yes! However, when chanting or meditating, I found relief and could measure the results on a natural feeling level. Throughout my life, until my 40s, I suffered from extreme emotions of anxiety and depression. These were the means for creating my true healing path aligning with the Red Road, or the right road in life.

As taught by Ogala Medicine Man Black Elk, all people on the Red Road are part of an interconnected circle that makes a sacred hoop. They say that to walk this road, you must practice and embody these seven values: Prayer, Honesty, Humility, Compassion, Respect, Generosity, and Wisdom.

In committing to this path, which many indigenous call "The Red Road," many may wonder why I would incorporate any other belief systems. However, when I began working with the Medicine Wheel system of wholeness and balance, I drew very strange and mystical visitations from higher beings from throughout the cosmos. This is because the Medicine Wheel is a model of the Cosmos itself. Luckily, my first Indigenous teacher, Firedancer, expressed her familiarity with these visitations from Masters such as Jesus and Green Tara, which allowed me to feel free to work with many beings.

You could say I am a Pantheist, since I believe in the Ascended Masters such as Jesus, Mary, Buddha, Krishna, and Tara. As a mystical "being" myself, I often felt that a backlash of labels could come from people who do not understand my medicine work. Yet others who work with me and trust in my abilities know that I intend to help humanity.

As the Bible says in Matthew 7:15-20, "Beware of false prophets, which come to you in sheep's clothing, but inwardly they are ravening wolves. Ye shall know them by their fruit. Every tree that bringeth not forth good fruit is hewn down and cast into the fire. Wherefore by their fruits, ye shall know them."

Call me a Record Keeper

While working at a spa in Sedona, a client on my massage table asked, "When was the moment you knew that you had past lives?" I used to get angry when clients asked me questions like this, because I felt they should know more about the soul. I took a deep breath and started to understand the importance of her query.

I paused for a moment, to recall a juicy memory. I had an image flash through my third eye, then I gasped for air. The smell of old worn paper from a used geography book in middle school flooded my senses. A teacher slammed this book down in front of me. The cover was a sienna-toned face of the Great Sphinx in Egypt. In that moment, my eyes peered at the Sphinx's head with awe. I thought I was seeing it for the first time, but suddenly I had an out-of-body experience.

I am not sure where I went, but the next thing I knew, I flew back into my body. When this happened, I did not have any visions about Egypt. I felt a surge of electricity and a cord of white light from my tailbone shoot through my spine to my crown. It upgraded my whole body, making a connection with Egypt's current timeline. I later learned that the Great Sphinx is the house of the ancient library, or Hall of Records, which stores the Akashic Records of humanity from the time of Atlantis.

As a record keeper, my Earth-temple-body matrix stores many histories of this planet. For teaching the "Rainbow Warrior Prophecy," it is important to share my Native American lifetimes with you. The lifetimes I have had as an indigenous person are encoded in my soul's DNA. I have been a male medicine man and Apache warrior in New Mexico, a male chief on the American Plains, and a Priestess that was captured and sacrificed on Red Mountain in Colorado Springs, Colorado by an Arapaho priest during the event "Coyote Lightning" 800 years ago.

The external color of a person's skin, or even the religion they were born into, is not the totality of a person's history. This is exactly why using the circle as a tool for transformation, is so critical. It is a hoop in which to REMEMBER what you have done in past, present, and future lifetimes. The soul has traveled and been many types of beings, whether Black, Yellow, White, or Red. NOW is the time we should live and co-create on this Earth in harmony.

The Medicine Wheel is a tool that unravels cellular memory binding me to the Earth. I found that using clear quartz crystals as a container for the healing circle accelerates the removal of pain and trauma. If we want to ascend, we need to release our karma and the memories stored within our cells. I want to create a future that is different from my past, so I release pain and trauma to create new stories. We need to know *how* to use the wisdom of our past lives to assist the shift of consciousness and planetary awakening.

My creativity is limitless, yet the feeling of inspiration has its peaks and valleys. The peaks for me are ecstatic and allow me to be a natural-born healer, artist, and poet. As you will read in the later chapters, I went on a ten-year journey from filmmaker to healer and then circled back to filmmaking again. The valleys often are filled with feelings of deep depression and have limited my production of any art for long periods of time.

In 2010, when I was studying Reiki in Grandview, Ohio, I had a vision of Jesus coming to me with a ball of light, which he put in my hands. It was 'infinite creativity.' Jesus telepathically came into my mind to illustrate that all the power I had previously put into painting and drawing could be translated into my work as a healing artist.

As I wrote this book, I often wondered whether people who lead very modern lifestyles would want or need what I have to offer. Yet you may have noticed how the popularity of words like 'tribe' and 'native' are not only more widely used today but are more triggering than ever.

More existential proof of how my ancient knowledge applies to the 'now' surfaces from time to time. When I meet mothers who have birthed a Rainbow Child, I receive another shock to my system and want to share this knowledge. I believe these children are souls who were warriors in past lives but chose to be peaceful warriors in this life. Some of these children were Aboriginal Grandmothers or Grandmothers from other sacred and ancient places on Earth. Many are gifted with supernatural abilities beyond my own. These children are teachers. We should allow them to lead us in this ascension, for their ancient wisdom as well as their playfulness. My role has been to reflect to the parents what these children know is 'ancient lost knowledge,' including rituals and songs.

Rainbow children know how to repair the rain cycles and balance the weather on the Earth. You need only look at the way their bodies remember information from their past lives. You can see it in the way they sit or stand. A Rainbow child that I know had a strong remembrance at a birthing cave in Sedona and asked 13 adults sitting around her to sing about flowers and pray. The shamanic work I do is ultimately for Mother Earth's children.

In 2021, on my website I advertised my services as an Akashic Records healer and teacher. I fully stepped into my power and purpose, including training Rainbow Warrior men and women to use the medicine wheel for healing their past lives and balancing the weather on the Earth. To bring my soul purpose to life, it takes courage to 'stand out.' The alternative would be living like the zombies I see walking on the streets of Denver.

I see and feel time accelerating. What we need more than ever is to slow down and match the vibration of Mother Earth. As you may now understand, our climate has become unusual and the four seasons have been disrupted by our thoughts and our actions. Now is the time for me to find all the Rainbow Warriors and help get my message out to the world. If we can gather 'holy people' together and do this work, we can help Mother Earth restore balance again. This is the focus for my website www.serpentbird.com.

Rebel on the Road

My spirit continues to crave rebelling against the grain of society and the cultural illusions of government structures. The journeys and pilgrimages I took to sacred places like Hopiland and Navajo lands allowed me to expand because the roads felt unknown. I had never traveled these roads in my current life. I was in a constant state of awe and wonder on my journeys. As I lived in a carefree, zero-point field of possibility, I was open to receive what I needed when I needed it.

I want to live outside the norm of the nine-to-five structure. I want to be a leader, showing people there is more to life than structure. You will hear me speak about capitalism in America as an antagonist. I believe that my growth has been put on hold because my needs are simply drowned out by the 'market economy.' The Matrix, which is also capitalism, keeps us from knowing ourselves and our history as a soul on this Earth. We are so busy within a construct that keeps us locked in fear, stress, and a lot more disorder than order. The vibration that the Matrix puts us in prevents manifestation towards our highest potential. As I experienced in the Medicine Wheel, the higher vibrations help regain memories from other lifetimes.

There is also a direct correlation between property ownership and the medicine wheel, having to do with greed and control. It is impossible to give yourself totally to an experience with creation and the presence of the Angels if you are constantly at war with those who own the land where you are practicing your sacred medicine.

As I remember my past lives, I see how they connect and how deeply the soul experiences war and peace. Through this range of experience, we cultivate deep compassion. Our Mother Earth is calling us to choose a path of Ascension, requiring the remembrances of our lifetimes to 'choose peace.' This is my mission. I am here to assist in your remembrances and to facilitate a path back to peace within yourself. This Peace will then help to restore our Mother Earth.

My mission in sharing and giving talks from these medicine journeys is how I fulfill the lesson of Chiron. I wish to be a leader within the field of healing arts. I see myself writing books and screenplays, making art and films, while also traveling frequently.

This memoir is a way for me to heal the karma from many past lives. I have multiple lives in which the power of my pen and words created irreparable damage. I have spent many nights crushing my hands, fingers, and sometimes my entire arm with my face and jaw, until I had to wake up to relieve myself of the pressure.

One lifetime, as a member of a royal family in the Mediterranean, I was forced to sign my name on multiple historical documents, one of them the Magna Carta. I signed humanity into slavery, because of my royal blood. I may have had the choice to move humanity in a higher trajectory, but the royals added many other parts to the document that moved us backwards. Someone looked over my shoulder as I signed the documents. If I had not done as they said, they would have killed me. I now offer this memoir to aid humans in choosing peace, freedom, and sovereignty.

Childhood and Karmic Ties with the Abel Family

I was raised on Caves Road in Novelty, Ohio, a small rural town east of Cleveland. I was very fortunate to grow up in Novelty with its creeks, woods, farmland, acreage of wild tall grasses and wildlife like deer, owls, hawks, ravens, and racoons. I grew up before the invention of the cell phone and there were no city sidewalks. I was comforted by raw nature and picturesque landscapes.

I find it interesting that Novelty means Origin, since as an Andromedan starseed I have always been on a mission to remember the roots of all my ancestors, past lives, and star origins. My mother practiced genealogy and created documents of our origins through family birth records and stories she collected from other relatives. My mother is a writer, which I always thought was interesting, but nerdy! I gravitated toward poetry, but never thought it would be in my soul's contract to write novels.

Before I was born, my mother had trouble conceiving, so she took prescribed medicine to help her. My father built a small "wishing well" in the front yard, over the metal covering for our natural water well. My mother threw a penny into the well and wished for a child to be born. I feel that perhaps it was a difficult type of soul lesson for her to call in. Her prayers and strong intentions were needed for it to happen.

Novelty, Ohio had no sidewalks like the suburbs and was quiet enough for me to experience a deep connection with Mother Earth in a serene way. As a little girl, the backyard behind my house brought me the most joy. I could sit in a field of tall green grass, yellow buttercups, Queen Anne's lace, and Indian paintbrush, which to me, was always a refuge of safety from the awful energies of my family life. Nature was *always* my salvation.

There were rivers, open space, woods, and small farms with horses and cows on them. My parents told me that Caves Road, a bit north of my home, had natural caves where Natives lived in the past. When I was older, I took long drives up Caves Road but never found the caves.

I clearly remember my father telling me about a flower called an Indian Paintbrush. The word "Indian" was so charged with life energy for me, it propelled me to have out-of-body experiences! This word resonated in my soul as a young girl, leading me to ask myself why this word felt so warm and familiar in my body.

Even at the young age of seven, my clairsentience alerted me when native ancestors were nearby. They assisted me as I was being raised by my blood family and cared for me throughout my young adult life. I remember them as warm and loving, surrounding my body as I sat in the wet grass in my backyard. This was truly the beginning of my Spiritual Path.

The experience of being with these guides connected me to God. I knew this had something to do with Native Americans, but at that age, no one had taught me about them. From time to time, my father took me on walks through the local parks in Geauga County, Ohio and he mentioned that native people lived here as well. I always thought to myself quietly and internally, "Where are they now?" Sitting on that land in Novelty, I felt the presence of Native People who had passed on many times. They were my family from the spirit world. They were more loving, present, and in a sense, safer than my blood family.

As a child, I felt very much alone. Most of the time I was not happy and didn't develop social skills, which furthered my loneliness and isolation. In photographs I smiled, and I know I did have good times, but the theme that ran through my family life was judgmental with lack of approval. I always felt extremely unworthy and that I constantly performed below their expectations.

I felt that I would have to measure up to what my parents wanted me to be, though they did not clearly express what it was they wanted me to be. As an individual, I know I make my own choices in how I choose to express who I am. However, I thought that following their suggestions would make them happy. What resulted was making many of my life decisions based on the fear projected onto me.

I loved the backyard behind my home, two acres of wild grasses, pine trees, and wildflowers. This backyard was where I found acceptance and peace. The massive clouds over the grassy field and clean air were normally plentiful. Big thunderstorms that crashed in the sky were followed by streaks of lightning. I often thought that the lightning brought a presence of "beings," which now I understand to be "Thunderbeings."

The smell of wet soil and grass after the rain stood out to me as a formative, notable impression in my consciousness, which led to a feeling of transcendence. The time I spent in nature was my way of keeping safe throughout my childhood.

It was strange to me having the backyard with our colonial style house in the front. The house architecturally represented conformity, structure, and of course colonization, which I did not associate well with. I did love my childhood home though. Later in life, when I discovered that I was an Empath, I realized that I had taken on my mother's pain. My mother's pain and anxiety was overwhelming for me, my sister, and my dad.

I am still undergoing more hypnotherapy sessions to reveal the hidden connections from my life as Queen Hatshepsut and how it connects to my current family.

Wanda the Medical Medium
Sedona 2015

October 17th, 2015. I was feeling intense pain and pressure in my throat chakra, so I sought out a medical medium and astrologer named Wanda in Sedona, Arizona. She helped me regress to childhood through meditation. I didn't realize that I needed to do inner child work and being with her was the first time I ever thought I needed a therapist for any reason.

Wanda revealed to me that as a young child, my mother controlled my energy to a point that it fragmented my whole body. I had soul loss because of her yelling and screaming with anxiety. At times my mother's 'fits' were so intense she would go outdoors, clench her fists and scream. With Wanda's help, I revisited the memories of my mother, who would bind my wrists and pull me with her hands. The cells in my right wrist were affected the most. As an adult, many times I felt so much of other people's pain I wanted to leave my body.

In the meditation, I saw what happened to me. I found out that the three- or four-year-old girl was traumatized. When my third eye read my energy field as a child, I WAS NOT THERE! Wanda patiently asked me to explore when and where I checked out. I had no idea!

She asked me to ask my young self where I would go if I could go anywhere in the world. I replied in a weak and cracked voice that it felt as though my head would disconnect from my body. When I saw my younger self, I saw her not wanting to talk.

Wanda asked me to play with her and take her to the park. She kept emphasizing that my refusal to speak at that age was a strength! All the people I trusted when I was young seemed to turn their back on me.

While I was at Wanda's office, she read my astrology chart for details on what happened in my family in early childhood. My sun sign of Pisces is at 28 degrees. She said Lilith, the asteroid of rage, represents my dad and that I carried his deep emotional pain. This resulted in PTSD and would absorb my mother's craziness. "I just wanted everyone to leave me alone!" But why? I felt disappointed in something, feeling it in my Throat Chakra. How did I take my mom's anxiety into my body and where? My neck and upper spine were where my body was hurting the most.

Another theme of my youth (and my life) was Truth. I knew in my soul that I was for truth and honesty. Many times, my mother accused me of not telling the truth and insisted that I was a liar. I felt that she was crazy.

Wanda suggested using my imagination to see if hurting myself would affect my mother's attitude toward me. How I could visualize my sister and I ending our lives, to hurt mom in retaliation? Maybe I needed to feel disgusted with my mother and disappoint her? If I found a busy street, a major freeway with a truck flying by, I could commit suicide. As I practiced these thought processes, I soon discovered that my mother wouldn't see how she was acting any clearer. She just grabbed her hair and screamed.

My therapist asked me to look myself in the eyes as if my adult self was looking at my child self. My five-year-old eyes were cerulean blue, yet were fried by the heat of fear as if struck by lightning. That is when my life with depression began. At 40 years old, looking back at that child, I saw innocence and purity. I had no desire to bring harm to others in this world.

I hated myself and this made the cycle worse. Instead of connecting with humans, I had a fear that they would hurt me. Looking at my eyes, my head was shaken so hard that my eyes were vacant. I had been stolen by my mother's need to take my energy. My ignorance and youth allowed her to take it. As a protective measure, my normal behavior in school was to ignore what was happening around me. I am not always shy, but I felt embarrassed to reveal who I really was from being shaken so hard and so often.

It was a shock that Wanda said was related to the spleen. I explained that my mom slammed doors in our faces and felt like whiplash. Wanda also informed me that when a door is slammed, shut in your face, it creates a line of shock through the body, which may have led to my schizophrenia. I just wanted to tell my mother, "I hate you." I had no idea going to therapy would reveal such childhood trauma. Until that day in Wanda's office, I thought I had a relatively normal childhood.

I have been misunderstood my whole life by my family. My experience was that their perspective of me was to follow their lead. In reality, I wanted to be heard and understood for my inner wisdom. I struggled with feelings of self-doubt, insecurity, low self-worth, and suppression while I was around them. The theme of having this great inner wisdom and truth but not being listened to or heard was connected to a bigger cycle of lifetimes, which were waiting to be uncovered from my subconscious mind.

As an adult, it was important for me to learn about the Akashic Records because this is my completion lifetime. I understand that the imprint from youth was connected to a series of lifetimes with my birth parents in this life. Their behaviors of suppression, violence, and betrayal were repeated in previous lifetimes with them!

The pain from these lifetimes formed a samskara in my solar plexus. A samskara is a knot of energy or psychological imprint that forms from multiple lifetimes and intersects its energy lines in a chakra. I came to understand that this pain was the root of anxiety triggers that happened later in my career as a massage therapist.

I can hardly believe that I lived in such density within my family, with the energy and lessons for almost half my life, because it stole so much of my life force. Most of the psychics I have spoken to made me realize this and told me that my childhood was stolen from me. They said that I had to grow up quickly around these adults who were emotionally unavailable to me.

A Talented Artist before Art School

Through my formative years and into my late 40s, I had such low self-esteem that I couldn't see what gifts were eternally mine. Once I started work with the Akashic Records in 2017 and with my regression therapist Greg McHugh in 2021, I learned how to overcome low self-esteem. The regression therapy sessions helped deprogram me from past experiences I had with my mother and father. Greg was able to help me separate my aura and energy field from the energy of my parents through prayer. This gave me a sense of finally being in my own energy.

I believe that ultimately, my art will bring me true wealth and fulfillment whether or not I generate revenue. My parents programed me to believe that money and art had to be tied together. This sent me down a miserable path where I failed at trying to be a Graphic Designer.

Before I went to college, I had an extensive portfolio of watercolors, life portraits, still life paintings, silk batik, and sculpture. Before I graduated high school, I created a fine art portfolio. The portfolio won me an $18,000 scholarship to CCAD (Columbus College of Art and Design) in Ohio.

My high school art teacher, Irene Sukle, was a key figure in my life. She spurred me on to take nude life drawing classes at Cleveland Institute of Art before I even graduated High School! She shot slides of my artwork for my submission to enter college.

One awful experience was when I stood against a yellow wall in my family's kitchen. I was holding the course catalog for CCAD, which was a prestigious private art college at that time. I was perusing a list of categories for majors, and without having to think, I chose Fine Arts. That was when my parents asked me what I wanted to do.

My mother immediately screamed "NO!" and they both chimed in, telling me I needed to pick something I could make money at, so I could have something to fall back on. I felt my heart break, my legs and feet froze in place like I had done something wrong. I felt I WAS NOT GOOD ENOUGH.

At 18 years of age, looking in the course catalogue of art majors, I used my inner wisdom to consider what these categories meant. The majors I had to choose from were Fashion Design, Industrial Design, Sculpture, Photography, Fine Art, or Graphic Design.

Something inside me informed my lower self that I already understood Graphic Design, so I chose that as my major. In a moment of tension, I felt my mom and dad pressing their intentions on me. I knew they would not send me to this school if I did not pick something other than Fine Art. During my second year of enrollment at the school, I wanted to change my major to Photography, but my dad refused my decision.

I hated Graphic Design and Advertising. I couldn't get into the computer classes because the school was growing and had not set up computer access for all of us. That meant I showed up to classes with watercolor paintings, and the students and teachers completely ignored my homework because it wasn't created on the computer. When it was time for graduation, teachers told me that I would not be able to find a professional job with my portfolio. This was a devastating waste of money! My mother paid for the rest of my tuition for art school, but in the end, I wondered how having an $80,000 degree could only get me a job at a small suburban newspaper for $8.50 an hour.

I completely shut down on the inside but persevered for a few years by finding internships at local graphic design companies. I soon learned that my computer skills were sub-par. Some of my childhood PTSD made it difficult to read the menus inside the Photoshop and Illustrator programs. It was hard for me to remember long strings of information inside the menus that would appear then disappear. My past traumas made my eyes flicker and my ability to focus impossible! I wouldn't understand how much damage had been done from my childhood traumas until I worked with countless healers.

No matter what life threw at me, I began to adapt 'like water' to the world and its needs, instead of staying with my unique voice and doing 'me.' One day my aunt revealed a hard truth. I learned that my mother was "living vicariously" through me. I think my aunt knew that at times my mother had vampiric energy as well. I had to think about it to see it from her point of view. I didn't quite know that it presented a danger, which meant I was constantly trying to please her, but whatever I did was never enough. This put a further "groove in my record" so to speak and left my wound even deeper with thoughts of "not being good enough." Now I know by following my parent's guidance, I cheated my real worth, my voice, and what brought joy to my heart, to LIVE!

One of the greatest lessons I learned under my mom and dad's influence is that I no longer needed their approval of what my life path should be. Healing on a soul level, I know that my talents are directly connected to my abundance. I constantly told myself that I couldn't generate an abundance of money through my talents because I accepted what my family was saying to me. In a sense, I was taught by them to fear my strengths. They were saying to me, "Work for the man, follow the status quo, and do what is guaranteed to make you money."

The words and experiences we exchanged did not let me STAND fully in trusting my talents. Even in adulthood, I find it difficult to trust in my talents to make a living, yet I know that is where my true joy is. Joy is what fulfills the soul and ultimately brings true wealth.

Until recently, I fought against fears of expansion. I went through many types of therapy sessions to deprogram from past experiences. In Sedona at age 34 to the age of 47 in Colorado, I searched for a significant change to my 'inner' landscape and spent more time searching 'outside.' I thought surely I would find happiness searching somewhere in the United States, rather than within my own heart.

My soul wanted to feel free to start painting again without the sabotaging voices of my parents or myself. After a lot of energy healing sessions to clear blocks around making my art, I began to feel free of these restrictive voices. Looking back, I can say, "I wish someone had told me that going to therapy is not a bad thing and needs to be done regardless of the cost." Once I had been through enough therapy, I realized that the money I spent was an investment in me being able to open the door to a joyful life.

Massage, Hands, Stop-Gap

Becoming a massage therapist was a stopgap, creating the time and space for me to understand that I needed to heal myself more than I needed to heal other people. This was a repeating pattern I learned as a child. I had to put other people in my family before myself because they were so dysfunctional. In reality, I had to protect my mind, body, and soul from them.

Massage therapy helped me to become a better person and learn how to heal myself in a greater cycle of mankind. However, it took me many years to reprioritize and stop accommodating people by putting their healing before my own. I also found out later, with the help of a healer, that I had some vows of servitude in the healing arts in past lives. These vows had to be removed, so that I didn't feel indebted to some of the spa employers I was working for.

I have worked consistently as a licensed massage therapist for ten years in Arizona, Colorado, New Mexico, and California. From 2014 to 2024, I touched more than 15,000 clients with massage and soul healings.

After ten plus years of being a therapist, I am amazed at how much I've developed my intuitive abilities and what my magic hands have done to help others heal on a physical level! Now I am ready to use tools such as quantum hypnosis and akashic soul healing, for an inside-out rather than outside-in approach.

The massage industry has changed since I began and is becoming less and less about therapy and more about money. The integrity of this art seems to be preserved more so in private practices and by great teachers of massage. I have not yet created a 'brick and mortar' private practice in massage, because it hasn't served me to stay in one place.

I have seen how the cult of capitalism and working for the dollar has wiped out our connection to our true selves and our talents. The idealistic lie that some adults try to sell the masses is that working will protect you from failure by giving you 'stability.' I have seen a hypnotic depressed state in most adults and even students I work with. Children have natural talents and abilities in the arts, like painting, singing, dancing, or playing instruments. Then, as they mature, they become convinced to be a damn Information Technology specialist or a lawyer or a Real Estate salesperson. This squelches their passion and pours their souls into the pit of smoldering white picket fences of corporate America!

Chiron in Aries, the Wounded Warrior
Healing the Wound of "Identity"

How does one know they are a "wounded healer?" Everyone has a Chiron aspect in their birth chart. It tells you what you must do in your lifetime to heal yourself. My birth chart shows that I am a wounded healer in the aspect of Chiron in Aries.

Chiron in Aries is the Wounded Warrior. In other words, Aries is the warrior archetype. I need to stand up for what I believe in and when I do so, move through fears that others may not approve of me.

This means I must develop a strong personal identity in the world with self-confidence. At times, I don't even feel like I deserve to be here on this planet, which is the wound of Self. Really the opposite is true. How does one heal the wound of not wanting to be here?

When I was a young adult, I did express myself but others in my family insisted on stifling my individuality. My choice to preserve my expression through poetry and the arts is what I feel makes me unique and gives me a way to express my individuality, as long as I am not just trying to please other people.

Other methods I have found to be successful in recovering from deep wounds are by using the medicine wheel, psychedelic mushroom journeys, past-life regression healings and the Akashic Records. These experiences have shown me my soul's fragmented parts. The most uplifting experiences I have had while receiving healing with regression and Akashic Records work is feeling the presence of angelic beings lift and transmute the pain from my wounds up into the light. If you want to experience your multidimensional self through this kind of transcendent healing work, I can assist you!

As you will read, my ancestors blessed me with harrowing initiations one after another, to test me and make me stronger. These showed me what needed to be healed, transmuted, and purified. I have found myself broke, even while holding a massage job and living in my car. I have traversed dark mental spaces to heal my self-hate with deep yogic breath in my lungs.

Part of my inner curiosity about practicing healing arts comes from my deep inner wounded physician. I'm deeply motivated to explore other's fragmentation because I can relate to having missing soul parts and have compassion in wanting to help them recover from trauma.

In my case, I believe the family abuse I endured in this current lifetime created PTSD in my body and mind. These experiences of shock and abandonment left me like a cracked vase that always had water leaking out. I hope this memoir will serve as a key in healing any starseed who is involved in toxic family dynamics.

On assignment from the ancestors in 2024 in Colorado Springs, Colorado, I've been able to feel more deeply my warrior archetype. The Akashic Records come to the surface when the time is right to work out the karma with certain characters to heal my tribe with love. I have always felt balanced internally as a male and a female essence. What is important about the discovery of myself as a warrior who shoots arrows and uses knives in war, is that by reenacting war, I find this enlivens my light-warrior / light-worker self.

Red Rocks Amphitheater
Denver, Colorado 2018

Chiron's Gold Key
Chiron's gold key sets the Samskara's free.

The yellow wheel beneath my sternum bone
contains a knot that triggers.
Nature pressed the button in my core wound.
Overwhelm, anxiety, and fear tremble through every organ
and sit on my chest.

Solar Plexus…
You are meant to radiate, yet you feel so unworthy
of the Sun shining on your own face.

Wounded Healer, please rise with the dawn!
Kill the pain by remembering your story.
Write your greatness over top
of the black and white lines with color.

The hate and the madness burn in my blood, but I create with
courage. Forgive their injustice and release the damage done.
Cellular release pours back into the grass and down into the womb
of the Earth.

I rewrite the story to build a new fate and claim my destiny.
I know my voice, my words and fated pen, can be
Chiron's gold key that sets the Samskara's free!

On a clear and bright day in 2018, I found out more about a particularly heinous past life spent with the same mother and father as in this life. I discovered this with the aid of my friend JoJo, a Reiki healer. She was able to assist my body in releasing the soul memory and trauma that I was going through. Suddenly, after showing her how to build a crystal medicine wheel on the land at Red Rocks Amphitheater in Morrison, Colorado, my head began to pulse and ache intensely. Out of nowhere, my heart raced and a trigger was pulled in my entire nervous system. At that moment, a mental impression was dying and desperately wanting to surface. Suddenly, my inner child felt a deep traumatic sensation that resonated and pulsed near my thymus in my soul!

I felt the 'samskara' rising to the surface of my skin and my blood felt hotter and hotter, wanting to be acknowledged and purged. As the heat pulsed through my body, my third eye illuminated a new awareness from a past-life where the wound originated in my sternum. I was in a lot of pain and it radiated into my skull, into an old head injury, which gave me a migraine. Even though I suffered with pain, I drove to a small park. Once we arrived, JoJo had me lay down on a blanket and laid her hands on me - or over me. I then saw a small boy, about three years old, next to me. He stretched out his arm and offered me an orange flower with his little hand.

The pain was bound up in my cells all the way from my right shoulder, liver, gallbladder, right ovary, hip, leg, ankle, and foot. I squirmed over the grass as JoJo guided me through the pain. She helped me to breathe and asked me, "Are you ready to let it go?" My resentment and anger said "NO." I was very resistant to forgiving my mom and dad. However, as I lay in the grass, I realized that my body would heal if I let go of my anger toward them.

Forgiving my family for the pain they inflicted was not easy, because my subconscious had been carrying this resentment since the 1800s! I felt sensations of metallic shackles around my ankles. I wanted to continue being angry with them.

During this past life in the 1800s, I was kept locked in an underground cellar. I was a handmaiden or slave girl to my mother, father, and Uncle Irwin in that life. My uncle raped me, and I conceived a boy child from him. The mother figure was a slave keeper. She kept me chained in a basement after the secret conception was revealed. When the boy was about three years old, he was killed and dismembered by Irwin. This explains why I never wanted to have children. I felt embarrassment and shame whenever I thought of having kids.

All my life, I have felt intense emotions when people ask me, "Where are you from?" This should be a normal question, but to me it is like the screeching sound of fingernails scratching against a chalkboard. My captors did not want anyone to know I had a child out of wedlock, or with the male slave owner. It was as though NO ONE wanted me to exist! I felt like no one liked me when I was growing up, because of this old story replaying in my consciousness. Henceforth, this is why I have a wound called "Chiron in Aries." I must heal the feeling that "I have no right to exist!" Finally, I found where the core wound came from.

This disgusting feeling has lessened a bit since the junk DNA and cellular memory have cleared out of my system. The event occurred near Savannah Georgia in the 1800s. Some of these memories had come into my mind in previous years, but only small pieces of what happened. The journey of being a wounded healer was not yet complete by just recalling those old memories. In 2018, I had to go visit my mother in Florida and confront her with our pattern of abusive power and domination. This lesson was about standing my ground. I had to stand my ground with her by being very present in my body. I told her that I had enough of her control and abuse.

While I visited, she even exhibited the same behaviors she had in the past life. Her home in Florida was locked up tight and she never gave me a key, which made me feel like she didn't trust me. She gave me the garage code 1492. "Columbus sailed the Ocean Blue," she would say, which further left me in disgust at her allegiance with imperialism and that old dominate and control matrix. She even had a metal device she used to bar the front door with. Everywhere I turned it felt as if I was being trapped inside, just like I was in the past life.

Unfortunately, this wound was so deep in my cellular memory that when I moved back to Boulder in 2021, the pain surfaced again. This time it was coming out of my sacral and root chakras and I had to re-enact the scenario of an abortion in that cellar room. Irwin came in while I was asleep and pushed my legs upward and must have had an instrument to kill the child with. The reason I am discussing this in great detail is because it took seeing at least eight practitioners over a ten-year period for me to be able to clear my chakras of that cellular memory.

This is something that no one taught me about Akashic Record healing. I had to go through painful releases throughout this 10-year period. Then I had the oddest experience. I was at my workplace and my spirit guides told me to put a pink calcite stone over my yoni and breathe deeply. I had to re-enact the abortion trauma once more to generate enough energy to get the final pieces out of my body forever! To this day, in my private practice I help women with transformational womb healing.

The Egyptian Ankh
Completion Lifetime Sedona, Arizona 2015

In 2015, I went to see Ray of Sedona, a seer and intuitive healer at the Crystal Magic store in West Sedona. He was instrumental in enlightening and widening my perspective of where I was going next in my expansion. For at least three appointments he helped me by reprogramming my body rhythms with Matrix Energetics and card readings. Once, he performed a 40-minute powerful channeled reading that informed me I have a "completion lifetime." Ray said because of my Scorpio North Node aspect, it was like I was fitting four lifetimes into this one! He pointed to one of the cards he was reading, which had the picture of an old sage on it. His eyes pierced into mine and he said, "NO ONE BECOMES A SAGE IN ONE LIFETIME - BUT **YOU** WILL!"

Imagine living a Piscean lifetime, where your soul recalls ALL the lifetimes you have ever lived. From the time I was seven years old, I knew I could embody many archetypes from artist, healer, filmmaker, to warrior priestess. However, it is important to note, I don't think total recall of every past life story is possible, though enlightenment is.

It makes sense why Sedona would give me this 'medicine' of being able to use the medicine wheel to further assist me in completing the contracts I have in this life and come full circle. One of the last phrases I remember my father saying to me was, "You should finish what you start." This was an eerie reminder, and his voice continued to echo in my brain even after he passed.

My initiation as a healer in Sedona went on for about three and a half years. During that time, I heard from a psychic, who told me that the ANKHs I was seeing were indicating that I was 'completing.' At times I would see scarabs as well. They reminded me of the power I was gaining in RE-membering who I am from my Egyptian lives.

Star Child Healing

Much of my descent into depression as a child involved blocking out everything I thought would hurt me. I was so adept at blocking life that I hardly remember my relationship with my sister. To this day I don't see clearly what caused the rift between us. Parents often take on the role of one who knows best, frequently the role of teacher. However, it is the old soul, disguised as a child, that comes in the form of a teacher.

I created ways to block life and close myself emotionally to the point that it hurt me into adulthood. At 41, I learned how to access what I was thinking and connect it to my speech. It is as if my heart and soul could not find the pathway to my voice. I imagine that my neural network had been cut during the times my mother told me to shut up or slammed doors in my face. How my mind operated was highly influenced by the fear and control mechanisms that my mother instilled in me.

Growing up, I never felt like I fit in with other children. I enjoyed movement and my mother enrolled me into gymnastics and dance classes in addition to public school courses. My inner wisdom knew that flexibility and symmetry of the body would be important throughout my life, even though I didn't consciously know why. I loved music, which helped me stay sane when my mother was around. I could spend hours after school listening to cassette tapes or the radio and exploring dance movements. Retreating into my silent bliss and remaining silent brought me closer to God.

On Sundays at the Jewish temple school, I felt the way I felt at my public school. I did not fit in and couldn't relate to others. I did not feel good learning about the Jewish religion, because it felt confining. My soul senses that the only real essential part of spirituality is to feel connected to God, without reliance on a structure. Feeling senses, extrasensory perceptions, or ecstatic states were more important to me than the finite details of dogma.

I had no patience or interest in learning Hebrew because it meant spending my weekends learning more in addition to my regular schoolwork. I did, however, feel a connection to God when I was in the Synagogue and singing in Hebrew. When the auditorium was filled with our young voices, I could feel God's presence. I could feel that there was an energy behind my back supporting me and at times could feel lower energies leaving my energetic body. I know that the Hebrew language has a fiery magic that can transmute feelings of unholiness through sound and vibration.

What caused me to rebel against learning at this reformed Jewish school was how my parents acted. They were not content with their middle-class lifestyle. On Sundays, when my father came with all of us to the Temple, our car rides back home seemed hours long. I heard my mom and dad laugh and cackle at the ostentation of people who showed up in their BMWs and fur coats. Being Jewish was always something I wanted to hide from kids at public school.

I know it was jealousy that made my parent's lives miserable. A turning point in my rebellion was when I absorbed something my dad said loudly on one of our drives home. He looked high up on a hill toward a large mansion and said, "It must be nice!" This became a constant phrase shared between my dad and mom. It was so unsettling that I decided then to rebel more.

I ignored them when they asked me to go through a coming-of-age ceremony like a bat mitzvah. I didn't even know what that was and they somehow assumed I did. I was busy in my imagination drowning out what they were teaching me in reform school. I stopped studying materials they gave me to read, all because of their attitude toward not having what they wanted. I thought that if this was religion, I wanted nothing to do with it.

It also caused disdain in myself about desiring wealth. In addition to feeling unworthy, I inadvertently programmed myself for failure in terms of acquiring wealth. Materialism is an institution I ultimately don't ascribe to, because I know in the end you cannot keep 'things.'

If my parents were not happy with their lives, then their religion could not be offering them any peace. I knew that following their example of obtaining material wealth for happiness would not work for me in my life. I continued to self-talk through my years as a teenager and beyond. Being 'different' or unique was what would fulfill me. Like the duality of a fighting fish, I battled myself as to how to handle being different while at the same time wanting to feel like I belonged in any social circle.

Mystical Poetry Rising
Columbus, Ohio 2002

When I finished college at the Columbus College of Art and Design in 1998, I found a new form of expression. I discovered open mic night at Victorian's Midnight Cafe and developed myself as a poet and performance artist. This required getting over my shyness and self-esteem issues by speaking on the microphone in front of my friends. The pivotal reality of this period was knowing that from then on, my voice would be instrumental in my healing. This provided tremendous growth in moving through my fears. I felt a new sense of myself, which expanded into infinity.

This feeling of the infinite and hearing my own voice on a microphone brought me to meet and activate my multidimensional self. All my life, I had quieted my voice just to avoid conflict and control in my family, so making it loud again took courage and a willingness to push my boundaries. As I wrote my poetry and heard my own voice aloud, I discovered that my multidimensional self was a 'cosmic woman' who transformed into many personalities. My subconscious found a new way to heal the fragmented schizophrenic parts of myself.

I created characters with costumes like "Freedom Eyes" and "Anarchy Rose." I was usually a one-woman act because it was an informal open mic. I always had a lot of pent-up frustration from working, but still not making enough money to support myself. I had a four-year college degree in Graphic Design that I was not able to use for reasons that I would understand later in life. Standing out from the crowd, companies, institutions etc. couldn't be right, even though my inner voice said it WAS right! During this time in my life, I found poetry as a way to recover from feeling like I failed at a Graphic Design career. Really, it took at least seven years to even remotely feel like I could forgive myself for my education being a waste of time.

Through performing poetry, I began to feel that I was more than just one person. I was Freedom Eyes, a sensitive gypsy girl with common sense, but no money. I was Anarchy Rose, the battered, exhausted, independent female who marches in the streets and protests the Iraq war. She works for the 'man' in art warehouses, painting plaid striped wallpaper. I had to conquer intense fear that would make me tremble when I got up to speak at the microphone. I needed to grow into a performer that could let the spoken word dance with 'Spirits' both good and bad.

As I amplified the energy of my characters and expressed myself, I would get so high that I entered ecstatic states. I created altered states but had no knowledge of grounding or protection from 'bad spirits.' I was subject to evil forces who would attach to my auric field and compromise the light around my body.

Sometimes I had out of body experiences just as I exited the stage. One time, when I got off the stage at Vic's, I saw myself from a higher perspective and standing on the ground in front of the stage, my Spirit re-entered my body. It was moments like this that I felt more alive and was entering a mystical realm. Performing on stage and being behind a mic put me closer to ecstatic states, which healed my soul.

At this point, I thought I finally met my 'tribe.' The people around me at Vic's were definitely a soul group, and I felt the connection in my heart and soul. For a couple of years, we all had what felt like a renaissance together. However, in 2007 I had to make a tough decision to leave my circle to maintain a more sober lifestyle.

The bohemian scene got heavy, from many of the artists and musicians using methamphetamines. This deeply saddened me, because I deliberately had to stop going to Victorians and stop being friends with them for a long while.

Tibetan Buddhist Retreat
Columbus, Ohio 2005

I retreated into my apartment space on Dennison Avenue, treating it like a Buddhist monastery and not having any friends over. I attended a Buddhist temple called Karma Thegsum Choling. Karma Kagyu, they told me, was a 'practice' lineage. I took refuge in a ceremony with this temple and made vows to the Three Jewels. I spent an incredible amount of time crying and purging my emotions at the temple.

Sometimes it was during talks from our teachers like Lama Kathy, or a traveling Rinpoche, sometimes it was during morning meditation or in Sadhanas where we read the transliteration of the Tibetan texts. These experiences enriched my belief in everyday magic. After going to some of the one-and-a-half hour long Tara Sadhanas, I had natural psychedelic experiences.

I felt more unique and powerful after chanting. The sounds I uttered in the Tibetan language created vibrations, which emanated ecstatic feelings. I felt more alive. More synchronistic experiences happened while I was going about my work week as well. The rituals at the Temple gave me more mind control. Chanting with a crystal mala allowed me to overcome obsessive thoughts. The completion of 108 mala beads is something I had difficulty with.

I received a "Green Tara Empowerment" while volunteering at the temple, which was very liberating and life changing. I felt even more connected to Green Tara as a personal protector. I still have the Carnelian stone crystal that mala gifted to me. I was able to use my Tara mantra practice to help cure my anxiety and battles with schizophrenia.

The experience of going to the Tibetan temple emphasized the kind of freedom I seek in my life. It is more than being free in relationships, but being free of karma, being free of wanting to be re-born on this Earth where there is so much suffering. During the teachings, the Karma Gagyu would often say, "All life is suffering." Looking back on it, I feel repeating the phrase "All life is suffering" is another bad program in my own psyche.

I have had conversations with people who don't believe that their actions/Karma have any effect on the world. Many people have an attitude that nothing matters. Yet I found while recovering my past life memories that even what I created in the past IS affecting me now.

During this three-year period, I spent most of my time alone. I worked for an agency helping disabled and autistic individuals for a while, which stretched my ability to have compassion for others who can't do everything they need to for themselves. Later, I started a house cleaning company called Karma Clean LLC. This allowed me a lot of time on the weekends to work on both my poetry and my performance art. I also got into making Silk Batik paintings and created my own art shows.

Still, I had trouble developing enough confidence to make a living as an artist, which was my ultimate dream. I was unable to connect with how to make money and put the correct value on the paintings I was creating, because I have a deep wound in this life around self-worth and self-confidence. My low self-esteem plagues me and is normally tied to financial strain.

While I developed my business Karma Clean LLC, I was able to work with a local business start-up group and save enough money for an Apple laptop. I hadn't owned a computer for a few years, and Macs were my favorite type. Soon after getting the laptop, I developed a dance and costume performance art group called Tribal Funk Shui. There were five members, embodying the five elements of Feng Shui. We performed for my friend Andrew's band at a CD release party for Mas Bagua.

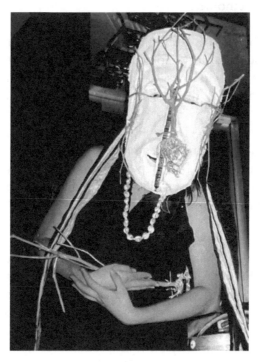

Serpentbird at Mas Bagua CD release party

PART TWO: THE WOLF SEEKS THE SERPENT

Lightning Strikes! Movies are Born
Columbus, Ohio 2005

During the creation of the Tribal Funk Shui group, I borrowed a video camera from my sister and a video transfer cable from my artist friend Matt. After the performance was filmed, I loaded the video onto the laptop using iMovie. While it loaded, my consciousness expanded with potent ideas and a new sense of myself flashed like a lightning bolt!

This unexpected breakthrough inspired a dream of becoming a filmmaker. I wanted to produce films that would help people to realize the beauty of nature and how man is destroying it. The theme of protecting the sacred poured out of me and became the basis of my life's work, which now in 2024 is being expressed through my Shamanic and group healing ceremonies.

The dream of becoming a filmmaker in that moment resonated louder than my previous goal in Graphic Design, because I knew that I could change people's consciousness on a wider scale. Right there in front of me on my desk were all the tools I needed, and community support was always available to me.

In 2005 I was successful, making good money from my cleaning business, and was able to move to a better apartment near Clintonville. I also found a way to buy an Apple Power Mac tower, giving me more storage space to create my art and films.

I met a woman named Amanda who agreed to work on a short film with me. I had a sense of what I wanted the story to be but had a difficult time explaining it. Gratefully, even though I couldn't express myself, she was open enough to follow my lead. All I knew was that I wanted to showcase the beauty of nature and have scenes in the film that showed our sensual nature.

When we were out in the forest, we filmed ideas that came to me as flashes of inspiration. The creation of the film flowed more like a river than any plan or storyboard could. Amanda was my muse because she was a dancer. I knew between the two of us we could create some amazing scenes. We went out to the local parks and filmed in nature when we were not working. This movie was my first attempt at creating a fictional dreamscape that would have the theme of women's empowerment and sensuality.

While we were filming one day in Yellow Springs, Ohio, a serpent slid up onto a large rock where I stood near the river. The six-foot-long brown and black non-poisonous fox snake moved over my bare foot! At that moment, instead of screaming, or reacting to the serpent like a damsel in distress, my higher intelligence told me to just follow the action with the camera. I filmed the serpent as it slid back into the water. I felt its soul spirit as benevolent and sweet, even though I was afraid of being bitten. I was able to follow him with the camera, focus and zoom in on it for a good while. It was this incident that inspired me to call the film "Creative Rituals and the Serpentbird." The experience I had making this film took my spirit to a place of transcendence. It solidified my passion for filmmaking because it contained so much natural beauty and magic.

One afternoon, I sat in an almost empty Hookah Lounge and scanned through the local magazine, Columbus Alive, to find a live band to go see. I vaguely remember someone mentioning a band, Mors Ontologica. That night Alexandre, a fiery Leo character, was working the door at the bar. Alexandre was also in a band that opened occasionally for Mors. The artistic synergy between me and Alexandre as we were completing my film "Creative Rituals and the Serpentbird," opened my heart to further expansion.

I began getting more and more stars in my eyes, and I received intuitive information about broadcasting my films behind the live bands in Columbus, because of my relationship with Alexandre. He had developed relationships with people at clubs and bars, which opened doors for me. He allowed me to show the movie at Skully's. My friends loved it, and as they watched, they could see the passion in my face, which was broadcast as large as a two stories high building on the film screen. I felt ALIVE!

For much of 2006, I filmed bands who played live in local bars. That year we saw the most amazing passionate and raw music. One sunny morning, we woke up on Clinton Street, and Alexandre exclaimed that we were going to make a movie! He inspired me to make a film about the Columbus music scene, which we had already began filming, but he wanted to see it on a larger scale. We easily filmed over 200 hours of live local Columbus bands, with interviews. But before I was able to get myself focused on finishing that film, I chose to apply to film school and leave Columbus.

In 2007, soon after watching the movie "The Secret," I got ballsy and borrowed enough money from the Sallie Mae loan company to attend The Los Angeles Film School program. From 2007 to 2008, it was my goal to finish the 11-month program. I was 32 years old, and I had a vision. I figured I could pay the money back when I was earning enough making films in LA. I thought that this career would be my last evolution, but I was VERY wrong!

Before Alexandre and I left Columbus, we had a yard sale to sell off our stuff so we could move to L.A. The rest of the story is a blur because I had a burning desire to live an important and artistic life in LA. At that time, I had a fairly new car and I was ready to DRIVE! We loaded up our belongings, tucking the large shoe boxes filled with the music documentary tapes under the seats in the car to protect them from the heat. I drove fast and furiously until we reached New Mexico, when I pulled over in Cimarron with driver's fatigue.

All I remember were the eerie run-down buildings of this ghost town as we passed through, but we parked when my eyes grew heavy with the pain of exhaustion. There were miles and miles of sage bushes all around us. Sage, sage, sage, the scent wafted into our noses and intoxicated my sleepy Pisces mind into a dream of a lifetime. I remember the texture of the seat belt cutting sharply across my neck, but the sage bush smells dominated my will to stay awake and lulled me into psychedelic dreamtime.

I kicked my seat back and slept. The Dreamtime produced larger than life technicolor visions of my movies floating on moving planes in my inner brain. Movie screens came down from the sky and floated like flags waving in the winds of the painted western desert. The visions were mainly colors, but had faces of old Native chiefs, perhaps Grandfathers, and large swirling eagles melting together high above the plains. When you are 33, you shake it off in the morning with disbelief and forget once again that ANYTHING is possible, while you hit the gas and drive off to Hollywood.

Film School Nightmare
Los Angeles, California 2006

When Alexandre and I arrived in Los Angeles, we rented a Public Storage bin and shoved my unfinished documentary tapes inside the air-cooled unit. I drove in circles around Hollywood until we found a hotel - stocked with bed bugs - to sleep in. The nightmare of being bit and left with bloody scabs on our skin just to afford the rent will stay with me forever. Regardless, we were both happy to make it out of Ohio and the comfort zones we had created in a small town. And we knew the bedbug saga was temporary.

We stayed at the Hollywood hotel for a week while I worked with the school to get the loan money to come through. I kept visualizing walking up the stairs to our new apartment with suitcases and setting them inside the door. We landed our dream apartment near Sunset Drive, which was walking distance to The Los Angeles Film School.

Ultimately, my goal was to save the planet from ecocide and destruction by making environmental documentaries. What I found in L.A. wasn't the harsh reality of Hollywood, but the evil film school itself. It was in the haunted old MCA records building on Sunset Blvd. A husband-and-wife team of lawyers had bought the building and started the school. The reality was, I felt lost again because I was conforming to an institution that didn't want to hear my voice. However, nothing would ever "happen for me" until I conquered my unresolved self-esteem issues at the core.

From the first time I entered the classroom, I was swallowed whole by students who wanted to make horror films and A-list Hollywood pictures. Teachers showed us hours and hours of films that were 'supposed' to teach us something.

Whenever people asked me what I wanted to do, I told them I wanted to make environmental documentaries. They laughed at me. I could hardly believe they didn't understand me. They passed a microphone around during the first week of school in the theater auditorium. When the microphone came to me, my voice trembled, but underneath, I knew I was strong. The response I got from the students and teachers was that women from Ohio should keep their opinions on reality to themselves.

This was obviously before environmental documentaries became widely produced.

During my enrollment at LAFS, I had ambitions to triple major in Cinematography, Editing, and Sound Design. It gave me a full load of classes that ran from 8am to 8pm each day. I had borrowed enough money to live on, which meant I had the luxury of going to as many classes as I could. Many of my peers told me I had to focus on one major, but I was too enticed by all the tools at my disposal. The excitement and power I felt holding a camera as well as being able to use edit bays for storytelling was something I was already doing back in Ohio. Why not add in sound design?

My idea was to work for a paycheck as an editor and use my spare time to work on my own documentaries. As time passed within the program, I isolated myself from other relationships. The teachers at the school often suggested that we had conflict within the student body. I found the MCA records building to be filled with ghosts and evil discarnate spirits and I was attacked frequently by demonic forces. Each day I found myself wearing more and more black clothes. I reverted to dressing like a 'Goth Chic' to hide myself from my environment.

Alexandre was indulging in alcoholic binges, which made me very depressed. Unbeknownst to me, he would leave the apartment late at night when I was asleep and play harmonica tunes on Hollywood boulevard to drink and flirt with women.

Jesus in Los Angeles
California 2006

Eight months into my film school program, I woke up in bed feeling crushed by the energy around me and through my body. I consulted a female psychic named Lee, who convinced me that my family had a curse and my money was cursed as well. She convinced me to jeopardize my finances. She told me to take out my student loan money, so she could cleanse it in a mirror-lined pyramid. I was so afraid of losing what love there was between me and Alexandre that I was easily brainwashed by this psychic. It helped that I was very young and naive, so was swayed by what she told me to do.

One of my visits with Lee, though manipulative and deceptive, simultaneously brought me to a new understanding. She would hold my hands in a kind and gentle way and call upon Jesus for my healing. This was something I would not have been able to deal with in the past, because of my upbringing. I was afraid to pray to Jesus, but I had to be open to anything that brought me out of the darkness. I had never thought that this Jewish girl would break down a barrier to Jesus in a tangible way. As Lee prayed and held my hands in her soft hands, I knew he was there because I could feel the static electricity in my energy field and I was enveloped in healing white light.

As her warm hands held mine, I knew that Jesus was with us in her reading room. This was a big awakening for me in accepting Jesus into my heart and my life! I needed his father-like presence because it brought me acceptance from a male father figure that I had never felt before.

One afternoon, Alexandre offered me a cannabis cookie. After I ate it, I laid down in bed, and he left the apartment. I felt my whole body being shattered and broken into millions of pieces. My eyes opened to the ceiling, and I gasped and cried to God himself. I thought, "Wow! I am in huuuuuuge trouble!" I asked God, "How can I get out of my mess?" He energetically found me and connected with white light, but the light was broken in striations like layers of rock. My body shook and filled with fear, grief, sadness, and pain. I knew that I had to make changes, but I didn't know how. I was in the eighth month of school but once I reconnected with God, I felt very different about being there.

During this time, I felt the planets moving and stirring my soul toward a new awakening. I was sitting in a room with the students watching a horror movie, but I couldn't watch the scenes they were showing because it affected me too deeply on an emotional level.

I had a magazine with me, called Topanga Magazine, which I pulled out of my book bag. I read an article about a woman who went on a vision quest to Hopiland, Arizona. After I read it, I tuned out what was happening in the classroom. I knew the only way to get out of this mess called Film School was to quit! I recognized in my soul that if I did not give way to my own expansion as a spiritual soul immediately, I would be even more overcome with the dark forces that the school was perpetuating.

While the horror movie played on, I had feelings of déjà vu and dark magic around me, especially since they kept showing us the same scenes over and over again. In fact, I started thinking about what they were charging per credit hour for me to watch this crap. It broke down to about $90 bucks per class. I wasn't going to continue watching a horror movie that the instructor claimed was teaching us which lenses were being used. When each shot changed, he would say in a hipster slack way, "Oh yeah, that was an 80mm lens."

I knew that the only way to reclaim my sanity and safety was to climb into the pages of this magazine. The holy grail of an article in this spiritual based magazine was called, "The Hopi-Tibetan Connection." As the article explained, the Hopi and the Tibetans are brothers. This resonated with me, because I had studied Tibetan Buddhism for two years in Ohio and had healed myself in profound ways with their Tara prayers.

I knew my soul was calling me to the desert, to do exactly what this woman did and find Grandfather Martin. Grandfather spoke about "Prophecy Rock," which led me to believe that he may have more insight into how to bring humanity closer to a new time of peace. Many people had sought him out and interviewed him on YouTube as well.

However, my burning question had more to do with how I could prepare myself and humanity for the shift that was to come in 2012. I also wanted to know…Who are the rainbow warriors?

The adventure to find the answers to my burning questions wouldn't be fully solved, answered, understood, and digested until I could write it all in the pages of this memoir. It was about more than getting answers, it was about listening to the land and being my natural self, trusting the Rainbow-Light-Warrior within.

I had much to accomplish during this phase of my life, including separating from Alexandre. However, he sabotaged himself. He threw my bicycle over the railing of my two-story apartment and as soon as he did that, my whole body experienced shockwaves of pain and release all at the same time. All I could think about was how would I get to my job without this bike? I went down and pulled my bike back up into the house. The handlebars had been slightly damaged and curled up around the frame. Alexandre and I fought physically with our bodies against the bedroom wall. I called the police because he had been on a rampage and throwing my bike over the railing was the last straw. Two strong women cops came in response. I stood in the kitchen while they held him down in the bedroom. They searched through the drawers of the apartment and cockroaches the size of a toaster ran out and up the walls.

The policewoman gasped for a moment and told me I should get rid of the roaches. All I could tell them was that Alexandre was drunk, verbally abusive, and tried to ruin my bike, which was all I had for transportation. I showed them the huge 20-gallon trash bag next to the stove that was full of empty liquor bottles of varying size. They met him in the bedroom as he yelled profanities and then restrained him, handcuffed him, and took him to jail. Soon after, I filed a restraining order.

I was still consulting Lee the psychic, who told me to meditate twice a day. I had to begin the process of getting a restraining order, which required me to get up at 5:00 am so I would make it downtown to the courthouse when they opened. After the restraining order was filed, I had to call a phone number that connected me to the county jail frequently, so I would know when Alexandre was to be released and when he might come to pick up his belongings.

Once he had been released from jail and came to get his belongings, I could kind of relax. Later, however, I found out he was staying with friends nearby and was spying on me.

After I quit school, I focused on getting a job and landed an internship and a job working for a tape duplication company in Burbank. It gave me a sense of freedom because I could drive their company car. The company consisted mostly of men, but I made myself fit for the part, because I could already drive a stick shift vehicle. I figured perhaps I could find a way to get a better job editing video, but unfortunately it never led to anything and every time I delivered a tape, I felt inadequate and unable to find the right introductions.

I had already sold my car, so I rode a bike for 10 or more miles every day all around LA. I even decided to go get counseling so I could understand my pattern of being attracted to men who were not able to care for themselves.

I spent a lot of time meditating on the upcoming journey to Hopiland and used the law of attraction to prepare me for what I wanted to experience. I posted a map of Arizona on the wall of my Hollywood kitchen next to my juicer and blender. Every time I made a smoothie, I studied the roads to the Third Mesa. Every day I would stand in the corner between the kitchen sink, the map on the wall, and my blender to bask in a strong vision of expansion and growth.

The journey out of Los Angeles began with a deep cleanse on all levels. I knew that if I didn't cleanse my insides, my external environment would swallow me whole. As I cleansed my body-temple, my thoughts were easier to control. Every time I had a fearful thought, I replaced it with a positive one, or just mentally stopped the thought in mid-stream.

Later, I realized that being on a strict diet of only green living raw vegetables and weeds was the right thing to do before embarking on a vision quest. I found a raw food group in Long Beach through Meetup.com for support on my raw food journey. The first event that inspired me to make the commitment was a class taught by Matt Monarch. Matt had been touring the USA in his minivan, giving talks, and selling his books and superfoods. He mentioned during his talk how he weaned himself off cooked food over time. He also explained that by not eating cooked food, he had many spiritual dreams.

The night after his class, I quit eating cooked food and had an established goal to be on a raw vegan diet for two months. I volunteered in another class, with a woman named Dianna, who taught classes in making gourmet raw vegan foods. This way I had support, new friends and new recipes that inspired me.

Jesus, "Star" of Hollywood
California 2008

Once I began cleansing my body with higher vibrational raw food, I had many spiritual dreams. One morning at four a.m., a bright light beamed through my bedroom window and straight through my crown chakra to my throat and heart. The light was no ordinary light. When my higher self was awake and my lower self was asleep, I could see this light was being broadcast by Jesus! I knew it was him when he spoke to me, much like a father, and clearly said, "I love you, Lori."

The light that descended upon me broke into thousands of pieces until it made a mandala. The mandala was round but had multitudes of five pointed stars, like a snowflake. The light-beam that was enlivening my top three chakras poured through me, and it expanded my body as if tethered to Jesus and his light-body.

A new seed of faith in Jesus planted itself firmly in my heart for my journey through a very dark time. Until that day, I had never known that Jesus could find me and support me, without me asking him! Yet, when he showed up and spoke to me, I knew exactly who he was. I believe my whole experience of being in Los Angeles led me to know Jesus. The darkness of my surroundings and choices forced me to delve deeper into my inner spiritual strength.

As I look back at all the times Jesus has been with me in times of transition, I feel a warmth that I never experienced in my family life. The encouragement he brings me gives me strength and support to keep going. It is a great honor to be visited by such a presence. He may always be by our side, but it takes a sense of attunement and listening to receive it. What a relief it was to have met him and make a deep connection.

I know it seems silly, but as a child I always felt left out amongst my peers in High School when Christmas arrived. In the Jewish family home I grew up in, the word Christmas and the name Jesus were scoffed and laughed at. I knew my parents weren't seeing the bigger picture. Later, when I moved to New Mexico, I found myself only ordering the 'Christmas' option for my burritos. What a celebration to welcome this new feeling of joy in having a real relationship with this master teacher.

You might wonder, "What is a Mystical Experience?" The story of being visited unexpectedly by Jesus was, in my opinion, a mystical experience - one that I want all humans on Earth to have. Even 'believers' I have met may not have had a mystical experience. I find this to be sad and even disturbing at times. Through my work as a healer and a ceremonialist, I am here to support our re-connections with the mystical. My definition of a mystical experience:

"A mystical experience combines a surprise happening and a synchronicity with a being of a higher order, frequency, and vibration. The experience creates awe and inspiration to aid the aspirant in knowing Divine Light on Earth is real."

Shamanka-Pisces, the L.A. Shaman
Woman Warrior at a Rebirth - Death point, California 2008

To handle the crisis of leaving the L.A. film school, I created a new name for myself. I wanted to become someone bigger than "Lori" that embodied the spirit of shamanism. Shamanka-Pisces was the alter-ego I created to rise above my current reality. This name helped me to manifest my rebirth as I was letting my old self die.

While walking around the streets of Hollywood near my apartment, I found some ugly, used brown sunglasses that had large shades. When I wore them, I looked otherworldly and much like an insect. When I put the sunglasses on, it became a shape-shifting ritual that promoted being in the NOW. As I became this urban shaman, I told myself to release fear and grow beyond it. As a result, I was able to stay in a vibration of joy, which was hard to maintain the entire time I lived in L.A.

My exit plan required me to propel myself straight out of L.A. as quickly and drama-free as possible. There were many stages of preparation to go through, which in my mind couldn't happen quickly enough. This technique brought my personality to a new height, and I felt relieved that my old self, resorting to fear, faded away and split off each time I wore the glasses.

During the summer of 2008, I tried making one last attempt to build myself up in Hollywood. After I quit the school, I called a company to see if I could work for them as an intern so that I could experience what a real-world editing company was like. I found that, yet again, my knowledge of editing software was not enough to get hired on as a paid intern. I found that the "fake it 'til you make it" attitude, along with working late nights, was how most folks made it to a dreamy desk job.

When I worked for the tape delivery service in Burbank, I was a delivery driver and was sent all over the L.A. area. I felt that surely these experiences would someday get me 'somewhere.' I was wrong.

I took enormous deep breaths as I rode my bicycle up Cahuenga Rd. to Burbank each morning. While swallowing deep breaths, I saw a Mack truck with a huge green cartoon Turtle painted on side, which inspired this poem...

Turtle Vision, Turtle Integration

The Ancestors gave me THE TURTLE.

As I hit the grey pavement,
I see the semi-truck with the big turtle drive past.
Huge and in living green colors,
the big rig passes and my mind brings answers.

My two bicycle wheels, my legs, pedaling Cahuenga Street.
I can choose to slow down, by softly thinking,
"They gave me the turtle."
Slowdown medicine for earthing.

Gift medicine for upward climbs and much needed stamina.
Slowdown Street.
I am small. I am smaller with longer legs, and longer breaths.
Taking time away from the game of time.

Aaaaaah, Breathe, little starling.
She makes the finish line, right where I am.

Each day, I returned to my home in Hollywood from Burbank by bus. Slowly, I got in better physical shape while riding my bike to work and back. When I decided to go to Arizona and created my exit strategy from Los Angeles, I made many pacts with myself. One of the strictest was to do a cleanse on raw foods, which meant eating fresh vegan food. Not only that, but I decided I would only eat foods that were green in color, with nuts and tomatoes being the exceptions. I incorporated cactus, aloe, and wild weeds like dandelion, purslane, and marshmallow leaves. The other pact I made with myself was to exercise intensely every day to prepare for rides through the desert.

The bike rides to Burbank were about six mostly uphill miles, and six miles downhill back to Hollywood. This was not a small feat, because I was out of shape and 20 pounds overweight in my opinion. As the summer moved along, I built strength and regained my beauty. I lost at least 20 pounds, and was almost too thin, but my heightened awareness and clairvoyant abilities thrived.

The Rainbow Phone
Burbank, California 2008

In 2008, while working in Burbank, I had a Samsung flip phone with a yummy plastic rainbow case. When I was planning the trip to Arizona, as a challenge I decided to make the trip without a cell phone and only take my MacBook Pro laptop. I planned to use other people's phones to save on cost and plainly as a way to meet an odd challenge. I could use my computer to post blogs to my live journal account.

One night, I left work and rested on a bus stop bench. I made a phone call to Pamela, while I could hear Angels whispering in my ear. Somehow, while balancing my bicycle in one hand, I left my phone on the bench when I boarded the bus back to Hollywood. At my stop, I got off the bus and as I walked with my bike back home, I realized the phone was GONE! I immediately tried not to panic. Instead, I broke out my Carnelian Mala and chanted Tara Mantras.

My mind went through many scenarios of what I could do, but my higher self told me to stay present in the moment. Eight or so excruciating minutes went by before the next bus arrived. I saw the digital banner at the top of the bus and it swung hard left. A window rolled down. One of the Hispanic guys recognized me from the usual evening route, smiled, and handed back my phone with the rainbow case! It was unbelievable! I attributed this good fortune to having said the prayers to Tara.

I Must Leave Los Angeles!
California 2008

When it was time to leave L.A., I clearly remember the emotional day of moving everything I owned out of the apartment and into the trash. Everything I owned was reduced to a backpack and two small bicycle pannier bags. I tried pretending that the bike leaning against the apartment wall was really a temple shrine with a bench. This is where I made my final offerings before "dying" to my old self.

Nopale Cactus Love
Nopale lovers stare at
ten hour's worth of thorns.

Green paddles glow with L.A. sunlight
burning down upon
ten thousand
city blocks of graffiti cactus.

Graphic sweetness, graphic bite.
Opuntia has pink fleshy kisses in her fruits.
Only if you can find opportunity
in between her pointed needles.

Oh, sweet Nopale...
you will never listen.
Oh, your touch is torture, and final.

No Nopale had a lover who made it out alive.
Yes, I will eat you again.

Freedom, Train, Bike
Los Angeles to Flagstaff, 2008

Departing L.A. was not easy. With my bike heavily loaded, I rode away from my apartment. It took several city trains to reach the AMTRAK station. The character Shamanka-Pisces made this flow much easier, and I used her persona and the magical glasses to persevere through the long, arduous journeys.

Upon arriving at Union Station very, very high on shots of espresso, I almost left my magical brown sunglasses at the ticket counter. The grand hallways were beautiful, with architecture of terra cotta and marble that shined. It was as if I skated over the floors partially disconnected from my body with the help of caffeine. The majesty of this rare historical building symbolized my rebirth/exit. It was breathtaking and life-giving with the promise of light in my life after being filled with so much pain and loss and disappointment in Los Angeles.

I was very nervous packing the bicycle box and sealing with the final tape. "There is always a chance you'll never see her again," I thought to myself after handing my 'Black Beauty' over to Amtrak. I departed Los Angeles on September 7th, 2008, on an Amtrak train, and arrived 12 hours later in Flagstaff, Arizona. The thrill of the ride on this train sent butterflies from my womb to my heart and throat, creating mind orgasms in sunrays from sunset to sunrise.

During my preparation stage at the Hollywood apartment, I researched many things about packing up the bike for the train trip. I found a place in Downtown L.A. called the Bike Kitchen. I learned how to pack the bicycle in a bike box before the trip and get everything I needed to the station. There were essential tools I needed, such as a pedal tool, bike pannier bags, and flat-resistant tires called Armadillos. I had to have these tires, because there is a thorny weed called Goat's Head that maliciously grows in the desert and is notorious for popping bike tubes.

The ride on Southwest Chief was exhilarating since I love trains! I love the rawness of their appearance with brown and orange rust colors, I love their industrial screaming wheels and sparks. The sound of the train echoes the sounds of the punk rock music I missed dearly in Columbus, Ohio.

I boarded the passenger train in the evening and sat next to a young woman who shared with me that she had just completed a retreat. She was a firm believer in Jesus Christ, and I felt very lucky that the universe paired me up with her for my trip. Even more than that, I knew I was on a spiritual quest.

I slept sitting upright in a leather seat for the remainder of the 11-hour trip. When I arrived in Flagstaff, I claimed my bike from the station and then realized I left my helmet behind on the train! That night I slept hobo-style in the soft damp grass in the park by the train station.

The whole idea of being free had settled into my system. At every moment I continued to be willing to transform myself by rejecting the norms that culture had handed me, not just for survival but for freedom itself. When I woke in the morning, I took out my Zoom H4 audio recorder and made a recording of a song with the screaming sound of the train built into it.

I went to the historic coffee shop Macy's in Flagstaff and found some hosts for travel on www.couchsurfing.org. I was awestruck in Macy's because the owner, an amazing photographer, has life-size portrait photos all over the walls of the cafe. The rocket-fuel grade espresso they served continued enhancing my feelings of freedom.

I planned to volunteer at the Raw Spirit Festival in Sedona, but I had about four days or so before I could pick up the festival van at the car rental place. I couch-surfed with some wonderful hippy girls at a farmhouse near the coffee shop. I enjoyed my new freedom of being off the clock of a 'regular job. I met a 50- something year old man near Macy's Cafe, who went bike riding with me and gave me an amazing army backpack. I originally had a smaller bag, but all my things could fit in this one better. I named the green army bag The Turtle.

The Turtle, like my brown sunglasses, became another method that helped me stay grounded. When fears crept in about feeling homeless, I saw and felt this bag as my home. I kept my focus as much as possible on eating raw foods, but I couldn't resist the amazing giant-sized mocha lattes made at Macy's Cafe. My body was clean from what I had done prior, but the espresso made me so high I couldn't stay grounded and eventually gave me some episodes of emotion I could hardly control.

When the day came to pick up the festival van in Flag, I loaded up my bike, most likely high as a kite on caffeine, and headed down 89A to Sedona for the first time in this life. As I drove down winding hills through the fir trees, I was overwhelmed with beauty whenever there were openings between the trees. Suddenly red rocks towered before my eyes. The power and the depth of these red canyon walls were nothing I had ever seen. Orange/red is my favorite color spectrum and seeing these opened my heart even further.

When I arrived at the Poco Diablo resort, where the Raw Spirit Fest would be, I parked the van. I was shown where to camp, next to Oak Creek on sparkling white sand. There were red volcanic rocks here and it was a wild and free environment where the festival volunteers felt free to bathe in the nude and sunbathe out on the rocks.

Sedona's Gift: The Medicine Wheel Vision
The Encoded Energy Packet, September 12th, 2008

It was during this special time in my life that Sedona herself spoke to me etherically on native Yavapai land. I could clairaudiently hear what she was saying. It was spoken more in a concept or energetic packet and I decoded this message with my higher self. *It took me years to recognize the gift and depth of meaning Sedona bestowed.* **My soul was destined to connect with Sedona's soul and it would take me the next 10 years to bring this lost knowledge back to humanity.** *She told me to learn about the medicine wheel.*

Before visiting Sedona, my soul or higher self already knew I was being called to the medicine wheels. I had seen pictures on tourist websites, but no one I met seemed to know where they were, or what was done with them! The practice of meditation in medicine wheels was a two-year search for a lost art. It was a medicine that I was hunting for subconsciously. This medicine was hunting for me!

I tried walking around Sedona, but there was a lot of construction on the roads and I couldn't easily find my way out of the Poco Diablo grounds. I was overwhelmed with the vast megalithic red rocks that towered above me. I was intrigued by the idea of the medicine wheel. I didn't know where to find one, yet knew they must be close by since I had seen aerial photos of them on the internet.

Biking or walking was not possible while the road was being widened on the 89A, because cars were tearing by quickly on exposed dirt roads. However, an opportunity quickly arrived to go into town with Carl. He asked if I wanted to help him and a few dudes pick prickly pears, which were in season in September. This gave me the ability to see the way the road unfolded from Poco to the center of town, and I might possibly spot a sacred medicine wheel on the way.

I piled into the truck with Carl, who I met through Katrina. I had to squish my ass on the seat between the door of the truck and two other guys. I was very disoriented because I had never been to Sedona and all the roads wound in circles around the Megaliths, producing a surrealistic reality. When we neared the destination, we passed the UFO Diner. A short way down Inspirational Drive, we arrived at a field with a huge crop of ripe, hot, pink, fleshy prickly pears. Carl gave us gloves and needle nosed pliers to pull them away from the cactus paddles, but we still got pricked frequently.

Being on a journey to Sedona and in the lands of the west required me to be open to new levels of faith. This meant taking a pause and being willing to change my plans quickly, to be open to new experiences.

While volunteering at the Raw Spirit festival, I met Katrina Blair of Turtle Lake Retreat Center in Colorado. She was the most real, down-to-earth and heart centered medicine woman at the festival. She gave some talks about wild foods and foraging in the pop-up domes. At Katrina's display table, I was intrigued by a stationary bicycle. It was rigged up with a blender so when the Turtle Lake kids got on, it churned up the prickly pears. The prickly pears were hot pink fruits that they made into high vibe juice. I bought some of their chocolate peppermint and magic bars and met her crew, feeling I needed to spend more time with them. She was surrounded by a curious bunch of from a heart-centered Tribe.

When I examined the labels closely, at first I thought it said CA, but it said CO. I knew there was no way I wanted to go back to California and being in Colorado was not on my original plan to go to Hopiland. I had to decide on a direction to go after the festival was over. I paused for a while, sitting in stillness on an old wooden rocking chair in the Poco Diablo hotel waiting area. I sat there halfway frozen in wonder. My small mind could only grasp that my heart was calling me to Colorado to be with these people, to continue feeling connected to them. My mind kept interfering with the order of things, which was vacillating between Hopiland and a spontaneous re-routing.

While saying goodbye to the amazing beauty of the red rocks, I wondered if I would I ever make it back to Sedona.

Durango, Colorado Bound
2008

I decided to take Carl's offer to ride with him back to Durango, Colorado, because I knew I needed to spend more time with Katrina Blair. This was an adventure inside of an adventure, which sometimes felt difficult to endure. I saw the most beautiful sunsets and sunflowers growing and glowing beside the Painted Desert highways as we sped past. Carl told me he was a triple Gemini, which meant he loved to speak non-stop. Sometimes he spoke so much I had to tune him out and stare at the landscapes instead.

When we arrived in Durango, I was introduced to many other wonderful people who welcomed me. I spent a week at the Turtle Lake Kitchen, helping out by preparing raw foods. When it was time to sleep I had nowhere to go, so slept in my sleeping bag in the alley. Once, the cops came at 1:00 am and checked on me. I didn't know whether I was in trouble or not, so told him I would just be there for one night. I had a hard time telling Katrina that I needed a place to sleep, which created an unsettled energy between us.

After I acclimated a bit to Durango, I wandered through the streets and into a local coffee joint, going through to their back porch room. It was there that I heard the most soulful, beautiful singing voice I had ever heard in my life. Once they finished their song, I introduced myself and asked if I could film them. Renee and Adam were a couple of young musicians, living beneath the radar of society. They lived in a huge tent up on the mountain hidden from sight. To my surprise, they had an enormous library of books in this tent. Renee read books to Adam late into the night with their big dog Bear beside them. I had plenty of time to ride my bike along the beautiful hills and roads of the town. I stayed in decent shape, but I was not as strong as when I was riding about 15 miles a day in Los Angeles. It was time for me to go see the Hopi grandfather, but I felt my courage waning.

Hopi & Navajo Rez

Black Beauty Rides! 🚲 *9/30/08 - Farmington, New Mexico*

Author's Note: The chapters subtitled Black Beauty Rides were handwritten dialogues of adventures riding my bicycle on a few Native Reservations. This was my first experience in this lifetime being on Native Reservations. The writings were originally penned on 8.5 x 11 paper that was folded in three columns. The data was later transcribed to my LiveJournal account at the Dine College computer lab in Dennehotso, Arizona. I traveled without my laptop to avoid any weather damage and to lighten the load on my back. My journal entries were written through my character Shamanka-Pisces, giving it a gangster punk vibe.

I asked Kyle from the Turtle Lake retreat center to ride out from Durango with me on his bike. At first, he was hesitant, seeming to weigh out the pros and cons. He said he had experience going to Hopiland, but it had been a long time. The look in his eyes had a heavy impact on me. His head hung down, as if he was revisiting an aspect of his soul that he hadn't seen in a long time.

Leaving Durango was sad for me because the Turtle Lake folks felt like my soul family. Leaving them made my stomach uneasy with the fear of not having the security of people I could call on for help. I also had to leave behind my laptop and my phone, because a bike tour requires being fully in touch with rainstorms!

The first town Kyle and I stopped at was Farmington, N.M., which was 40 miles away and roughly three and a half hours on the bikes. We visited some Indian ruins in Aztec. Kyle and Carl asked the attendant at the ruins to let us in without paying admission. Magically, she offered to let us in for free, but only if we did not mention it to anyone. She clicked a counting device that denotes how many people visited the ruins each day.

I sat in the different stone rooms and Kivas alone and away from the guys. The Aztec energy was certainly the most alien and cosmic energy I had ever experienced in meditation. I felt bombarded with orbs and sparkling lights. It was difficult to process what I was feeling in those moments. I knew it was important to feel what was happening, yet at the same time I resisted going too deep into the meditation, because I almost felt I would be consumed by it, which made me feel like it would be impossible to return to this reality.

After leaving Aztec, we went back to Farmington to spend more time with Carl and his mom Cleo. I knew the next stage of our tour was going to be epic, as we headed into Navajo land.

The next morning, September 30th, 2008, at 7:00 am I woke up to toast and chokecherry jam. We had coffee with cream and honey for fixins. Kyle needed to adjust his bike tires and told me about putting the valve facing the top away from me when changing a flat. He really wanted to share his bike mechanical knowledge but got a power trip over it. He also wanted to fix his disk brakes, which required riding to another bike shop.

I was growing anxious and impatient waiting for him because I just wanted to be on the road biking. In the meantime, I headed over to a coffee shop and bookstore. They didn't have too many books, but they did have good food. I bought a coffee and a bagel but felt tired after consuming it. I had to go to another spot down the street to access the internet, and we finally hit the road around noon. My impatience didn't end then because he kept wanting to stop! We went to a grocery and then to a Wal-Mart to find deionized water so he could fill all his water bottles. I told him we should stop looking for this type of water.

Later down the road, Kyle discovered he left his wallet at the Walmart. He freaked out for a while because Katrina had just paid him money and he had several hundred dollars in it. I wasn't worried for myself, even though I only had 600 dollars to my name for my entire journey. I was concerned for Kyle about losing his wallet and didn't know then that journeying through Hopiland and Colorado it would be about six months before I'd be working again. I trusted God and the kindness of strangers during my pilgrimage.

For once in my life, I wanted to practice receiving more than giving and relied on Spirit and God for abundance. After the long period of heartache and loss in Los Angeles, that is all the money I had saved. In the spirit of receiving, I used this autumn bike tour as a harvest time!

Down the road, Kyle thought he spotted an apple orchard. I could see a huge fence full of grapes of every color against it. We stopped after we coasted down a big hill and Kyle decided to ask the owner of the orchard if we could look around and take some apples. The owner said sure, we could pick fruit but told us they didn't get apples that year. So we tried their varieties of grapes - Niagara, purple, and red. I pulled off each kind to try them and stuck some grape leaves in my bag to consume later. I rolled some of the grapes in the leaves and ate them like a grape taco.

A while later, I ate a raw zucchini that Cleo had given me. It was sweet and sooooo good. When Kyle stopped to buy some "Kneel Down Bread" from the local Navajos, I kept on riding. This was when he realized he lost his wallet and when we stopped in Shiprock, he told me about it. I was pissed, because at this point, here and there it seemed he wanted to provide for me when he could. He also said he didn't 'believe' in money, so it really wasn't a big deal to him that he lost the money and the wallet.

Then he asked if I wanted to stop for lunch. I took this to mean "You are buying." So, I submitted to buying a foot long Subway chicken sandwich.

There was a lot of tension between us now, because he judged me for veering off the vegan diet. I was not only eating meat at this point, but the bread too! I was thinking I wanted to be prepared for the next leg of our journey into the desert but also binged on chips. Wow, what a sin it was to eat Jalapeno flavored chips and Doritos! I told him if he wanted to eat some of the sandwich he could, but when he found out about the cheese, let alone the chicken, he scoffed at me. What a priss. He ate his dehydrated apple chips in the sunshine outside the Subway restaurant, which overlooked the highway where semi-trucks were flying by. "This guy ain't going to make it on just dried apple chips!" I thought to myself.

I was losing patience more and more. We headed out again, but I was slower than ever on the bike, feeling bloated from the bread. We had been eating vegan and raw meals, so my belly wasn't used to it. I wanted to escape the previous confines of our diet, because I felt so free on the open road! Instead of feeling abundant, I often played the role of a scavenger.

Grand Entry into the Navajo Reservation

Black Beauty Rides! 🚲 *9/30/08*

As I rode my bike, the giant orange ball of sun on the horizon was my point of focus. I watched the yummy orange light drip down onto the desert sand and melt over the whole landscape. Everywhere I looked, there were discarded beer cans and glass on the roads. We headed out of Shiprock and into the Navajo Reservation. Kyle disappeared completely. We met up where the turn joined onto State Route 13. He was with a group of people who had camper vans, and they were packing up whatever they had been selling that day.

Kyle asked if I wanted to take a break. I said "Yes," but ended up passing out completely and went into a dream state. Just as I was slipping into deep sleep, he woke me up. This was very annoying! I tried to bike more, but with my stomach so full of bread, I could hardly ride. On only the second day of riding, I was losing my mind. Then I got my Tibetan Mala out, a rosary with 108 beads, and prayed Tara mantras. I had to wear the beads, rather than hang them over the handlebars, to avoid breaking them.

Experiencing fear and fatigue, I gave up and walked my bike deliriously into the sunset and desert sand.

Kyle found me sitting, doing nothing after a long round of prayers. My body froze. He said people were coming to take us to Red Rock. He yelled at me to get up. I tried to speak my piece, but he kept on. I hated him, but then I gave up. I was tired and frustrated, scared because I had never been to a Native Reservation before!

We headed toward Shiprock as our goal for the day. I felt the Navajo Reservation energy was deep; sometimes dark and twisted. I really hoped there would be acceptance toward us riding through their lands. People warned us of the ghost hunter spirits, "The Skinwalkers." I trained myself to ignore the fearful things people told me on this journey but did not let the warnings from locals deter me.

When we reached Shiprock, I was in awe at the red rocks that looked like alien angel wings stretching on for miles and miles. Kyle rode his bike faster and further than I could keep up with and the sun was going to set soon. The desert would grow cold for the night, and I was going to be terrified sleeping alone in the desert. I again pulled out my carnelian crystal mala beads and chanted to the Goddess, Green Tara. Suddenly, my road companion came back down the hill on his bike to tell me that some young Navajos would come pick us up and we would go to their grandmother's house. I was stunned and amazed that Kyle arranged this and came back for me.

In a flash, a young Navajo girl and boy arrived in an old green and white Ford pickup. Kyle and the boy threw my bike into the back. I felt like I was being captured and thought perhaps they were happy to smuggle in some white peeps!

Why was I feeling afraid of these kids? Intuitively I sensed something was off. Next, there was a series of weed handoffs by groups of Nav-Gangsta Punks. Going over 40 miles an hour into the sunset, I held on tight to the metal truck bed. We sat on some weather-worn foam seating against the cab window. It was comfy. They smoked a stogie and it smelled like a clove cig.

I love the smell of clove and immediately wished to have one of my own to take my mind off Kyle being a bit domineering. The scent of clove calmed my anger. I tried to enjoy the open air of the truck and observed the shapes of the enormous rock mountains that looked like sculptures. We passed "Ship Rock." I saw what Kyle told me were rocks in the shapes of wings, like on a spaceship. He said there was a story that the rock was an actual spaceship and that the paper-thin looking rocks, stretching out for miles, were the wings. I saw the big sun-ball setting over the expanse of angel wings at Shiprock. It was a sight I hoped I would never forget. The beauty was unmatched to anything I had experienced before.

The truck made a series of stops and starts along the main Highway 64. Jonah's mom was in another car ahead of us, so he was concerned that she would find out what he was doing. After his mom pulled off, we saw a drug transaction taking place in a white sedan that pulled up behind us. Then we picked up another Navajo boy, who I thought was super gangsta-sexy. We turned off the main highway and wandered past dead trees, bramble, and large wild dogs. We parked next to other run-down old Fords from the 1950s that served as weed dealing substations.

The drug drop-offs took way too long, but we made a couple more stops at dwellings that were only halfway built. We stopped at a house structure with striking red soil. It looked like a boneyard or a punk Navajo style compound. There were little kittens and dogs everywhere. There was another Navajo in an old truck weighing out the weed, while I smoked a stogie with a young lady accompanying him. He had a light rigged up in the truck, making it a 'professional' weed office.

The young Navajos took us to Jonah's mom's place, in Red Valley, but it was originally communicated to us that we were going to a Grandmother's home. Upon arrival, I saw a menacing rusted swing-set and even more threatening, several large pit-bulls on long chains. I had images flashing hard in my imagination, that I slept near a life-threatening dog. We were told to be careful what we say, since Jonah's mom was "very religious." I said, "Not a problem."

I locked my bike to the swing set and asked where the bathroom was. Jonah asked his mom if I could come in. Just at that moment, the wind pierced through my clothes and chilled me to the bone. Once we got inside, I was offered coffee to keep warm. After washing up, I sat at the kitchen table and felt like the rest of the night would be easy.

Kyle came in and we all sat around the dinner table eating fry bread. We were offered mutton, but I passed, only because Kyle seemed to be watching over how far I was straying from eating a raw vegan diet. Rose-Ann, Kyle's mom, made the dinner, mostly for her boyfriend who entered just a bit after we did. I knew in my spirit that this gift of homemade food offered by the Grandmother was not to be refused. Everyone left after dinner, but I declined going to some party with the kids, because I knew I'd probably witness some lame pot-smoking hang-out and thought I would be cranky and bored.

Rose-Ann and I talked. I told her that I was working only on my dreams now, and that I was not as concerned about finding work. She was a writer and said that was HER dream, but she teaches now and doesn't have much time to do her writing. She told me her son Jonah was going to graduate from High School and all her other kids were in college or had received their master's degrees. Then she told me her husband had been killed by a drunk driver not far from where Jonah picked us up.

She prayed she'd find someone she always dreamed of. She remembered praying once. "Lord, if I am meant to be lonely and alone and that is what is meant to be for me, then that is alright." Soon after, she met her new boyfriend at church. She said they were going to get married, that they plant flowers together, and that they built a greenhouse on her property. I was happy for her but was dreaming of the possibility of my own romance - which was nowhere to be found.

She gave me two phone numbers, her email address, and directions to her sister's trailer in Chinle, Arizona, which was going to be my next stop. She let me sleep in a room once occupied by one of her kids and I had a dream about visiting Grandfather Martin. In the dream, I made him some frozen banana ice-cream and showed him some things, while he also wanted to share important information with me.

The next day, I headed out with Kyle in the early morning, making further progress toward the Hopi reservation. We went down Route 13 from Red Valley to Lukachukai, about 20 miles. We barreled down large hills and sailed past beautiful rock formations on our bikes. It was bitterly cold, but very sunny, and I had a scarf wrapped tight around my face. We stopped at a place where natural spring water flowed out of a mountain. Kyle took off his clothes and showered in the spring falls, acting as if it wasn't at all cold in the water. I stared in awe but couldn't do what he did.

My soul was loudly screaming that my journey into Hopiland needed to be taken ALONE. I wanted to hear my own heart, restore my sense of self, and hear what God wanted for me. I had to develop my self-reliance and freedom, since I was always sheltered and controlled in my childhood. We stopped at a remote and barren gas station, where Route 13 and Route 12 meet at the fork. It felt like we were in Afghanistan or some war-torn country, not the United States. This gas station and the land surrounding it was like a place you would experience after bombs shatter buildings, with feelings of desolation and decay permeating the air. The corner gas station was suspicious to me and at that time in 2008 had a name so generic, I couldn't remember it.

I stood just far enough away from the station corner to have a wide view of the whole scene. My heart raced because I knew I had to tell Kyle I needed to go my OWN WAY. As much as I enjoyed his quirky personality and good looks, I knew I had to leave his presence immediately, my skin was crawling with the need to cut loose! Kyle bought me a map at the gas station and then we split.

Gypsy dogs and more Indian folks were walking around as I tried to calmly breathe in my independence. I scribbled on notebook paper that I had folded up into many parts. When we left Durango, where I left my laptop, I decided to make all my journal entries on paper and log them on the computer later.

I knew that the moment we parted in the middle of this foreign land, I needed ultimate courage to travel this desert alone. My paper maps and journal writings became my comfort in the unknown.

Generous Navajo - Navajo Rez, Chinle, Arizona

Black Beauty Rides! 🚲 *10/01/08*

When I finally left the gas station, I rolled downhill from Lukachukai and pedaled 26 miles to Chinle. The day was sunny and clear with few clouds in the sky. The terrain turned from desert brush to pine forest, surprising me with its diverse and extravagant beauty. I rode my bike through a small herd of white goats that startled me, but managed to breathe calmly into my heart and they let me sail on between them.

The miles were grueling even though it was somewhat of a coast downhill. The land was breathtaking. I knew I was getting close to Chinle and Canyon de Chelly when there were three overlooks of the Canyon. The views were spectacular, with red rock cliffs everywhere. I didn't take much extra time to explore, since I wanted to make it to Rose-Ann's sister's home before dark. I went to the visitor's center at Canyon de Chelly National Monument to track down the elementary school where Louise worked. A guy gave me a map of the town, but there was not much to note...a few stores, schools, laundry-mat, etc.

I found the elementary school just as a ton of Navajo kids poured onto a group of busses. I went to the front desk and asked a lady to page Louise Benally. They called down to her room on a little intercom after I told them that Rose-Ann sent me. They directed me down a few turns of the hallway and I found Louise sitting at a desk with an enormous mess of papers surrounding her. It turns out she had no knowledge from her sis that I would be showing up, so I was a complete surprise explaining my situation to her. I had to call on every ounce of courage and a deep well of humility to even be standing at her desk.

I explained that I stayed with her sister the night prior. She asked where I was staying tonight, so I clarified that I really didn't have plans and that was why I sought her out. Her sis wanted me to stay somewhere dry and safe, and Louise agreed to host for me. She said they didn't have much room, only their living room floor. I said, "Yeah, I don't need much," and she drew me a detailed map to her trailer park.

We agreed to meet at 6:00 pm. Then I went back to the front desk and asked where their public library was so I could use the internet. There was no public library in Chinle, but she directed me to Dine College. I tracked the library down in a shopping plaza that was super 'sketch' with Navajo drunk beggars and meth heads hanging around. There was a sign on the door to go around to the back of the plaza. Naturally, I was worried about leaving my bike anywhere where people might be inclined to steal it.

I knocked on some steel doors that were locked. Then, just as I was about to give up, a guy opened one of the doors. I said that I was traveling and wanted to use the internet. He welcomed me into the clean computer lab and logged me in right away. I stayed there, wrote my journal entries, and even arranged with him to come back the next day.

After journaling, I headed out to find Louise's trailer. She was in a monster 4x4 truck near her place and said that she and her daughter had to run to a meeting, so I should just head over to the trailer and someone would let me in. I rode through the parking lots and had a bit of a time trying to find it from the sketchy map she had given me.

On the way there, I met a guy named Verl. He was happy to direct me to another lot of trailers, but first I got the hundred questions about my travels, since everyone who noticed my travel-rigged bike had to ask. I was both annoyed and happy to share my story of WHY I was traveling alone through the desert. After explaining my roots and travel whereabouts, we talked about the Navajo culture and I soon found out he was going to be able to take me closer to my next destination, Second Mesa.

I continued through the trailer park with dogs barking at me. I walked very slowly to avoid dog attacks and found Louise's address. Joel, dad to a six-month-old, was at the trailer. He calmly greeted me while smirking with 'the weirdo girl traveler' attitude. I said my hellos. He was packing up bottles with milk or formula for the baby. He seemed a bit weirded out by me but continued his tasks while I sat in the kitchen and studied my map.

Later, Louise came home with La Princessa, one of her daughters. She had two daughters and a son. We talked for a while, then La Chipita came home. She shared the story about her baby's Navajo cradleboard. She and her mom explained that babies only cry when they are not tied up. I found this super funny, but if it meant that parents could sleep soundly, I'd tie my baby up too. It had soft leather, which laced up the board. They say this also helps the baby's spine stay straight.

La Chipita told me that when a baby first laughs, they have a big celebration with food and offerings. She showed me her baby's first Indian turquoise bracelets and leather footie cuffs. She also showed me her massive turquoise bracelet with a rosette pattern, bigger than a normal belt buckle. They let me take a shower and sleep on their couch. The laundry dryer buzzer went off every 20 to 30 minutes all night long. It seemed they were up all night, too. Each time the buzzer went off, I remembered my dreams. The buzzer seemed to help me remember the sequence of symbol imagery.

I got up at 6:30 am to be off in time for a Navajo guided tour through Canyon de Chelly National Monument. Once there, I purchased a ticket from a Navajo man named Merlin and soon after, he organized our tour group. We hiked up and down amazing, rippled rocks. He said we were on a man-made trail, which consisted of little depressions that looked like people's footsteps embedded in rock. It was curious; I had never seen anything like it. He said these trails were still traversed with cattle and sheep at times.

It was pretty hard-core. French and American tourists, plus myself hovered on these mountainous cliff paths and I thought, "NO WAY! Modern folks are such wimps." It seemed these paths couldn't be taken by livestock to settle in the canyons for a summer stay. Merlin said the canyons below were still inhabited by local Native Americans, growing corn and fruit trees.

Merlin was a very sweet tour guide but didn't reveal much to us in the way of the historical past, though he did point out some of the local vegetation. At the end of the tour, we came to a wall painting that he said was Anasazi. It depicted a raid. The stone petroglyph wall carving/painting was pretty lame. There was no description from our guide that piqued my interest. Meanwhile, the tourists snapped pictures and I laughed to myself.

After the tour was over, I rode back to town and almost passed Verl, who was waiting for me in the parking lot. We were supposed to meet later in the afternoon, but his plans changed, so he tracked me down. Mysteriously, he had to pick up his paycheck in a town named Dilkon. We looked for a new route for me to enter Hopiland and agreed to meet in front of Bashas, a local grocery chain, at 2:00 pm. I headed over to the computer lab around the back of the plaza, where I printed out my master phone list and another copy of my Goddess of Vision manifesto.

I went into the Wells Fargo Bank like I was finally headed into a developing nation in the midst of vast devastated lands. I took out $40 to make sure I had enough for the Hopi journey and beyond. I bought some Jif peanut butter, some Swiss chard, and sprouts. I ate almost all of it in the truck on the way to Dilkon because I had starved myself all day prior to meeting Verl. He and I had really interesting conversations.

He discussed his views on spirituality and generalized about how things are in Navajo culture these days. I tried to explain why I want to make films and covered how I was born an anarchist who hated 4th of July parades and the United States in general when I was a child. He said he had an idea how he would build an all-magnetically powered car. Later he said he thought we could have sustainable homes built underground to always remain at a constant temperature. They would have reflectors to gather needed light and energy.

When we got to Dilkon, I shopped again at Bashas since I needed water and more food for Hopiland. He took me up Route 87 near the Montezuma Chair Mine to make sure I didn't get lost, then dropped me off with my bike. I was alone again.

I rode past a series of pyramid-like rocks that looked as though the hand of God effortlessly placed them there as if playing with Legos. They were small mountains that looked like monument faces or masks, lying like turtles on their backs with their faces toward the sky. I had 25 miles to get to the Second Mesa. It was 4:00 pm and my goal was to make all those miles by sunset. The sun and flat brush landscape was all I could see anywhere.

Eventually I saw the purple mesa directly in front of me. I was slow, tired, and could barely ride anymore, so I got off the bike to pray for guidance. I held out my palms facing up to the sky for answers. I called in my guides and the four directions. I asked if I should camp out in the desert sand and grass or keep riding until I found a camp and people. The answer that came was "Go have fun." On I went, after strapping one of my glow lights onto my backpack.

Hopiland, a Wide and Mystical Expanse

Black Beauty Rides! 🚲 *10/1/08*

Prophecy Rock Painting

One of the first things I noticed arriving in Hopiland were large old billboards, still intact from perhaps the 1950s. The huge signage indicated that NO PHOTOS were allowed to be taken on this land. Remember, it is said that photos can steal your soul. When I reached these lands, I felt another surreal sensation, as if my brain literally fluttered and turned upside down in my skull. My cranium was filled with the sensation that America was here in Hopiland, and everything outside of Hopi was a farce.

The energy of the land was telling me that this place is where life is birthed from the sand and dirt into beings that make existence more beautiful. The colonial concepts that exist outside of this place represent extraction and death.

Nightfall - Third Mesa & Gangsta Hopi

Black Beauty Rides! 🚲 *10/2/08*

When arriving on the reservation, the first sight I saw was kids playing on a basketball court. They waved to me in a friendly but oddly menacing way. I rode past but considered stopping to talk to them. The song below was inspired the moment I saw them all dressed in black clothes:

Oracles
A song by Serpentbird

"Sing to me purple
Blue Star lady
Oracles!
Blue sky, blue sky.
One-time rains,
and two ways to take my freedom.
Take my freedom and run with a smile,
power hungry takes a dive,
in my words of swords,
in my belt of nails,
bed of feathers in these days of sand and dirt.
I dream of ladies dressed in furs,
wild western leather, new cowboys of coal
leave me in wonder.
Dogs wander and scrape,
pilfer the mind of Satan.

Bring down the mind of humans.
Sing to me purple
Blue Star lady
Oracles!
Blue sky, blue sky.

Live in ecstasy,
Live in blur,
Coo at the full moon and shooting stars.
Juniper scent waves to my nose
hoo hoo hoo
the whistle blows,
Metal and steel track over my heart.
Wallet in the ditch, never coming back.
Love the dawn now,
Love the sun set.
Swing with the Indian children,
all dressed in BLACK."

All the fears I had about speaking to Hopi people came from people I met along the way. They said the Hopi people were very strict about spiritual practices. I biked up the hill while it was still light outside and warm and asked them about the campground I heard was nearby. They pointed to the top of a tall mesa that I had no energy to climb in the dark. I said I'd go up the next day and would also go to the visitor center then. "Where can I camp tonight?" I asked. They laughed and said, "Right here!" A gangsta-Hopi pointed to a sandy spot beside the basketball courts. I was fine with that since I like sleeping on sand.

I guess hip-hop has penetrated even the most remote cultures. Wearing black and hats with big logos and brims made you cool!! I locked my bike up and walked over to a double-wide trailer to write under the lights. I could hear them coughing and smoking weeeeeeeeeed!

After finishing my writing, I spoke with Raymond, who had a great laugh. Then I walked over to three of the kids in the dark and told them about my journeys. We all laughed when I told them about ditching Kyle.

There was a young girl like a butch gangsta...possibly lesbian. They told me I could sleep on their roof, then picked up my things from the picnic table and told me to come to their house, so I got the bike and rode it through the sands. They giggled and I seemed to get a contact buzz from their ganja as we hopped through a patch of magic bushes on the way to the house. I felt like I was floating with them above the sand and was happy to have new Hopi friends.

A family of seven lived in this little ranch house. A five-year-old named Karlee nearly attacked me at their kitchen table with her coloring books and crayons. The mom of the house, Molly, came out and told me I could sleep in their living room. They were watching a movie called "Urban Legends" on a massive big-screen TV. The kids were making a 'stoner high' late night dinner. It included peanut butter and jelly, which I said "No" to during their stoner party. I was tired but mesmerized in front of the TV and kept coloring within the lines of a coloring book with Kylee. I was in love with her dark hair and eyes, plus she was so intensely loving and maddeningly friendly, she reminded me of my own bold techniques in reaching out to people.

She pretty much sat on my leg the whole time, while the others kept trying to call her away from me to go eat, leave me alone, or go to bed. She totally ignored them and I found that entertaining.

Grandfather Martin Gashweseoma
Hopi Elder and Guardian of the Sacred Stone Tablets of the Fire Clan

Black Beauty Rides! 🚲 *10/03/08*

I woke up and Molly said her daughter had to go to Kykotsmovi. I asked if they had a truck and she said they did. Thank the Lord for the land of PICK-UP-TRUCKS!!! I met the husband, who was super nice. They explained that I was on my way to find Martin and said he lived in the Village of Bacavi, in Hotevilla, but there was a huge wedding celebration happening across the street today, and he might be there.

We loaded the truck with my bike and snacks and headed up the mesa. I saw that it would've been quite a hike without their help. It was still a climb getting to Hotevilla from Kykotsmovi. I hiked upward and upward and felt tired as usual, but OK. When I got to Old Orabi, I decided to stop and meditate there. Ants crawled up my legs and bit me, so I only managed to meditate for 15 minutes.

More climbing. I stared at the huge rock boulders and thought about where I would hang out if it rained. There was some wind and my sweat got a bit cold, but other than that I did well and finally reached Hotevilla. I was still adjusting to the altitude but walked up a dirt road searching for "the biggest store," where I read you could ask where Grandfather Martin was staying.

I went into the convenience store in this "third world" village, which proudly displayed a huge sign out front for Monster Energy drink. The place was positioned and built to suit a gas station, but there were no gas pumps. The guy working inside was the only other white person around. He directed me to the next store over, 'cause he didn't know anyone around...let alone a guy named Martin.

I met Betsy at the counter and she said, "Yeah...just go down the dirt road into the village and ask around since it is too difficult to explain where his home is."

I rode my bike a little way past the post office, school, and water tower. There was even a graphics/print shop, yet this place seemed like I was on the top of the world. My bike at that point couldn't go through the sand, so I walked until I reached a disgruntled woman standing next to her huge white pick-up. I asked her if she could help me find Martin's house. She asked me why I wanted to find him. I said that I had read about him on the internet and in magazines while in California and I wanted answers about prophecies and 2012. She said that Hopis don't tell people about it, so he may not tell me anything. I immediately felt disappointed and sad. I knew, though, that Martin DID want people to know. I walked back to the store to get the real info on his whereabouts, like a dog with his tail tucked between his legs.

I asked a man near the store to tell me. He drew a picture in the sand with a stick, like you see in some old cowboy and Indian western sitcoms. I didn't want to walk down there yet, because he wasn't even certain if that was the right guy. I politely asked Betsy to set this all straight. I told her about the mean lady, and she asked me if I got her name. I told her no, I hadn't, and she said, "You should leave!" I was delighted to hear this because it meant she'd help me out. She drew me a map of dwellings, trees, forks in the roads, and square kivas.

The dogs that roamed up there were more chill than those in the Navajo lands. I think they felt the serenity of the altitude, which is something that makes your head feel numb. They didn't bark or move very fast, they just sat and kind of smiled at you, just looking content.

I walked back down the dusty road on a cloudy sunny day, feeling a bit nervous because I knew I was about to meet the holy man! I stared down at myself and tried to imprint a memory of what I was wearing and how I was feeling. I thought I would look out of place to Grandfather Martin.

I was wearing my bright blue shirt with the hot air balloons on it, and all my geek necklaces and my Tibetan mala. As I got closer and felt more nervous, I ran into a couple men, one who looked like 'Colorado' next to his Honda jeep. He pointed me toward the right home, where I would find Grandfather.

I knocked on the outer screen door and opened it, while saying "Hello." I let myself in the door, knowing he was going deaf and wouldn't have heard me knocking.

He was alone. He sprung up from his chair and delightfully exclaimed, "Nice to see you again!" He held my shoulders with his big square hands and his blue eyes blazed out at me. It was as if beautiful lightning bolts came out of his eyeballs. He looked at me to see if in fact he had met me before. I think the Tibetans and Hopis believe in reincarnation, so maybe that's what he meant. Either that, or he says, "Nice to see you again!" as a funny joke to everyone.

He tried holding me there to look straight into my eyes, but his blue eyes threw me into a shyness. I couldn't bear the fullness of the moment, so I looked off to the side with some regret. His hair was bluntly trimmed and squared to his chin, but he had a longer silver ponytail in the back that was bundled with bright red yarn.

As he put his hands on my shoulders, I saw how happy he was to see me. His wonder and excitement was like that of a child. Even though there was a lot of excitement swirling around me being in his ancestral home, I felt at peace. I feel his essence brings peace to all he relates with.

He had a huge, lined notebook on the table for visitors to communicate with him. He's going deaf, but of course can still sense your movements. He explained that I should write in big letters so he could read it easily. I wrote. "Hi, my name is Lori." Then, "I am wearing my Tibetan prayer beads." I told him I wanted to know about the Blue Star Kachina prophecy. He said something as I was writing, I think referring to his amusement of the bright colors I was wearing.

In the notebook, I saw that people who visited him before came from South America and they also discussed the Blue Star Kachina (Sasquasoha). I was there to see him because I genuinely felt a sense that the world might end in 2012. As a Rainbow Warrior, I wanted to know what "WE" were going to do about it.

He didn't really answer any of my burning inquiries, but I detached from these desires, since I wanted to enjoy the fact that I actually found him and take in the experience of being in this strange village.

I wrote that I came on my bike and he wondered where it was. I explained that it was locked up near the store, and that I'd bring it down after we had our talk. But then he whisked me off, saying very loudly, "It's time for lunch!!" He walked me over to a little stone dwelling, where a mom and grandma and grandpa were sitting. The granny was cooking and they all spoke to each other in their Hopílavayi language.

Teresa, who was cooking, introduced herself and told me the other names, which I have forgotten. We were in a kitchen which had a gas stove, but as in most Hopi homes there was no electricity or running water. We had Ramen soup with Zesta crackers and yellow watermelon.

This kitchen was curious and sad at the same time. There were mountains of laundry baskets and kitchen items piled up chaotically, and my internal jaw dropped when I noticed a few cat skins on plastic hangers in the corner of the room. The ceiling had corn and Coleman camping lamps hanging in various places. I didn't dare look at the floor since I cleaned houses for a living in the past and felt my heart sink into what it would be like to live on 'impoverished' Hopiland for a longer time.

Grandfather repeatedly set watermelon slices by my right hand on the table. As soon as I finished one, he followed up with another. "Papa thinks you're too skinny," Teresa said. He laughed with a great silly laugh and continued this laugh throughout my two-day stay. My stomach was full, and I really enjoyed their company.

The family didn't say any prayers over their meals or seem to have any strict practices around their food while I was visiting. We did, however, put all our watermelon seeds into little piles directly on the corners of the table. There was a bucket to throw away the rinds and little bowls designated for saving all the seeds for the next planting of the Hopi fields. At the end of lunch, we scooped the seeds into a Styrofoam bowl.

The little stone home was packed with regular grocery items, so I didn't feel much separation from the encroaching modern world. They had a jug of Kool-Aid on the table, which repulsed me.

Grandfather and I walked back to his home, and then he demanded, "It's time. Go get your bike." I unlocked the Kryptonite lock from the fence near the store and walked the bike 'home.'

Grandfather, Belt Weavings, and Prophecies after Dark

Black Beauty Rides! 🚲 *10/06/08*

I immediately went into a food coma after lunch from the overload of bleached flour in the Zesta crackers and Ramen noodles. Grandfather was weaving a belt on a home-made wooden framed loom that was about six feet long. He knelt on the floor with a low chair or stool to prop him up.

He had a finished belt laying on the floor to the side of the loom. I stared at it intently. I had seen this kind of craftwork before, but never witnessed the skillful artisan beside it. This simple looking activity was something that awed me. I had made looms myself to bead necklaces on. It is soul-satisfying to put your hands and mind to work in this way. I wanted to know how he felt about this, but we couldn't exchange many words because of his hearing, so I merely watched in awe. As he did his weaving, I took out my papers to journal the previous days.

Three Square Meals with Grandfather

Hopi Reservation 1st Mesa

Black Beauty Rides! 🚲 *10/4/08*

I had three 'square' meals with Grandfather, which consisted of beans and fresh baked bread. I asked Grandfather Martin if he was going to the wedding in the next town and was surprised when he said, "I am too old." He seemed pretty sassy and a bit too sharp to even utter those words. I was even more surprised to see that no one came from his family to scoop him up and take him there. So, I accepted that we would be each other's company and was content in that.

Black Beauty Rides! 🚲 *10/5/08*

After dinner, Grandfather told me to bring my bike in. Some things he voiced in a definite and demanding manner. Other than that, life was heavy but also general and simple. As I went into an after-dinner food coma, I tried to go to sleep on the couch and Grandfather exclaimed. "It's EARLY!!!" He lit a gas lamp after striking a match on a seashell and began explaining the prophecy rock down the road in Old Orabi. Then he went into his piles of stuff in the back room and brought out something wrapped in scarves. The inner cloth was red, tied with red ribbon. I immediately understood that 'nighttime' was the proper 'storytime' for sharing secret mysteries and hard-core prophecy shit!

He explained the little tablets that were wrapped in the cloth. He said very loudly that "THEY" have the originals down there. This meant that some organizations of the Hopi were preserving the REAL rocks in a safe place, but Grandfather had copies. There were drawings inscribed on the tablets that I had seen on the internet. Grandfather went through each symbol, explaining them to me. He said that China and Russia were going to take over the whole U.S. Then there would be great purification time. Then he said. "We will have LOVE." Then he took my arm and pointed to the picture of him and Kimberlee Ruff standing arm and arm in front of the larger prophecy rock.

He told me to go the next day, make an offering, and bury the little tablets under the rock, "Like tobacco. Bury them so no one will take or steal them." I was a bit shocked, because I didn't know he would actually put me on such a mission. I felt fulfilled and honored to follow his wishes. I was beginning to feel the tension of the other supposed "spiritual" community of the Hopi, who seemed to have lost their faith in such rites - though I had only spoken with a few of them and couldn't judge what percentage of people still jive with the old ways.

I found such a mix of strange ancient and modern architecture there. It baffled me to see outhouse bathrooms mingled with solar paneled roofs. Later, when I journeyed out of the village toward Tuba City, I stopped at a Navajo Chapter House. I will explain later, but a man there told me that since 1908 or something crazy like that until just a few years ago, there was a governmental freeze on any modifications to Hopi or Navajo buildings. I was beginning to see the macro- and microcosms of so many corrupt ways that governments create chaos. I can't even begin to explain it all so quickly in this journal.

Grandfather drew a map for me to find the prophecy rock the next morning in Old Orabi. I felt a bit uneasy knowing that I would be looking for it alone and felt sad that he wasn't going with me.

Prophecy Rock - Old Orabi, Arizona

Black Beauty Rides! 🚲 *10/4/08*

I woke up for breakfast at 6:30 am and realized that sunshine on the Hopi rez was a form of food! Grandfather brought me to the realization that 'sun on the mesa' means you actually see the sun on the horizon. There are no obstructions to block our views of such simple natural occurrences that we are so separate from. As you walk the sandy paths, take in the breath of the life giving and happiness granted by the sun fire ball. This is breakfast, you see?

After breakfast with my new Hopi family, I headed out to Old Orabi with the tobacco from Grandfather's table. I could hardly believe that the Prophecy Rock I had seen in photos was here before my eyes.

I needed to pray immediately, since calming my confused mind was a priority. I meditated with the tobacco pouch in my hands beside this amazing mega rock, saying my no-fail Tara mantra on my mala for three rounds. That's 108 x 3. This was my own way of connecting and drawing in willing positive spirits.

My intention was to bring in peace and to thank the rock for all the "beings" who have made pilgrimage here. People come here to think about what the rock is trying to tell us, which is that we are in serious wars and conflict, have suffered greatly, and will continue to until some fine day as Grandfather says, "We will have LOVE." I believed that Grandfather and I both felt that at least something was still sacred.

I dug a deep hole in the sandy soil as far underneath the rock as possible. My whole body could fit under there when I laid completely down. I'd like to think that I put my whole heart into doing these rituals, even rolling around in dirt!

While I lay there, I tried sleeping for a bit to see if I'd receive a vision. The wind was pretty cold, so I just rested a bit, then headed back down to Hotevilla and hung out at their brand-new community center. They had a big computer lab with internet that I would have used, but since it was the weekend, it was closed.

I hung out with a woman named Roberta who was watching her niece and nephew. Roberta's husband, Bear, had just moved from Wyoming. She told me her uncle had been missing since January and there was a Hopi search party out looking for him. She was making lunch for them at the center.

Meanwhile, I wanted to nap. When rain arrived from California, it created a heavy pressure that folded my eyes down so heavily I had to sleep. I slept for a while on the seats in their van. I didn't want to hang out with Grandfather because I thought he'd think napping wasn't cool. Then came a point when it was time to say goodbye to him, but looking back I have no idea how I tied up loose ends before I left. I do remember needing to ride my bike off the Third Mesa toward Tuba City and then back to Durango, a distance of 235 miles. In my young mind I did not think about the time or stamina I needed to get there. I just knew to keep pedaling and TRUST.

Death by Peanut Butter - Navajo Rez, Dennehotso, Arizona

Black Beauty Rides! 🚲 *10/4/08*

Earlier, on the journey through Navajo lands, a woman at the chapter house between third mesa and Tuba City told me that people drive too fast on Route 160. She said it was the Highway of Death. Well, I did die on the Highway of Death! My body went into anaphylactic shock after eating rolls of Swiss chard with stale Jif peanut butter inside.

I managed to send a clear message of distress by laying down in a death meditation posture amidst the dust and dirt along the roadside. First, a Navajo policeman showed up and got out of his truck to tell me that he had received a call. He asked, "Are you OK?"

"Yeah," I said, "But I can't move and need to hang out here and drink water until my body wants to go again." At this point, I didn't care if I couldn't move until the next day, since I knew I had enough water. I surely didn't want to eat anything at this point, and the cop said he'd check on me later. In the back of my mind, I was thinking that life should be slow, but it was messy out here.

I also knew and trusted that someone would pick me up at some point anyway, or I'd just continue riding down the road as planned. No one wants to be humiliated by forfeiting their plan to ride hundreds of fun-filled miles. However, at that point, my search for the meaning of the prophesies and desire for fun on the reservations was satisfied. I probably rode a stretch of 150 miles from Tuba City to Dennehotso, but at this point, I just wanted to go back to Durango.

This is what happened: I was rescued by a guy in a blue minivan. He picked me up only because he was familiar with touring on bicycles. He said he didn't normally pick up hitchhikers, but I bet he didn't realize had a divine mission that day! I made it safely back to the sweet arms of Turtle Lake Refuge in Durango. I retrieved my computer, which was a big relief. Ahhhh Durango, I loved your rain, hail, sun, clouds, and bohemian gypsies! Throughout the travels on my bike, about 20 days total, I never had a flat tire thanks to my Armadillos.

Journey Home
Return to the Heart, Alchemizing the spiritual elixir of eternity
Columbus, Ohio 2008

Originally, I thought that the "elixir" in my heroine journey would come from my Hopi experiences at Prophecy Rock or with Grandfather Martin. However, Sedona had planted a dormant, yet potent seed in my subconscious that took time to germinate and bloom.

I moved back to Ohio from Los Angeles after going to The Los Angeles Film School and touring through the west on my bicycle in 2008. I showed my bike map to many of my friends, but very few of them fully engaged with how much my soul-seeking adventure meant to me.

When I reached Ohio, beyond wanting to learn more about the Hopi and the Navajo lands, I came to understand that my passage to the old worlds was more of a global prophecy, relating to the Eagle and the Condor. I had found and lost myself many times over in relationships in Ohio. I craved to be in a Tribe where my heart could open up again.

Soon after I returned to Ohio, I got a job at Donatos Pizza, which was boring and obviously low wage. I was very fortunate that I had friends who lifted me up with their hearts and gave me a bedroom to sleep in until I manifested employment that would satisfy both my physical needs and my thirst for knowledge.

Serpentbird Is Born!
I Commit to Create my final Avatar Name

In April of 2009, at the art collective "The BOG," I sat alone in my bedroom and tried to figure out how to reinvent myself again and integrate back into the Columbus community as an artist. My close friend and spiritual teacher, Pamela Thomas, told me that as an artist, I needed to be more consistent. She told me that changing my poet's name over and over again would not generate a following.

I invented the name "Serpentbird," based on the God Quetzalcoatl and on a previous inspiration from the movie I made with Amanda. There was a strange phenomenon of me "forgetting" that I had already created the name, but here I was, creating it again! I had read about the prophecy of the Eagle and the Condor, the brothers of North America reuniting with the brothers of South America in ceremony. This would unite our traditions and culture while also uniting the mind with the heart.

At that time in 2009, I understood the urgency and meaning of the Rainbow Warrior Prophecy, but I never believed I would see it develop and become real, like it had with the rise of Standing Rock in 2016. I didn't have much of a 'costume' type of character, but I felt that the name represented me. 'Serpent' meaning Death of Ego and Transformation toward whatever shape or multidimensional self I needed to embody to bring about positive change and a greater light. 'Bird,' of course, because I knew that Quetzalcoatl was basically a flying Feathered Serpent. I felt that 'Bird' fit generically when I broke down the meaning of 'flying serpent' etymologically.

If you read my natal astrological chart, you would see that I will go through many deaths and rebirths as my Pisces Sun is in my 12th house. My life in this incarnation will be as a seeker, climbing through the jungles of mysteries of ancient civilizations, unearthing my past lives while craving to understand how to heal this current body, and releasing cellular memory and pain from all my hundreds of previous incarnations. My goal is to attain liberation from the death and rebirth cycle and incarnate in another galaxy. In essence, I am not just seeking bliss or Nirvana, but to be fully liberated into Moksha or Enlightenment.

I purchased the website www.serpentbird.com, a major commitment. I envisioned making it a premier Art and Environmental online magazine, but this was easier said than done without start-up capital to pay people to produce content.

One spring day while living at the Bog, I was determined to paint a logo of what this flying snake bird should look like. I had a small glass dish, a flat Golden Taklon paint brush, and some black tempera paint. That afternoon, I painted a stack of 40 black tempera paintings on office white paper.

Serpentbird Media Logo

While I sat at a circular wood laminate table, making the paintings, two Mormon evangelists rapped their knuckles on the front door. These young 20-year-old guys were almost giddy and had huge smiles across their faces. I hesitated to open the door at first but was too curious to walk away. I let them into the living room, and their enthusiasm soon spilled over, touching my heart. They showed me very clearly the testimonials of Jesus.

They opened a small pamphlet to an illustration that made me laugh. Jesus was standing in a white robe in front of an Incan pyramid in South America! I thought to myself, "What are the chances these guys would be showing me this drawing in their pamphlet, while I was painting a representation of Quetzalcoatl?"

Quetzalcoatl, by some mystic's definition, was also Jesus! The logo design process brought in such strange synchronic order and validation for the direction I was heading in with this mission.

Death and Transformation Medicine
Spring Romance with "Crow" Columbus, Ohio April 2009

One of the most important components of being able to facilitate others in their healing, is "letting go." Serpent medicine is an energy that means many things but is undeniably useful and effective in transmuting energy. Receiving healings from other healers is just as important as giving. It helps me develop this power when I assist others.

Returning to Ohio, I left my relationship with Alexandre behind me, even though I did feel bitter about it. I searched for new romantic connections and one evening while at the Shi-Sha Hookah Lounge, I looked in a newspaper and saw that Mors Ontologica was playing in Old Town. I went to see their show and was mesmerized by Marc, the lead singer.

That spring, living at The Bog, was a pivotal time for me. I wanted to invite a deeper human love into my life and felt frustrated that I didn't have any romance on my travels. I decided to paint my room pink as they do in Feng Shui when a mother wants her daughter to get married. I even furnished my bed with a beautiful pink and green bedspread. I also found some American goose feathers from molting geese, which were plentiful, and put them in the little holes in the Masonite boards that were on my walls.

I often took walks through the neighborhood on East Tompkins Street. I would see Crow, also walking, and thought, "Hmmm. It's interesting how we synched up at the same time." He was skinny and tall, with long hair and tattoos. He wore black work shoes with buckles, which were worn through and distressed. His head was bowed down and his gaze held punk angst as he marched down the sidewalks.

I later learned he did this to appear inconspicuous, because he had been attacked once as he walked down the street. He wore a faded black jean jacket with a leopard print on the back with studs and a patch with the words, "Do Yourself In." He was my 'Mr. Rock and Roll.' When I saw him from afar, I sensed that he walked with purpose. Marc was always thinking hard about some conflict and had a strong desire for all people to get along. The trees that lined Tompkins Street were budding with pink flowers and the sun cast a light, yellow glow through the morning.

I invited him to my room at the Bog soon after. He told me his arm hurt. I wondered, but didn't ask the real reason behind the pain. Perhaps it was heroin needle marks. I knelt down to massage his inner arm and took his hand. It felt sweet and healing in mine, surprising me. He had Grateful Dead tattoos on the front side of his hands, which I thought added mystery and excitement to his already magical and beautiful musical hands.

That spring, I think we both felt lonely and in need of nurturing. The day I was painting the Serpentbird logo with black paint, I invited him over to eat with me. I made brown rice and vegetables that we ate with chopsticks. When I got back to Ohio, I volunteered at an event at the Clintonville Community Market to help re-integrate with my local community. An elder woman was designing a raffle of prizes, which I could see on a shelf in the store in small colored baskets. One of them was a book called "The Sacred Tree." I knew I needed this book, but she resisted giving it to me, since it was part of the raffle. I had to convince her in a stern voice that I really needed it. I told her I would buy it from her, and she finally gave in.

While reading the book, I discovered that Medicine Wheels are a tool for reflection and a way to understand the cycles we travel in our lives. At that time, I didn't really know how to practice a ceremony on the land, because the book didn't illustrate it. I was dumbfounded and confused as to why Sedona would have attracted me to this without providing a teacher to show me the ancient knowledge connected. The call of Sedona and her etheric message was only a tiny seed growing in my consciousness. I would be traveling in consciousness from a world out of 'time' back into the world of 'time' and density.

By spring of 2009, Marc and I were closer and our love was stable enough that I felt I could move into his townhouse on Clinton Street. I remember the beautiful pink and lavender tree blossoms that year, colored with true love. We took long walks before sunset and everywhere we went the sides of our hips were glued together and our arms wrapped around each other's waists. There were dandelions and violets in the grass, apple blossoms, pink blossoms, and magnolias.

When I moved into his apartment, I had some strange feelings of being trapped and felt that I didn't really know Marc. One night I smoked a tiny puff of weed with him and looked around the walls of the apartment. I noticed several Grateful Dead posters on the walls. I could feel Marc's energy expand and almost felt as if I was re-living a Grateful Dead show with him. It made me feel odd and embarrassed to be in his little world that felt behind the times for me.

During this phase, I was very happy because I felt like I was a part of the band Mors Ontologica. I also felt very much part of a community of highly charged creatives, who made music in what they now call the

SoHud district. I encouraged them and nurtured them when they had band practice at the house. I convinced Marc that feminine energy was what he needed to finish their next album. I remember us having dinner, just the two of us, and the album playing. I would dress up for him and we would dance together in the living room.

That fall season, the band finished the double album. It was also a great time for me to bask in attention after making the MORS music video called "The Party!"

Marc and I went to a healer's group that met regularly at John's apartment. We studied Aura Meditation, which really helped us while we worked through difficult times. It was great how Marc was open to so many kinds of activities I was already involved in. I had no idea that Aura Meditation and healing with colors was something I'd use to assist people in healing themselves.

Apartment Life
37 West Tompkins St., Columbus, Ohio 2011

In 2011, our apartment on Clinton Street became infested with bedbugs, so we looked for other apartments. While we lived in Tompkins Street, I felt excited to have an apartment where we could collaborate on music and filmmaking. My friend Dawn called us the "Ultimate Power Couple." It is rare to have such a pairing of talent to influence the world!

Marc and I were involved in the music scene and I was making music videos. However, the call to help Mother Earth came back to me strongly after we moved from Clinton Street to an apartment on West Tompkins. The rush of the Olentangy River could almost be heard, and was definitely felt, from two blocks away.

The "call of water" was made clear to me as I read an article online about the brine, or wastewater, that was collected from fracking fluids, then transported from Pennsylvania to our rivers in Wayne National Forest to be dumped in Ohio. In 2011, 3.6 million barrels of the waste was sent to treatment plants in Pennsylvania and emptied into Ohio rivers for 12 months.

Marc and I worked together five days a week at the TextbooksRus warehouse, so we spent a lot of time together. It was intense physical labor most of the time, but not much of my mental space was required. I used my imagination to get me through the day. Not long after, Marc proposed to me. I was wearing his engagement ring and remember opening a book on African art called "Flash of the Spirit." The book contained a picture of a man from the Abakua tribe. He had black and white diamonds painted all over his body, which symbolized communication. He held a pipe that was on a long stick with smoke coming out of it. I felt such an overwhelming connection to this image that immediately I had a psychedelic vision of myself painted in those diamonds. I used that image as an inspiration to develop my new persona as Serpentbird.

I had an interest in Shamanism for many years and spent time with a few Shamans. I believe that a Shaman is a being who can be a channel for the Cosmos. They ground their energy into the Earth and have connection to the stars and galaxies. Most importantly, I feel that Shamans are connected to the forces of Nature. They are in tune with the seasons, the weather, the elemental spirits, and ancestors. **The African version of Serpentbird would help me portray myself as a wild feminine being yet would also embody a masculine drive that was explosive and raw!**

I also saw a nude form with body paint that would express the idea of Tribe. However, the tribe has gone missing or died from environmental destruction from humans. This being would yearn for her Tribe but bear the burden of feeling isolated and alone. She returns as a Goddess to a dying and desolate planet. She dances at Mother Earth's funeral.

I adapted the African character as Serpentbird, a female. I describe her as a being who incarnated on the Earth before, but as Goddess returns to inform humans that they are destroying nature to the depths with irreparable conditions.

Refusing God's Call to be a Priestess
July 2011

While working at TextbooksRus, I received a vision in my third eye to make a movie protesting fracking. Serpentbird would be the star, but it posed the challenge that I would not be able to film it myself. I tried to find a team of people to help me produce it, much like a music video. I could have found some musician friends to help, but since I wanted to star in the video, I could not find any videographers to film ME!

I wanted the video to be about fracking and how Ohio was going to be destroyed by it. I read articles and watched YouTube videos about how the fracking brine was being transported from Pennsylvania and dumped into the rivers in Athens, Ohio.

I made several attempts to find a skilled videographer by going to a 24-hour film fest and meeting other videographers in my community. I met a man through Facebook and had a short meeting with him. He liked my video concept but told me he was thinking of going to NYC for a while to work on a Zombie pic. In that moment, I felt the weight of my sadness and realized that without paying someone to shoot, there would be no movie. I halted the project and felt as though I was having an abortion energetically. I needed money to pay for someone to shoot the video, when I hoped my community in Columbus would pitch in for free!

As the autumn season approached and leaves changed color on the trees, I knew I was running out of time to fulfill this project. I had to stop and ask God, "What am I really trying to do? What is the planetary mission of Serpentbird?"

In these moments of abandoning a project that would show others why we should stop harming the Earth, I made an enormous shift in my consciousness. I was willing to let go of that approach and see clearly after praying and surrendering the energy of battle, to an approach of creating peace. The lesson being instilled in me came up again and again. This was God intervening and telling me, "Don't tell people what not to do, instead show them what to do." Years later, while living in Colorado, the theme presented itself again. What *to* do, not what *not* to do.

After feeling so deeply about not producing the movie, I realized it would be more powerful to create something real. That something was a group of healers called the "Serpentbird Seven." This group would be a core to lead ceremonies for an even larger body of people.

I wanted people to learn how to respect the Earth by feeling connected to her. I knew that I could show them how to observe nature, such as trees, grass, the river, birds, deer, insects, and more, by slowing things down, by walking slowly, or speaking prayers slowly. I would exemplify reverence and connection. Essentially as my dream had shown me, I would be 'walking in new shoes,' like I had worn in many lifetimes as a priestess. Leading ceremonies was a natural talent but trusting and believing in myself as a leader felt new to me in this lifetime. Creating medicine wheels felt new to me, yet a healer friend of mine told me that I had known how to make them in past lives.

Fast Forward, Television
Colorado Springs Pilgrimages, May 2018

In 2018, I created a video for my Serpentbird Activation show that made explicit points against the oil and gas industry. It took me two long months to produce a video that was only 10 minutes long. I had already posted episodes I and II of Serpentbird Activation on YouTube, and then aired them on Comcast in Denver.

When I finished producing episode III, I went to Denver Open Media and had Jesse Lockwood help me upload it. Later, Jesse notified me, my still photos and videos were scrambled and the imagery was pixelated on the screen! We would have had to adjust some of the settings to make everything air correctly. I told him hold off on posting anything live just yet. As usual…God had other plans and illustrated clearly what NOT to do with my art.

On a trip to Colorado Springs, as I was driving up Gold Canyon Road in my new red Kia Soul, I began receiving guidance. On my way up a steep hill, a Red-Tailed Hawk swooped across my windshield. It seemed larger than life. I pulled over to the side and as I walked toward an overlook to sit and meditate, he flew down over me again.

I was running away from myself because I was afraid. I also needed food because I hadn't eaten all day. I went back to the car and opened my phone wallet. The number was 144, the sign of a lightworker. I thought, "Oh man, I am in trouble." I went back to the edge of the cliff that overlooked the pristine wilderness of pine forest. I prayed, offered tobacco, and ate some sardines from a can. Then I offered some sardines over near a tree, so hopefully the hawk or other animals would have food.

I attempted to meditate there at the power spot but felt overwhelmed and scared. That night back in Denver, while I was dreaming, I had a profound clear vision and warning. I heard a group of ancient voices speaking to me in the dream, with a backdrop of starlight draped over a dark indigo tapestry. Then a Red-Tailed Hawk swooped in and filled my third eye, as big as a movie screen. As I slept, my consciousness said, "How can he do that?" The ancients replied, "This heavy energy you are feeling is not you! The battle has been going on since the beginning of time...and THIS is the last battle for Earth!" I woke up with incredible relief, thinking, "Man, I thought all this was just me." I had three experiences that shook me to my bones until I heard God's warning call.

The third warning came when I went on a psychedelic medicine journey in a different part of Colorado Springs on the Red Rock Trail. For several hours, I sat in place by the Grandfather rocks. The vision descended from the heavens and then into my third eye, when I heard God speak directly to me. I saw my video footage draped in front of me with the squares and pixelation of my face and costume broken into thousands of pieces.

God said, "Do you see this?" and I replied, "Yeah." He said, "Don't do this." When his stern voice intervened, I knew God was saving me from being trailed by the oil and gas monsters who had been following other Colorado Rising team members. I let Jesse know I wouldn't be showing the episode on TV.

After this experience, I couldn't produce another episode until I took time off to reimagine ways to show people "how" to honor and cherish the Earth by example. So there I was again, running in loops and circles, infinity signs through time.

I was feeling unsupported by humans and without a movement of people who were on MY side. As I stood between the ancients and the future, my inner fire burned, but my inner warrior cowered in fear! How could we salvage the beauty that the Earth still embodies and save her unscarred landscapes from the hands of the oil tycoons?

This story continues. (Choose your own adventure style on page 165, Serpentbird De-Fractivisation.)

Heeding the Call to be a Priestess
July 2011

From my womb, I drew up a new intention after feeling a loss with the horror film camera guy and the abandonment of my anti-fracking movie. As I prayed with God, I felt my sacral chakra, my 'womb of creating' with a new intent. I felt a resonant shift in my body as I re-visioned my plans and downloaded the new vision. In that moment, I knew bringing people together in real time and integrating them with nature, the way I experience it, would be more fulfilling than making the movie. I knew I wanted people to reconnect to the land and nature while respecting Mother Earth.

When Marc and I lived on West Tompkins, I convinced him to save money to take a Reiki course as a means make a living. Yet upon this decision, I saw within myself another void that wanted to be filled. I saved money as well, so that I could study Reiki 1 in Grandview. Days before my first class, I had a dream where I saw myself in a white wedding dress. This wedding, however, symbolized the marriage of a new part of myself coming forward into my consciousness.

Call of the Pleiadians
Galactic Federation of Light - St. Augustine, Florida 2010

On October 1st, 2010, I traveled to Florida where my mother was willing and able to buy me a used car. This was a pattern with her that played out for many years. After receiving the car, my plan was to quit my warehouse job, start a new housecleaning business, and have more time for my creative projects on weekends. I went through challenges with my mother, of course. I felt that I was purifying many layers of old energy and prayed to Jesus frequently to protect me from her. She would offer to buy the car and then she wouldn't. She feared that I was not appreciative.

I prayed and saw in my meditations that Jesus and I made a rainbow over the house. I finally got a car but didn't have the best feelings about it being a solid car for the money my mom spent. It was a strange gold or sand colored Hyundai Elantra. To offset its muddy brown color, I decided to call it the Vision Quest, because it looked like fine sparkling sand you would see in the southwestern deserts.

Egypt Future Calling and the Completion Lifetime

While I was with my mother, I took many long walks and went running around the neighborhood. One time, as I ran past someone's home, I spotted three palm-sized toy pyramids, marking the outer rim of a yard. They seemed kitschy and out of place to me. All of a sudden, as I ran past them, my guides mentioned the name Hatshepsut. I had no idea who this was, or why I heard this one word so clearly.

My life as Queen Hatshepsut connects to my current life with the Abel family but is still being uncovered with the help of my current hypnotherapist. I hope to write a separate book about that lifetime in the future. The ancient past self is also my future self, dancing and merging in and out of the sands of time. My soul had already been programmed with knowledge that was needed for humanity's ascension to 5D unity consciousness.

Once I had the "Vision Quest Car" in my possession, I was finally free from staying with my mom and sister. I was very excited to leave by myself to and headed to Saint Augustine to swim in the ocean! Driving down I-95, I cranked the stereo up as the 70s rock tune by the Steve Miller Band "Fly like an Eagle" played. As I drove, my sense of hope and aliveness came back, because I knew I would have the ability to get out of the warehouse job soon. I could also feel pulses of electricity swirl around me, communing with my Galactic self. My new car, the Vision Quest, was definitely being driven by the light-beings surrounding me.

On my way to the beach, I had my little poetry journal on the steering wheel and drank a Java Monster energy drink. The feeling of being so high helped me raise my vibration and opened my psychic abilities.

The Pleiadians were giving me ideas while I got exceptionally high on guarana and other stimulants. They wanted me to write a book about Metaphysics and healing. I don't know how I knew it was the Pleiadians, I never had an awareness that could differentiate who they were until this convergence happened. A lighter frequency continued to swirl around my body and my car. The Pleiadians spoke as a meshed together team of feminine voices and urged me to start a group called the Serpentbird Seven. Holy Wow?!!? I didn't quite know how to process all of this, but I knew I was creating a new phase in my life that would help lift myself out of the mundane existence I was experiencing at the warehouse. I think the Pleiadians knew that the time was ripe for me to start a tribe of healers.

When I got to the ocean and dove in, the water spoke to me in beautiful poetic phrases. I was challenged since I couldn't write it down! I received an initiatory healing from many beings of light and the ocean knocked me over many times. Each time, I could see my chakras in my third eye. A lot of blockages were released, and green light replaced them.

While I was in Saint Augustine, I visited the Fountain of Youth Park. A clear-cut example of the intersection of native culture and white colonizers was shown to me. When I arrived, I paid the park entrance fees and showed my new AAA discounts. While I stood at the gate, I felt the old power structures of man fencing in the expansive primal energy that radiated from the glorious and stunning 15-acre waterfront property. In this strange place, where Caucasian and native converge, I was reminded again and again of who I was. I felt it, but it wasn't until years later I saw how my being was the center of these diversities, from the past version of me with Native lifetimes to the current version of me, raised from middle class life in a colonial pillared house.

I was astonished to learn that this place was home to a 5000-year matriarchal culture, the Timucuans. I found the land to be beyond ecstatic energetically and could feel it empowering me to step into my new ceremonial role as a priestess. I knew that the Timucuans were a matriarchal culture, and it opened my eyes to see the patriarchy as an invasive species, who wound their parking lots and roads around the women, the flowers, trees, and the sacred waters of the "Fountain of Youth."

I found myself wandering past huge peacocks. They opened their "eyed" wing fans and led me over to a planetarium, where I could watch virtual stars and planets. I can't remember what movie was playing and I was very high on an energy drink, but I do remember that there was Pleiadian energy around me, lifting me up. I had been feeling stifled without a car, but now knew that I could go to another level spiritually, as I processed and shook with love and life and purged old energies with my light-team.

Crow and Serpentbird Engagement!
Ohio 11/11/10

I got back to Ohio in the Vision Quest car just in time to experience the 11/11/10 gateway. When I arrived, I met up with Marc for a party with his band at O'Reilly's Pub on High Street in Columbus. I could see something secretive had been happening between him and his friends. They encouraged him to head home with me, but when I looked at Drew, I could see he was hiding a secret in a crooked smile.

When we got back to 37 W. Tompkins, Marc got down on his knees in our kitchen and presented me with a beautiful antique diamond ring! In that moment, I clamored backwards, feeling very unsure and unloving. We had talked about getting married before, so I kind of knew this proposal was coming. The problem was that I had some unresolved issues with him. As he went down on one knee, he proposed to me while in a state of drunkenness. I accepted, but felt that this scene was all wrong. The energy flooding my body was scattered and made me tremble and shake just as much as Marc was. But even in my fear of unknowing, I accepted his proposal.

In the weeks to follow, I decided to write a contract for him to sign, showing me that he could be and stay sober if we were to get married. He took the agreement seriously and changed his habits to meet the requirements for the marriage. I always felt burdened with the need to keep overpowering him and convincing him to surrender and heal. I knew if I was patient, he could overcome his addiction.

During this chapter of our lives, we practiced the medicine wheel ceremony together. I felt we should get married in one, because other areas of religious expression did not feel good to me. I had spent a lot of time at Phoenix Books during the past year and knew of a medicine man and minister who had his business card on the bulletin board at the bookstore.

I called the number on the card and explained that my partner and I were seeking a Native American elder who would marry us in a medicine wheel. When we interviewed him, he explained how he would do it. I spent a few sessions with him alone because Marc was still working during the day at the warehouse. This medicine man, I will call him "Eddy," wrote that he was of a Cherokee band. He told me that it is possible to get married in a medicine wheel and that it would be created over seven days, because he said it would take that amount of time to bless the land. I was enchanted both with his stories and the new knowledge that the medicine wheel was something that could be cultivated over time, not just in one day.

At one of our meetings, he told me he frequently had disputes with another local 'medicine person' who held sweat lodges in town. Eddy told me he threatened to kill the other local medicine man and mentioned he had a gun. As Marc and I sat across the table from him, we felt our stomachs turn.

I consulted my tarot deck for guidance. I didn't know much about the Akashic Records or about asking my higher self, because I was still heavily reliant on external sources of divination. Over the course of writing this memoir, I realized there were many actions I took that were not aligned with the will of my higher self. I used the tarot cards to pull past, present, and future readings. I received the Judgement card multiple times. For several weeks, I couldn't figure out what this card was telling me. The lessons that screamed at me from the heart of the cosmos and from the etheric teachings of medicine wheel were about PEACE! I knew that the person who would marry us needed to stand for Peace, the primary lesson of peace.

The Call to be a Priestess - and the Power of Ceremony

It was clear that I was entering a new phase of life. My ecstatic love affair with "Rock n Roll" had its place. Now the power of the medicine wheel was taking the forefront; I knew I needed to focus on it and let my passion for the music scene subside.

I had to tell Eddy that because of his gun toting, he would not be our wedding officiant. We asked Marc's sister to do it instead. I kept asking God, in sorrow, "WHY? Why can't we rely on someone to guide us in these old medicine ways?" As this lesson ended, I stared into the image of the Judgment card over and over and felt a greater initiation being enacted by the cosmos. I had hoped and longed for a spiritual mentor who would be Native American. After this lesson, it was clear that Spirit was going to lead me and I would be taught by higher mystical forces through my channeling abilities.

I channeled much of the guidance from ascended Masters. I committed to NOT carry any weapons, to bring the teaching of peace. I didn't NEED to carry a weapon to defend myself, because I trusted that I was divinely guided and protected. My lifestyle would soon become a distraction from "the mission." In fact, every time I went to a show, there were signs all around that told me to refocus my attention on my bigger calling to be a priestess and teacher of unity.

I was following Solara An-Ra on YouTube. She is a Pleiadian channel and meditation teacher. Solara influenced me to strengthen and ground myself with her meditations. In 2011, she was traveling around the United States, building medicine wheels everywhere she could, to heal the land of the past where there had been Indian wars, bloodshed, and violence. She explained that it was important to anchor incoming light for the 2012 gateway. On her website, she had explicit instructions on how to make medicine wheels with crystals. She encouraged people to make the medicine wheels themselves to help anchor the light. After reading the page on her website, I had dreams about stepping into 'new' shoes. Who knew that I would have to absorb and contemplate, then enact the role of priestess? The information on that page resonated so much with me that I made a conscious mental shift to believe in my power to lead within my community.

> **Rainbow Warriors Reader's Note:** *What is a priestess? The role of priestess is one who can decipher the hidden realms and mystical forces of nature. She is a channel for the cosmos and has a vital role to embody the energy of the divine. She embodies the divine feminine and brings the sacred energy of the Goddess to her community by creating practical experiences with ceremonies. She is a guardian of ancient wisdom, rituals, and song. She has the ability to identify the talents and gifts of her community and helps to illuminate them.*

Later in my quest for lost knowledge, I questioned how 'white' folks could feel comfortable using Native American based ceremonies. I found information on the star system of the Pleiadians and their connection to medicine wheels. I thought that if "I" am Pleiadian and "Solara" is Pleiadian, this system must go beyond the cultural ties of blood and native-born ownership. The Pleiades system is also referred to as the Seven Sisters because we can see the main stars from Earth.

The Pleiades

The system of working with cardinal directions and totem energy was a way for me to express a calling of my heart through ritual. Up until this point in my life, I had no grounded expression for my devotion to the beauty of nature. Medicine wheel ceremony practiced over a seven-day period gave me a foundation for surrendering and creating outdoor devotional events that would be held in local public parks. This gave me the added challenge of seeing how I could work with people who were not necessarily invited by me personally or with members of the community that might be in the area, but unknowingly, subconsciously called to the ceremony.

Original Serpentbird 7 gathering in Ohio

PART THREE: SERPENTBIRD THE HEALER

Birth of the Serpentbird Seven Tribe
Columbus, Ohio 2010

After many dream confirmations, the call to action could no longer go unanswered. It was time to assemble my team of healers. I informed them that I had held them in mind for a long time. I had my poetry notebook from the trip to Florida with all their names already printed in blue ink, where I had written the names of people who had interest in developing themselves spiritually. Many of these friends had clairvoyant abilities and were already on a journey of awakening to higher truths. The thought of gathering friends with these abilities inspired me to move forward with the project.

I followed my gut feelings to make medicine that would relate to the prophecy of the Cree "Rainbow Warriors." This was a vision of unity that allowed the blending of all people's beliefs and traditions in one harmonious circle. This can also be referred to as "The Whirling Rainbow," symbolizing unity and harmony. I always had a deep desire to 'belong' and now I had an opportunity to create a cohesive community of light.

The Serpentbird Seven Tribe members were Dawn, Alex, Crow, Michael, Melanie, Nick, and me, Serpentbird. The idea I had in mind would be for the core members to hold a ceremony for healing that could be attended by a larger community in public parks. This project spanned about a year and a half of ceremonies.

I chose Dawn and Alex, who were in a partnership at the time. Dawn had many extrasensory and clairvoyant powers. Alex had a background in visual and digital video art and was studying yoga as well. I frequently looked to Dawn for intuitive life guidance, because I did not yet know that my natural psychic gifts could be strengthened like hers.

My partner Crow had the ability to see ancestor spirits on the other side, with his eyes open. He was gifted in playing piano, song writing, and Reiki healing. Michael was a talented poet and had the ability to see into past dimensions while we were in the medicine wheel. My friend Melanie was in tune with the elemental spirits, and it seemed we both had the power to bring on the sun or thunder showers when we put our mind and intent into it. My friend Nick, a Shawnee Indian, was a talented dancer and poet. He had tattoos on each inner elbow depicting the medicine wheel with feathers coming off it. He always brought his passion for the ceremony, prayer, the land, and the people. This tribe I called together created a microcosm, where the living, breathing rainbow prophecy could be seen, felt, and explored. Together we made magic.

The medicine wheel ceremonies gave me the opportunity to explore my own soul's latent wisdom, gathered from past and future lives. I rediscovered talents that help me identify a 'crystal cure' for the needs of individuals and groups. In general, I realized that 'magic' generates a feeling of freedom and opens my heart to infinite potential with the Divine. Often, I would surprise myself by having an etheric download from the 'Crystal Kingdom,' which gave me precognitions about which crystals I needed to heal the people who would be there.

What is magic? I feel that magic is about diving into power that comes from my imagination. I have always been excited and stimulated easily with this power from childhood. Creating paintings or drawings also helps me access this power, because I am in a state of joy. Becoming ecstatic is also a place of power. With every ceremony, I have the intention of bringing people to that ecstatic state. I'm always amazed at how quickly I can bring people from a traumatic wound or those carrying a fixation dominant in materialism to a place of peace, gentleness, and ease. The power of holding a circle as a priestess is an honor and a gift that I appreciate within myself. When joining hands and hearts, with facilitation by crystals, we experience an acceleration, much like a wheel in motion.

The most beneficial tool I had in creating ceremonies that followed the Native American medicine wheel layout with the four directions was using the Jamie Sams medicine cards. I learned spirit animal medicines by giving people readings based on the book Animal Medicine. I even had a totem party and did a long reading with a sign-up sheet. I began to understand that a totem helps you connect to your personal power. KNOWING what powers you are working with in the first place is what helps you awaken to latent energy that you are not using. Through her card system, I was able to assess what was happening with my group and how to best offer the type of energy they would be able to respond to and receive. Becoming a leader is many more times humbling than empowering, because there is sacrifice in creating with many people working toward the same goal.

During the process of organizing the groups, I repeatedly had to surrender to the Divine and feel this was ultimately my biggest lesson. No matter how much I wanted someone to be at my ceremonies, it was up to a higher power to decide who needed to be there.

Psychically I began to see and feel undercurrents of Indian guides, masters, and other unknown beings working their powers in tandem with me. The circle became a sacred Temple, in which only those who really needed the medicine could even attempt to step inside. Again and again, I found myself surrendering my ego so that I could affirm that all was being taken care of for the highest good of each person. I needed to deepen my capacity for unconditional love between the group members and the participants.

I was always surprised and overwhelmed when I realized how people at the ceremony needed to share their deepest feelings of sorrow and loss. Many times, people very close to me having lost a grandmother would stand in total surrender and reflection while they shared with the group.

Early in my practice, I found myself stunned or shut down. In those moments, I was at a loss for words to aid in their healing and could only hope that the community we were with would allow those who needed love to receive it through intense listening and presence.

The experience I had with creating medicine wheels allowed me to back away from my own desires and wants within my capitalist agendas and enter a realm that felt lighter and more positive. The experience of being able to travel between realms gave me more fluidity in how I 'un-planned' my days and my life. For many years, I trained myself to plan out my days and weeks. I planned myself into rigid routines, which sometimes took me out of the possibility of possibilities. The way in which I was able to exit the matrix of capitalism was the way I could help others see what we unconsciously agree to in our culture. The medicine wheel reconnects us to a living world that is harmonious with the desires of Spirit.

Serpentbird Seven Tribe in Action - Columbus, Ohio
Fall Equinox Ceremony, September 23, 2011

I learned how to set the stones at Northmoor Park, situated along the Olentangy River. This part of the park was my first choice for the fall Equinox ceremony. There were six-foot-tall grasses in this area, which I knew would keep most people from interfering with the ritual. For seven days I prepared the land with stones and my prayers. I encountered fairies and had an experience with a magenta orb, which was Mother Mary.

To my surprise, I was monitored many times by military helicopters flying directly over my head as I set out quartz crystals. I had to surrender my fears while in the wheel because thought creates form. Years later, I learned from my Native Cherokee grandmother and teacher that when we create a huge vortex of energy, it creates a signal on radar. The military must investigate when they see a spike go across the radar screen. This happened during my very first attempt at creating a seven-day ritual in a public park. It didn't scare me, it perplexed me. I kept going and laughed at them inside my own mind as they flew away over a field of tall grass and trees.

I was reinventing myself from filmmaker to priestess and had to rely on what I read in books about the medicine wheel. How I built a medicine wheel was based on diagrams from the book "The Sacred Tree" and the direct communion I had with the Creator.

We didn't always know what we were doing, but Marc was supportive and came with me to pray with tobacco before our final seventh day. I wore silver and black and sneakers with the five-pointed star on the sides. It was cold and wet from rain. The clouds were grey, but at least ten people joined the Serpentbird Seven for the ceremony. At the East gate, I had my friend Bree hand out seeds of corn to the participants as they entered the sacred circle, representing the promise of new beginnings.

During that ceremony, we had a person stand in each direction with a special offering and a ritual of their own. Crow's offering was a sound healing in the south with a Djembe. Dawn did a third eye anointing and activation in the west. Alex taught yoga, setting up an entire blanket in the north to represent the Elders. He always came with many offerings and outshined us many times, which makes me laugh in hindsight.

At the end of the ceremony, we danced to represent the movement of the Hawk totem. I had made ribbon sticks that we could flail and move around with to express our joy for life. We also had a water bucket with a huge ladle, so that we could bring water from the river into the circle and then at the end, offer it back to the river to charge it with our ceremonial blessings.

An Incan Priest Challenges the Zero Point
Autumn Medicine Wheel, Columbus Ohio 2011

My friend and spiritual mentor Pamela ruffled my feathers when I was planning the fall ceremony. Upon assembling the Serpentbird Seven tribe, she tried to convince me to make her a key part of the core group. She went on and on about manifesting things and desperately wanted to bring her knowledge to my group. However, forming this group with people I chose myself was my time to be a leader. Her intention was really to come in and direct and control the members. I followed my instincts and told her that she could not be a core member. When I made a medicine wheel on the Autumn Equinox, she kept asking if she could lead a manifestation segment. I told her she could have ten minutes during the ceremony, but she didn't want that. She wanted to be the star and center stage.

My friend Dawn told me she could see how Pamela would come to the ceremony and push my buttons, so I would have to stand my ground. Pamela showed up in a taxicab and brought all kinds of chairs, crystals, and ceremonial objects, as if it were her event. She wore a magenta-colored poncho that was from Peru. When she walked up to my group of friends, her presence emitted a strong masculine vibe.

We argued about her disrupting the event. She shook and trembled with anxiety and anger, and I couldn't tell if she was just suffering from her meds. Anyway, I figured out later through my meditation that we both lived in a past life where we were in an Incan ceremonial temple. I was her teacher, and for some reason pushed her off the edge of the stone floor. She fell into a fire. The medicine wheel was apparently to heal this lifetime we had and restore balance between us. It was after this ceremony that I saw and felt everything that happened during my dream time. I also learned that this medicine wheel went beyond the limits of the "now" reality. It encompassed the transmigration of the soul. Therefore, the medicine wheel is the ultimate healing tool for humanity during this ascension.

Ritual is "Grounding" for a High Priestess
Columbus, Ohio 2011

As I embarked on learning the process of developing the rituals of building medicine wheels, I read Solara's instructions on her website and discovered how to use different types of crystals. I often used rose quartz, Apache tear, amethyst, and citrine. These stones were anchors for the center of the wheel and the four directions.

It wasn't until I met Firedancer and took her class inside a bookstore that I discovered the power of using clear quartz crystals. I found them to have a greater uniformity and were easier for me to program with my intent. However, she taught us that we could even use hairpins to make a medicine wheel, and that it is really our intent that is important. She also spoke about the crystals being akin to the element of fire, and that a crystal grid will warm up any space. I felt and saw light travel in a spiral around the group at the bookstore, fiercely zipping through the crystals like a lasso of lightning.

Through my entire life, I have had difficulty focusing my attention. It is not like having a limited attention span, but more about concentration. I feel that the practice of ritual and working with the ascended masters has helped me with this.

When setting a medicine wheel, it is important to have a pure heart, mental clarity, and intent. Each time I create one, I feel like I am starting over. It is an eerie feeling of emptiness, but also where creation is in my hands, ready to begin. The memories of past rituals and medicine ceremonies seem to be totally inaccessible in my mind. I often wonder how much of this is me and how much of it is the universal mind intervening with my own.

With each ceremony, I have developed ways to use stones and sacred objects differently. Each medicine wheel, I feel, needs to be built with the clear quartz, tobacco prayer, and lots of sage to build the dome of energy. I use tobacco smoke to call in native spirits to help with the ceremony.

Ritual is a practice that allows me to witness the presence of the supernatural, and to transcend the laws of nature.

Serpentbird and Crow Wedding
The Broken Bride of Boston, Summer 2011

Marc and I searched for a good date to get married by going to Phoenix Books, where we had a special astrological synastry chart made. We took Bob Peters' advice and got married on July 30, 2011. There were a lot of positive aspects that the planets were making, allowing us to share in future endeavors that we could accomplish together.

After meeting with Eddy, we decided to make a medicine wheel. According to him, we only needed to bless the land, and to practice for seven days leading up to the ceremony. While planning the wedding, we knew we needed to work more so with Marc's family than mine, and we had to decide between having the ceremony in Ohio or Boston. We chose Boston because his family had a lot of private land where we could have a large medicine wheel and the freedom to use the land in a sacred way, completely undisturbed.

The planning issues that kept ringing in my mind were issues of old and new merging, our old selves from native lifetimes merging with timelines of colonial mind constructs. Marc's mother wanted us to have a legal marriage, but I did not. I felt that it was too confining for us. I think subconsciously or consciously, I wasn't sure how Marc could ever support me financially because of his attitude toward money, but his mother insisted on a legal marriage. Francesca, Marc's sister, had to get a minister's license to help us out. Most of our friends could not afford to fly out from Ohio for our ceremony, which made me sad, but we were able to have some key friends come and represent the four directions in the ceremony.

We drove the Vision Quest car across Ohio, Pennsylvania, New York, and then to Boston. I didn't take any time to rest and didn't get a hotel because we didn't really have the money. This set me up to have my entire body-system crash, and my brain chemistry couldn't recover, even by the day of the wedding. I tried taking Melatonin, which helped a little by day five.

Marc's parents surprised us by having a man build a stone platform in the shape of a wheel, where we were going to have the ceremony. I was concerned, because the stone prevented my feet from having direct contact with the Earth. It was difficult to get some of the celestial subtle energies grounded, because the stone platform was dense and prevented the earth's energy from rising. All I could think about was the man setting the wheel, and somehow his masculine energy was too much to have the energy set right. No matter how beautiful his craft was or the intention behind the gift that Marc's parents were trying to give to us, it wouldn't work. I was pretty self-centered.

Between Marc and me and his parents, we also had conflicting views about our choice of bridal fashion. We were being pressured, mainly by Marc's mother, to dress in traditional wedding clothes. We didn't want to wear modern clothes for the ceremony, so we wore white cotton garments for the medicine wheel ceremony, and then changed into traditional American wedding attire afterwards.

I wrote vows for the both of us and found myself writing something beautiful and poetic, but I could NOT reveal a purpose of solid commitment. I even told Marc's mother that the vows would be secret until the ceremony. This need for secrecy was wrapped up in a past life karmic contract that I would later see in my Akashic Records when I was in California in 2022!

As I look back, none of this wedding journey was aligned in complete integrity with what my higher self was saying. I feel that my ego took over the need to be aligned with the will of the Creator. However, what made sense to me was to serve the Earth and help humanity evolve. The power of serving medicine to the people overcame me at every turn. I was drunk with the power of my newfound magic, converging with the forces of nature, angels, native guides, land guardians, and animals, creating a microcosm for transformation within the cosmos.

Whether or not our marriage was going to last, I knew that I was making sacrifices of my heart to create a bigger gathering of diverse peoples with diverse beliefs. Ultimately, I felt that the wedding ceremony healed lifetimes between me and Marcello, but additional healing would be needed years later when I had more skill in uncovering 'dark truths' in our soul history.

There were circles within circles converging, threads of souls being re-stitched and un-breaking mistakes, iniquities, battles, and harmonizing purpose beyond their small-minded understanding, including land guardians, colonizers, ancestors, white people, boat people, and native Indians! How do I know these things? Healing souls, healing their lifetimes without their conscious understanding? Somehow, I feel it. I feel the energy and I know that the past must be healed for people to evolve. There is Grace in the wheel. Group healing is possible with the medicine wheel. I feel that a higher intelligence was haunting me to take on this practice!

The night before the wedding, clouds and rain came in, so I called Pamela to get her advice on what to do. She said we could move the clouds. Marc and I tried not to be sad about what tomorrow might bring, so we just went outside in the dark to perform some rituals. We picked up sticks and talked to the clouds above us. Marc was silly and tapped the sticks in the air and on the ground. We offered tobacco prayers and smoke while moving clockwise around the circle. Marc was always great at getting the smoke to rise and become thick, because he had a better handle on the fire element than I did.

At one point, he stopped in his tracks and told me what he was seeing. With his own eyes he was seeing 80 native people sitting in the white chairs that had been put out for the wedding ceremony. I was frightened at first, because I couldn't see them. Eerie feelings and chills came over me when he told me what was happening, but then I was moved to tears, knowing that there was so much spiritual support from the ancestors of the land. I could still hardly fathom the fact that we connected the spirits that we were calling into the medicine wheel, that it was real.

When our wedding day arrived, I took a long walk around the streets surrounding the property. It was a sunny day and warm. As I walked along Lee Road, I watched to see what animals crossed my path, because I knew it would be important to the medicine that the wheel would bestow on me. A blue heron flew directly above my head. This was a sign of self-reflection from what I had learned about totems. However, I felt it also indicated there was something within myself that I wasn't being honest about. I felt that commitment would be tough because our ways of being intimate were difficult. I was still feeling wild inside and did not know if I could be completely committed to one person sexually.

When I was getting ready for the ceremony, I felt alone. Even with Marc's sisters around to help me, I felt eerily alone. I went outside in the basic white outfit and thought I looked pretty. I also thought my whole life would change once I headed downstairs. I was going to feel different.

Everyone asked afterward if I felt different, but the answer was, "No." How could this be? I was not a whole individual to begin with, so how could I merge with another soul? I couldn't. I would not be an individual until I underwent my solo journey of traveling over the next ten years.

Firedancer, My First Nations Teacher
Firedancer! Prayer! Tobacco Spirit of Gratitude! - February 2010

My heart longed to find an elder Native American teacher to learn firsthand about the medicine wheel. Beyond the longing was a need for validation from someone of native blood, who would help me feel comfortable in my current incarnation with a climate where many people are screaming about appropriation. After many years, I came to the conclusion that the bottom line is whether this medicine works or has ever hurt anyone. The answer is that it has never hurt anyone because only the people who need to be there come to receive its natural power.

I always interpreted that since I found it so difficult to find a native to teach me about this ceremonial art, my consciousness and evolution as a soul needed to experiment and trust my instincts, as well as learn from ascended masters and the Pleiadians. I also needed to remember that in past lives, I was a high priestess with access to ancient knowledge.

The burning question was, "Why?" Why don't you see natives practicing this ceremony if it has so much potential for healing? It was illegal for them to practice any of their ceremonies in America until the American Indian Religious Freedom Act was passed in 1978. The truths of our history and times were and still are difficult to integrate into my consciousness.

In 2012, I was surprised, grateful, and even shocked to see a flyer posted at Phoenix Book store announcing that Firedancer would be teaching a workshop called "Living the Medicine Wheel." Firedancer is a Native-born Choctaw Indian who would be in Columbus for a whole week. Grandmother Firedancer was a medicine teacher, elder Choctaw,

Cherokee, and adopted Lakota Oyata, a pipe carrier, minister, counselor, and White Bison meditation facilitator from Colorado.

We were approaching the sacred 2012 gateway and Firedancer was determined to help us prepare. I had always dreamed that I would be part of a prophecy outside of the modern matrix of capitalism. In my soul, I felt a strong urge to leave all I had created in Columbus, Ohio and move to another city. I wanted to find funding for my environmental art films. While Firedancer was in town, I hoped to meet with her privately and see if she could help me figure out whether I should make this big change and if I should move to a city that offered more support for my art.

During the week she was in town, I attended her medicine wheel class at Phoenix Books. She created a wheel inside the store with huge clear quartz crystals. She taught us many things about the wheels and explained that you can create different kinds besides the basic four direction wheel. She also used different totems than the ones I was using. The clear quartz crystals she used helped me understand that I could generate a greater energy for my wheels by using clear quartz as a base. To this day as a medicine wheel teacher, one theme I have difficulty with is that I am not a native in this lifetime. Firedancer began her talks by saying that many cultures such as Celtic, Christian, and Native American have made and used different types of medicine wheels.

She also told us that she created medicine wheels with her teacher Sun Bear. Vincent LaDuke was an activist and environmentalist, Winona LaDuke's father. He was the one who wrote "Dancing with the Wheel," a medicine wheel workbook. I found it very interesting that Sun Bear was identified as a 'new age' author by Wikipedia because he brought native wisdom to ALL races.

Firedancer taught us that tobacco was a great amplifier for our prayers. She gave us a ritual that I use in all my ceremonial work to this day. First, she said all prayer is to give thanks. Begin with, "Thank You," she would say. This teaching helped me solidify how I approach my spiritual mind set. She told us that many religious folks will pray, "Gimme, gimme, gimme!" The creator has your best interest at heart and will give you what is best for you, not necessarily what you ask for. She said that we never have to light the tobacco on fire, we can put it in between our palms, say our prayer with intent, blow our breath into our hands, then make an offering to a tree or a crystal.

Firedancer's tobacco prayer has become a primary ritual that I use daily. It helps me so much because I can do it anywhere, giving gratitude, grounding, and clearing my thoughts. Usually the wind comes as I give thanks to sweep my aura clean of stagnant energy. She also told us that she almost died, which was why she became a teacher. She said during the time she almost crossed over, God told her not to go and to promise to tell people about him.

The use of tobacco in my medicine wheel ceremonies is very important to me. I know that if I use it, I can center myself more. I can get aligned with my truth in a quicker and stronger way. Once I make contact with the plant in my hands, I say my prayers out loud, so that I can hear the beating of my heart. The words then seem to come from my heart as well as my mind. Tobacco becomes a higher dialogue. I always make a prayer shape with my hands and put a small pinch of tobacco there. The prayer mudra itself is powerful in that it aligns all the chakras. After I finish praying with the tobacco in my hands, I blow my breath on it and then offer it to the stone or crystal.

While I was cleaning houses, I saw what I thought were signs. I kept seeing dragonfly totems on couch pillows, towels, and shower curtains when I was working. So I slowly began to prepare to move across the country.

What is a Serpentbird Medicine Wheel?

After working with Firedancer, my First Nations teacher, I developed my medicine wheel ceremony process. I studied books about medicine wheels before I practiced and led 10 group ceremonies outdoors in Ohio from 2010 to 2012. This self-initiation period proved to be healing for my community in Columbus, Ohio.

This book is NOT a replacement for study and deep understanding with Indigenous elders or personal initiations with me. I do not reveal the entire process here for safety reasons, because it contains the elements of "*high magic.*"

I invite people who want to study in person with a human being of integrity and good moral ethics to learn this ancient lost knowledge. It is a gift and ancient technology that not many make time for in this day and age. I have initiated people by invitation, but most successful medicine wheel practitioners were chosen by *the Creator*.

There are seven directions in total for a traditional 'sacred hoop' embodying the four directions.

You! Creator and Mother Earth in the Center
  To the East is the Eagle and the Hawk.
  To the South is the Wolf.
  To the West is the Serpent.
  To the North is the Bear.
Then you are back at the East again.

This is a tool I use to measure my progress in phases that include a place I live, a career I am in, and life in general. It is a sacred conversation with EVERYTHING. It is a way to find any lost parts of the self and pull them back into a sacred circle.

Reiki Crystalline Transformations
Grandview, Ohio February 2012

Originally, in my mind, Marc was supposed to be the energy healer in our partnership, but soon I had a shift in consciousness and a fire of desire burned within me. We started tucking away cash in a paper envelope, which we taped to the back of the closet. I knew that I needed to save money and wanted to take the level one Reiki training course.

I was having dreams about myself in a white wedding dress. This symbolized a marriage of my soul parts wanting to reunite. A marriage of soul to soul, self to self, lifetime to lifetime as a high priestess.

My experience at The Reiki Center awakened more parts of my feminine personality and enhanced my sensitivity to subtle energy. At the Reiki Center, we drank water from a glass pitcher that had rose quartz and amethyst in it to help amplify our intuitive powers. We attended lectures, then practiced laying our hands on different students. We learned a sequence of basic hand placements on the body. We learned about the human biofield, the Usui Reiki prayer, and were attuned by the end of the weekend.

When Marc and I worked at the book warehouse, my attitude was very masculine. I took the lead in our decision making much of the time. I was transitioning from working in a warehouse to building my own house cleaning company so I would have more time to create art.

In 2011, we had several parties for our metaphysical friends, along with the medicine wheel ceremonies. However, I wondered about living somewhere outside of Ohio, where we could find more support with government grants for our projects. I grew tired after noticing no one from our fabulous parties ever called to thank me. I get a lot of pleasure making the offerings but felt that something in the cycle of giving and receiving was unbalanced.

Four Months of Death
Portland, Oregon May 9, 2012

I flew to Portland with my bike, alone without Marc. I had the idea in my head that I was scouting out whether we wanted to live in Eugene or Portland. Using the www.couchsurfing.org website, I couch-surfed at stranger's homes. When I moved to Portland, I thought people there would accept that my mission was all about creating medicine wheels and saving the planet from destruction and fracking. However, during this new chapter living in Portland, I found that I really hadn't accepted myself. My ego had completely died and the strength I had built with my friends in Ohio was gone.

I discovered that moving to Portland had more to do with discovering who I was, rather than fitting in with a community. If anything, I would have needed to stay there longer to develop relationships and again lead the community. When Marc arrived, I was already volunteering in a kitchen at the church where a Permaculture festival, called the Village Building Convergence, was taking place.

I unexpectedly found myself looking at other men and craving sexual and romantic experiences outside of my marriage, but I knew I would not act on my urges. Marc arrived with our orange cat Abigail about two weeks after I decided we should live in Portland. When our eyes met, Marc looked at me with a solemn but passionate gaze. I felt extremely hesitant to even hug him, because I was lost in my own head trip. I could not come to terms with the new parts of my own expansion and sexual desires for other experiences.

For four months, we lived in the basement of a huge Victorian house, which also housed five or six lesbian women. It became apparent that Marc and I were becoming two different people, but at the same time we were mirrors of each other. We bounced our unprocessed beliefs of low self-esteem, lack of self-worth, self-hate, and worst of all poverty mentality between each other. When we fought about our ideas and I felt that he was wrong about something, it would spring back intensely and hurt me, like knives twisting in my wounds. Sometimes it felt like a flash of lightning flooded over my face to illuminate the lies I said about myself.

Marc continued to grow his dreadlocks very long, another rebellious act that added to his deeper study of Rastafarianism. He told me he was healing his body after taking Reiki Level II. He rolled around in bed with all his organs hurting intensely. I knew that my income at a Starbucks would not support us and I was fiercely angry with Marc for telling me he couldn't work during this transition.

I spent hours looking at a computer screen, staring at the jobs that were on Craigslist. There were janitorial jobs, nanny jobs, then I saw written in blue text that stood out to me, the massive amount of massage therapy jobs to be filled. Something lingered in my brain about that, but at the time I never thought that kind of work would be a possibility for me.

While Marc was healing, I had flashbacks of every other time I pulled the weight in relationships. He went deeper and deeper into his Rastafarian ideals and I didn't understand his new beliefs. The way we came together in the past to collaborate on the medicine wheels seemed lost with the simplicity I found in connecting to nature. Marc made his spiritual life into something so complex that it seemed to banish my sensuality. I felt like I needed to meet my needs with other men. I was sick of this. I wanted to die.

It would take me years to find out that through my life, I would have the feeling of wanting to die and invite it in. These death cycles brought in heavy energy around me and invited spirit attachments, who fed off the energies. I remember wearing two jade rings on my middle fingers to help me manifest more money. When Marc and I fought one day about money, I shattered one of the jade rings as I closed the sliding doors in the basement apartment. I knew this was an omen.

Multnomah Falls on Mushrooms
Multnomah Falls, Oregon July 2012

Note: the name Multnomah is Chinookan - toward water or toward the Columbia River, known in Chinookan as "the great water."

Marc and I went to Multnomah Falls and did a magic mushroom journey together. We prayed over the mushroom chocolates and wandered around the national park. I noticed huge amounts of people using iPads and cameras to photograph the tallest waterfall in the world. I thought it looked strange because I felt much like a human. This water was being over- photographed, like a runway model. It was being looked at as something novel, but at the same time not being respected. They were not putting themselves in the moment, they were just capturing an image that they could enjoy later by looking at their photographs.

That day, Marc and I both had amazing connections to the land. I felt called to sit near a little waterfall called Wahkeena. Afterwards, we sat together in a field. The mushroom medicine rose up inside me and all of a sudden my intense emotions blew, like a cork shooting out of a shaken champagne bottle. I remember loudly chanting sound syllables, "OH YE HE AYA HA." I became a version of myself that was more like a native of the land than my small consumerized self, working for Starbucks!

I don't know from what lifetime I was finding this information within my being. The clouds in the sky told me they were the 'cloud people' that you hear of in the Hopi and South American creation stories and even formed a "Serpentbird" in front of us! I felt as though I was being held and saluted by Quetzalcoatl himself. I sensed from the Cloud People that they knew we were on a sacred mushroom journey and they were assembling in the sky, like millions of souls collecting and grouping together to form the Quetzal in the sky. I felt closer to God in this experience than many other times in my life. I felt like my body, mind, and spirit were all participating fully in the tapestry of nature.

We saw very large crows and ravens all around us. There was one in particular that looked like Marc's Spirit Animal, which was crow or raven. It looked like a Chief in my multidimensional 'dragon vision.' I was seeing the bird as a person who was guarding this land. He swooped and flew across our line of vision. His spirit jumped out of his body slightly and what I saw was red and blue emblems on his body decorated by stars. It was as if he had been waiting for us to arrive, to celebrate the land and the animals in a way that would help the people who had lost touch with their souls integrate with the land.

The land and the crows cried and begged us to make a ceremony. I couldn't get over my discordance with Marc and I had no way to overcome my negativity. I had feelings of low self-worth beside the feelings of how we could be fully empowered with the versions of ourselves that could honor the land and people. There was a definite disconnect between modern life versus a simpler time on the planet and it just didn't seem like a war we could fight. We barely made enough money to survive, even living in the small basement in Portland.

One day out of desperation, I called a psychic hotline while I was in my car alone. The woman on the phone said I had a chance to start over. She said I could live my own life there without Marc. She told me I was there to meet a whole new circle of friends and that they would help me reach a new level with my photography. I kept thinking to myself that I had just promised to be with Marc for the rest of my life.

However, our belief systems around religion and money clashed so much that we couldn't stay together. I couldn't believe it. Why? We had just gotten married, and it was over, just like that? I felt so bad about myself I just wanted to die. I felt it every day, JUST DIE!

I was no longer cleaning houses and making good money. I was working for a Starbucks inside of Barnes and Noble, so I called it a fake Starbucks. The boss who hired me said that I was the lowest on the totem pole, which shook me to my bones. Just because I was the newest hire on the team, in her mind I was lowest in rank. A totem pole was traditionally a pillar that represented family lineage. The word "totem" comes from the Algonquian word "odoodem" meaning (his) kinship group.

I was using Jamie Sams' medicine cards, and I kept picking the Crow medicine card, which represented LAW/Karma. I stared at the image of the Crow looking at his reflection in the water, and I was filled with sadness and rage! When I meditated on the meaning, I realized later that it was unavoidable and that I needed to find a shaman who could help me with shadow work.

Now that I am looking back at this chapter in my life, I see I also missed an opportunity to understand a native past life I had in this area of the country.

Mount Shasta Mission to Find a Shaman
Mount Shasta, California July 2012

Somehow, even with my fears around money, I was able to take a four-day trip and drove to Mount Shasta, California. I had never been there before and rented a room at a hotel. I was using the Jamie Sams medicine cards, which told me that I was working on my self-esteem.

I searched for a female shaman. I saw a brochure for a vortex tour guide, who used energy to heal people out on the land. I called her while I was in my car. When I spoke to her, she told me in a very pompous tone that she was very booked up. She said she could do a "distance" healing for me on the phone for $120.00. This was a total rip off! I exclaimed to her, "I am *in* Mount Shasta!" This experience left me in disgust, but encouraged me to serve people in need, in person when at all possible.

I continued to search the bookstores and crystal shops in Mount Shasta while feeling helpless and alone. To escape my feelings, I got high on caffeine and attempted to meditate at a shop with crystal bowls of every color of the rainbow. While in meditation, the only thing I could figure out was that I needed to create more art, but I didn't trust or believe in myself.

As I left the store, I found a woman's business card with an East Indian sounding name. I knew there was something different about it and went to my car and called her. I was in tremendous fear that she would not meet with me in person, but she set an appointment with me. On the way back to the apartment, I drove past an "I AM" temple. When I met with her, she said she had her training through the "I AM" community. She told me she would use sacred mantras and holy names to clear my energy.

She welcomed me into her home and her husband pulled my astrological chart up on their big screen TV. She told me that I was using the totem of Leo the Lion today. To begin, I didn't understand why there would be no laying on of hands, but instead we sat in two large pink sofa chairs across from each other. Through my tears, I told her about what was happening to me. She was able to look into my past lives and pull up information.

She told me I was in China for many lifetimes and that she saw many red dragonflies spinning around my body in gold. I had a lifetime in which I was a powerful singer in China, that I had been embarrassed deeply, and that someone cut my throat.

She also said I had several lifetimes with Marc, and that I was from a Shoshone tribe. She said I would dance until I was exhausted and then fall on the ground. She screamed the holy names of gods and angels, to crack down walls of energy that were around my body. I specifically felt my wrists burning. When she used her voice emphatically by screaming, "Vairochina," I felt my wrists break free and my shackles loosening, but the grip of the shackles did not leave immediately. It was extremely painful!

It sucked that even after finding a shaman to help me to heal, I was still experiencing so much self-hate and pain that I couldn't love myself and STILL wanted to DIE!

Drum Call! Spirit Called
Back to Ohio, then to Boston 2013

I continued to work at Starbucks in Barnes and Noble until one day, while cashiering and making infinite amounts of iced lattes, I became aware of the escalator. I could hear it clanking and crashing, kuthunk, kuthunk, until I heard it like the sound of a medicine drum. Dum dakka, dum dakka, dakka dum. I clanked my hands on the silver counter and beat on it like a drum. I missed my friends in Ohio and knew that summer solstice was upon us.

I had to beg Marc to call his family, since we were one paycheck away from living in the car! I actually MADE HIM call his father, in Lowell, Massachusetts, who said we could move there. I was too afraid to separate from Marc yet, because I felt insecure and unsure of myself. I was ashamed that the marriage was failing and tried to hide it from my own family while I processed it all.

However, my ego had no issue with creating a power over Marc that deep inside, I knew was immature. I had him drive the Vision Quest car solo, with our cat Abigail, back to Ohio and then all the way back across the states. I flew out to Ohio and attended my sister's wedding without him. When my family asked where Marc was, I acted as though we both just needed time away from each other.

We eventually met up in Columbus, where we assembled on our sacred park lands and called our Tribe together again. This medicine ceremony was very large and very powerful because we could spend all our time preparing as we weren't working at the time. We stayed with Zoe Boyolus, who hosted us for two weeks. The ceremony was so powerful and our journey back across the country so intense that we couldn't move from the single extra bed in Zoe's living room. The bear medicine had conquered us. Our bodies recalibrated and we slept many times during the day.

On the way back to Boston, we stopped in upstate New York to stay with my friend Logan, so that we could share the medicine wheel knowledge with him. When we finally got to Lowell, Massachusetts, I needed to be alone with my feelings to face great loss. I was isolated in Lowell, where there wasn't much nightlife or connection. I tried my best and landed another job at a Starbucks in Arlington, downtown Boston.

Marc and I tried discussing long-term plans for our lives together, but we argued at every turn. I really wanted to live 'in community' or have a tiny home on wheels, but Marc wanted a camper van.

Marc was entrenched in reading the Bible. I would wake up in a twin bed, with a series of 14 books called The Apocrypha stretching the length of the wood antique dresser. It loomed and stared at me with its own eyes, as if it knew that I was trapped in a sexless monastery. Marc and I differed in how we wanted to experience God. I wanted to travel and take journeys for growth and enchanted mystical experiences. He wanted to read sacred texts and not share any of his wisdom with the world, which frustrated me until I wanted to shake my fists at him.

Serpentbird Answers the Call
Brew'd Awakening! Lowell, Massachusetts April 2013

Later that year, I was hired at a place called Brew'd Awakening. It very much lived up to its name. A woman named April liked to chuck sharp knife spreaders behind my back and have them land in the metallic industrial sink behind the Baristas. I kept telling myself that was my 'shaman in-training' experience. In reality, I knew it was unacceptable. As usual, I didn't speak up for myself for fear of losing my job.

However, working at Brew'd Awakening and being centered in Lowell wasn't all bad. I discovered that right down the street from me was a public access TV station. I quickly enrolled to be a member there so I could once again pursue my interest in filmmaking. I found out from the director that I could apply for a scholarship to their video and business program. I was able to relearn Final Cut Pro and began putting a group together in Lowell to help me produce a TV show called Sustainity TV. It would be about the insanity of trying to save the environment. I realized, after the business program, that my small video business was going to be too difficult to lift off on a shoestring budget. It was a much different scenario than starting my house cleaning businesses.

While working at the coffee shop, I met a man who needed ideas on places to visit. I told him about Sedona and how fascinating it was because of the vortexes there. I conveyed to him that this was really a call from my higher self, asking me to get out of my current situation. I prayed for answers from God. Why was I stuck? How could I get out of here? One day, a woman came in wearing a navy-blue lab coat. The coat looked more like something an auto-mechanic would wear, which made my head turn sideways in wonder. Then I saw the tag on her coat, with the word "MASSAGE" embroidered on it. The word MASSAGE instantly broke apart into particles of magical fairy dust and hit my left eyeball while the cash register drawer swung open and I handed her some change.

One day, on my way home from work, I rode my bike to the Romario Land Trust. I brought some poke weeds to transplant to the property and have my own patch of edible weeds. As soon as I dug my hands into the turf, my male Spirit guide barked loudly in my ear, "You can't plant anything here!" This message was so loud and clear that it made me cry. It made me angry to be such an unwanted bride here on the land.

Soon after this event, I went to see a psychic who did a card layout on my upcoming changes. She said that for my whole life I tried to be an artist, but now I was going to be a healer. I was landslides away from knowing that my journey to become a healer would be more about healing myself than others. The psychic said that I was co-dependent in my relationship with Marc. She said I would only be living at the estate for a few more months, but I was still very afraid to leave. Soon after my meeting with the psychic, I visited my mother in Florida. She said she would help me change careers and asked which school I wanted to attend. I told her that if there was a place I thought could make me happy, it would be Sedona. Her 300 days of sunshine and beautiful cloudscapes called me, and I would answer. When my mom and I looked up the cost to go to school, it was $6,000. This was the exact amount my mother told me my father had left in a CD account. It was through this synchronistic event that I knew that I was on the right path, led by Spirit.

I would not have predicted that massage therapy would be able to support my living and travel for seven years. Granted, it is not much to live on, but I am proud that I provided all I needed for myself with my own two hands. At times it barely provided, yet I always recovered by the hand of God.

Golden Dragonflies - Sacred Passage
Lowell, Massachusetts 2013

From the end of 2012 through the end of 2013, I worked to save my marriage to Marc. When I got back to Lowell from Florida, I told him I was ready to leave Lowell to go study massage therapy and figured out a plan to move to Sedona. It was the height of summer in August and the air in Lowell smelled sweet from fresh cut grass. There were beautiful days out on the land, but they were drowned in my sorrow. I cried for whole days sometimes because I had been so close to Marc.

One day, I noticed something phenomenal was happening on the chain link fence. There were at least twenty beautiful gold dragonflies perched on each post, looking like a fleet of air force pilots. I stared at them in wonder and disbelief. There were 20 of them landed perfectly on each post, as though they were expecting me to take flight to Arizona.

In the same week, I was laying on the couch on the porch, when a gold dragonfly flew up onto a long chain under the ceiling fan. My cat Abigail was on the porch watching it and was at first hunting it with her eyes. Then she took a big leap into the air and miraculously got high enough to grab it with her paws and mouth, to eat it. What were the chances I would be aware enough to witness this scene? I was proud to see her be able to jump so high and catch it in one fell swoop.

I had financial fears about being able to support myself while going through massage school and was in fear of not finding a home because I ruined my credit when I went to film school. I had to believe and trust in myself and in God that I would be able to support myself. Seeing the dragonflies gave me strength and hope. My original thought was to drive the Vision Quest car to Sedona, but one night, when Marc and I were driving back after enjoying a nice dinner together, I'd had one glass of wine and slammed the Vision Quest into the back of a Jeep. The front of the car buckled like a cheap soda can. After that, it was clear I would be flying to Arizona.

Most cars I owned during this 10-year journey lasted long enough to get me through a cycle of transformation. Then somehow, the car would die and propel me into the next chapter.

Massage School Mission
Sedona Bound 2014

When Marc dropped me off at the Boston airport, I was angry that we could not make the marriage work. I reiterated all the ways he could have focused on making a better living and being more open to making money. I had a total of two oversized backpacks with me for my departure to Phoenix - the Turtle bag from the man in Flagstaff and another enormous black Army backpack.

When I arrived in Phoenix, I was suffering from a sinus infection, so my whole head and ears were plugged up and blocked. However, I was feeling excited about my new life, even though I only had about $600 in my bank account. I took the airport shuttle van to Sedona, where they dropped us off at the Super 8. It was a rainy and cold day, but my excitement was activated seeing the towering red rocks.

Right next to the Super 8 was a place called Java Joe's. Upon entering the cafe with this awful head cold, I could see a man standing in the center of the cafe entertaining three women. His name was George Pierce, or Silver Wolf. I asked him a question and the next thing I knew, with all his might, he held my head with his big palms and sent intense Reiki healing through my entire head. This counted as my first Sedona miracle!

As if a miracle wasn't enough, a strange phenomenon known to many locals followed. Sedona decided to wipe out my computer. After booting it up a few times, it came up with a pink screen and locked me out of it. I knew that this had to correlate with the magnificent power of this small ancient city.

I couch-surfed with John who was willing to host me for a few days. He was very much about positivity and positive thinking. I slept on the couch and continued to pray that I would find a cheap room for rent quickly.

I went outside and wrote a list of three things I wanted to manifest on a piece of paper. Room for rent, job, and joy. Within a few days I manifested a room for rent on Inspirational Drive, and in a short period of time received everything else.

Becoming Turquoise with Uqualla
Sedona, Arizona - New Year's Eve 2014

Note: In 2024, James Uqualla, a Medicine Man from the Havasupai Tribe and his family actively participated in protesting Uranium mining, to protect their drinking water and to shut down Pinyon Plain Uranium Mine in Arizona. You can contact the Sierra Club Grand Canyon to get involved.

I celebrated my first New Year in Sedona in a sweat lodge with Uqualla at the Walk in Balance Center. We prayed, sang songs, and rattled gourds. After the ceremony we were gifted with handmade medicine bags. When Uqualla presented it to me, I could see it had a turquoise bead sewn onto the white leather. He said the blue represented the water clan and that we would be healing others this year. Once we were given our medicine bags, I entered the house, where my Cherokee grandmother gave me an Eagle feather for the pouch. The Walk in Balance Center was the home of Joseph "Grey-Wolf" and my "Cherokee Grandmother." They were my closest friends in Sedona. I would not have made it through my time there without their love and unwavering spiritual support.

After we had dinner, I met a handsome young man named Puma. I introduced myself as Serpentbird. He came with me on an adventure to Hopiland where we met Grandmother Rowena and we watched the Buffalo Dance on second mesa.

Massage School Begins
Sedona, Arizona - February 12, 2014

I sensed that this time of my life was more about an initiation and rite of passage, rather than a time of being in school. The Sedona School of Massage teachers emphasized that the five-month course would be for and about our own healing as much as it would be about training to heal others. I needed this time to help my transition in separating from Marc, my husband. I had left everything and everyone that was familiar to me to be in this sacred land.

Once I began the classes and was in the presence of Nancy Mathews and other amazing teachers, I knew I was in good care. When I was in the classroom, I could feel warm orange megalithic stones all around us in the distance through the soles of my feet. I kept trying to remember my feet while being ignited in the vibration of high vortex energy. Spinning on this gigantic ball of quartz that is Sedona, she helped me 'remember' but still I had to consciously remember my feet!

One of the first classes offered at the school was about the medicine wheel. As my teacher Nancy said, "It is a model of holism." I had to sit still and quiet, while my whole being ached to share my first-hand experiences leading medicine wheel ceremonies.

I was restless as I watched 12 students sit in wonder looking at the dry erase board. I could see question marks of stale energy and blank stares floating in the room. The teacher used a blue marker to write the characteristics of psychological states in different quadrants of the circle on the board. I really missed the smell of sage and the feeling of grass and dirt beneath my bare feet, while all I could smell now was the xylene fumes wafting from the trail of dry erase markers. At graduation, I was standing at the ready when the question was posed, "Who will lead us in a medicine wheel ceremony on Rick's property out in the middle of the Sedona desert?" That's right, Serpentbird!

My first Medicine Wheel ceremony in Sedona was with the graduating class on a very beautiful property in the middle of the desert. It was tucked away in the National Forest off Route 525. Large stone slabs had been placed in the dirt around the wheel. Unfortunately, I could not spend my usual 6 six days preparing on the land, because the site was on private property and we were only invited to be there for that specified time.

One of the most prominent and spiritual awakenings I had in massage school was when studying polarity therapy. My teacher explained that we would draw upon different systems of energy medicine within this system. Without doing any meditation to achieve an altered state, I started receiving visions. They happened during the daytime as well as in my dreams.

The image I remember most clearly was that I was in a photograph, somewhere between seven and ten years old, and there were many gold ankh shapes floating downward from heaven, as though the still photo also had an animated quality to it. The ankh, a symbol of life, was there to help me understand that I was connecting to a past version of myself in Egypt. As time went on, I met souls from Egyptian timelines that were called to go to Sedona School of Massage to heal from past lives as well.

Later during my time in Sedona, I spoke with a psychic guide about the ankh. She said that it meant 'completion' for me. My dad always told me, "You need to finish what you started." This was always such an eerie statement. It left an impression because he was not a man of many words.

Looking back on the massage school experience, I can say that what my soul longed for may have been better suited to other internal healing sciences. The fields of hypnotherapy, psychotherapy, and past life regression, combined with my clairvoyant ability, may have made more sense as a career path, though many elder women folk told me they felt doing bodywork was what kept me grounded. I suspect they were correct.

I struggled to remember anatomy terms or even hold the attention span needed to learn it.

I was working at a grocery when I wasn't at school, so all I wanted to do when I had downtime was sleep. I quickly learned that my 'gift' wasn't as a 'medical' massage therapist, but as an intuitive healer.

Earthship Arizona - Chevelon Canyon Ranches
Holbrook, Arizona 2014

Before I was able to leave for this trip, I had a major slew of shit storming my dimension. First, Whole Foods bought the company I was working for, so I was stuck in town till Thursday just to file 10 minutes of paperwork with them. Next up, my friend Hosh couldn't travel with me because he had more work to do for his company. Soooo, I had to relearn how to drive his manual transmission Honda. Well, THAT was fun...ooooh yeeeeeah!

On Friday, April 25th, 2014, I FINALLY left Sedona after six months of intense times. After loading my friend's tent, two sleeping bags, my camera and tobacco pouch into the little blue Honda Civic, I was off to Holbrook, Arizona. I took some reasonable directions down on paper. Driving up and away from town was fun and exhilarating, winding up through the switchbacks toward Flagstaff. I stopped off at Macy's Coffeehouse, hoping to meet a new face while slurping a Macchiato. It wasn't glamorous, but I enjoyed the Flagstaff people vibe more than I did the Sedonians.

On the road again, smoking tobacco and purging boredom, I drove 90 miles through Coconino to the Petrified Forest. Without any radio, I was mildly entertained with flat desert land views. The quaint town of Holbrook on old Route 66 was bustling with tourists taking pictures of fake wigwams, the Safeway, and some cafes. I picked up a bottle of Cabernet, and two bottles of coconut water. I knew in just a bit I would be entering no man's land, so I attempted to save myself from non-civilization where there wasn't much water.

I arrived at Hutch Rd, 15 miles from Holbrook. I could see miles and miles of flat land, sun-soaked earth, twisted pinyon pines, and scrub brush. There were high winds. I was told to find the Chevelon Canyon Ranches signs and then follow the pink flags. I got to the signs and saw that the pink flags were not marking off the kind of road that I was looking for. I drove and drove far down Hutch Road past many roaming cattle herds and hoped I would find the Earthship compound.

Finally, after stopping to pee a bunch of times and driving without really knowing where I was going, I turned back around to the Chevelon Canyon Ranches entrance. I got out of my car a few times to ask directions from strangers who were driving in. The second truck that stopped to help happened to be a couple who knew where the Earthship build lot was and had a detailed map of all the roads and lots. So, we made a directions list backwards. Eeeeeeek. They said they were out on the land scouting some property of their own so they could build Earthships as well. I asked the woman if I should head back to Holbrook to get more gas, but she said that I had come pretty far already. They were a super sweet pair...and gave me two eight-ounce bottles of water. They were very compassionate.

I followed the rest of the road signs with intense anticipation and some confidence that I would actually find the ranch. However, only about a quarter tank of gas was left and my personal water was already gone. Later, I realized that I was driving into oblivion and kind of losing my mind, while facing dehydration and cotton mouth every time the wind blew. I was thoroughly excited about being on the street Arapaho Drive, since I believed that it was still the thoroughfare for the native spirits.

I thought I was finally on the right road to the Earthship but soon realized that it trailed off into a pile of rocks. I drove back out to some now-familiar roads, feeling like leaving this territory entirely and turning around to reach Holbrook again. I was thoroughly lost. I parked the car and looked for a trailer, so I could find someone who would be able to direct me. Somehow, I went crazy and started shouting for Jesus. I was being totally ridiculous and walked away from the car without drinking enough water. The wind was blowing at 30 mph and drying out my mouth until I could taste the dirt and sand. After getting somewhat close to the run-down abandoned trailer I saw, I realized I had to find the nearest sane person immediately!

After trying to follow the directions again, I opted to follow the driveway I kept seeing with a white mailbox at the end. I drove down the driveway and parked my car, then met a woman named Lynn who was in a trailer on the land. I said, while shaking, "I'm so sorry, I am lost!" She spoke with a very warm heart, smiled, and said, "Well, don't be sorry about that!"

Next, I told her that I was there to find Ullyses and the Earthships. She said, "Oh yeah, I know him." She looked for someone's number on her cellphone. She offered me a beer and said I should relax for a while, that it was taco night. She told me about Al, her landlord. He lived in the nearby trailer on the land and knew how to get out to the ranch. Lynn said that everyone meets up for taco night anyway. I said, "Everyone?" and Lynn replied, "Yes, the whole community is invited."

I jumped up into a truck with a hillbilly and he took me to taco night. I was nervous because I didn't have Hosh's car, but they assured me they would show me how to get to the Earthship later, after we experienced Taco Night. When we arrived, a young man named Jordan noticed me and said, "Oooooh a new intern!"

As the night went on, I realized that Jordan wanted me to seduce him. I mustered up the courage after watching him at the party and noticing how joyful and beautiful he was.

I also met Ullyses and Beau, builders and organizers of Earthship Arizona. I offered Ullyses the wine and was redirected to the kitchen, where there was plenty of wine, beer, wine coolers, and liquor, along with chips and taco supplies.

Beau and Ullyses were discussing chemtrails and the looming issues of the scarcity of rain. The leader within me wanted to interject my knowledge of crystals and prayer to manipulate the weather. Ullyses raised an eyebrow, since he himself was familiar with prayer through his devotion to Tibetan Buddhism, although his willingness to listen further was limited, since it was apparent I was sitting at the 'men's' table.

After indulging in just enough Cabernet to make me tipsy, I went outside just before sunset to find Jordan with his friends. I managed to separate him from the boyz with a few words. We quickly walked into the sunset, I threw him down into the grass, and we kissed. Finally, I felt some relief from the boredom of school, work, and other routines!

The next step was to make it back to the car and then drive to the land where the actual Earthship was being built. When I arrived the next morning, Hosh's little blue car was almost out of gas. I humbly asked Ullyses to give me some fuel to make it out of Chevelon Canyon.

When we arrived at the job site, there were at least 30 people with rakes and shovels pounding dirt into tires. I met loving souls. We endured heavy winds and had lunch.

Jordan's brothers were there at one of the tipis. Out in the distance beyond the tipi there was a windblown tent, held in place by an old, discarded tractor tire. Jordan and I had 'user vibe' sex in the darkness of the tent that evening. The winds on the plains were haunting and kept me from fully sleeping, but for a short while I slept and had a visitation by a female Arapaho land guardian wearing yellow-beaded bracelets with the Zia symbols. It was clear this land wanted more acknowledgment and healing between the community, the elementals, and land guardians. I was honored to receive the acknowledgement but felt at a loss to help the people hear my voice as a seer for these land guardians.

Rainbows on the Run
Sedona, Arizona 2014

After the Earthship adventure, I returned to Rita's house on Inspirational Drive. Rita tormented me by slamming the microwave door closed every two minutes while warming her coffee. The microwave shared the wall where my bed was, which was very frustrating, but somehow despite all that, I managed to graduate from massage school.

I found out Rita felt the need to warm her coffee one minute at a time. She was so volatile and scary that I had to move out of her house in secret, without notifying her. I called my friend Nico and he helped me move all my stuff to Hosh's house. I manifested a home in the Village of Oak Creek, which lasted a few months. Then I had to move back to West Sedona because I couldn't get to work on time with just my bike.

One morning at dawn, I got my red dragonfly bike out and walked up a mountain through the rains and mists of monsoon season. I had no other option but to TRUST that I was manifesting a new home. There was a rainbow in the sky on my way to a 'Sacred Geometry' house.

What a confirmation of God's hand blessing my life. I felt that Sedona was teaching me a lesson about instant manifesting. As long as I prayed with all my heart and my friend tobacco, things came to me quickly.

I had a sweet room on the first floor of a little blue house that felt nurturing for a time. I tried dating through an app, which was mildly successful. I was still working at Whole Foods and then at Body Bliss, my first massage job. Paul and I started dating after a year of seeing each other in passing at Whole Foods. One night after he gave me a massage in one of the rooms at the blue house, I felt that I wanted to have a sexual relationship with him. Within a few weeks we had our first kiss outside the house in the garden. During our time together I laughed more than I had in years. Paul encouraged me to live outside on the land, along Forest Road 89B where he camped out a lot.

At the sacred geometry house, I realized that I needed a deeper understanding of the Akashic Records and how to access them. I thought the only way was to use a drum and other healing tools. Later, after moving to Boulder, Colorado, I learned it was more about tuning in to your body with strong intention around what you want to heal, and with deep meditation go into the vibrational feel of the records.

Raven Reflections - the Healing Industry

Sedona constantly gave me crystalline doses of increased self-worth and self-esteem. Even though I tried two previous careers, graphic design and filmmaking, I was determined to make it 'stick' in massage and the healing arts. My first job with Body Bliss right out of massage school put me into an environment filled with crystals and heavenly essential oils. They had an interesting menu of services that gave me enough structure to be a challenge. The first step in an interview is massaging a body. When you are nervous or intimidated, touch doesn't hide your feelings. I implemented too many of my techniques into my massage with the shop owner, but the ladies hired me anyway.

I was meeting tourists coming to Sedona from all over the world. I kept my personal life as separate as I could, which helped me excel in that environment. Wearing black at work, though, could sometimes be a curse, but I used my imagination to tell myself I was the Raven super-heroine! Why did we wear black in this industry? Wasn't it time to change this? I had to wear grey for the six months I worked at Massage Envy in Denver, Colorado and wearing grey was confining and repressive to my Spirit.

New Day Spa opened, and I thought, "How am I going to work there?" I felt intimidated working at my first 'real' spa. The decor and music followed a Native American theme, but it wasn't run by Natives. I went online to view the massage rooms, which were filled with very large dream catchers and impressive company logos. At this time in my life, I didn't have a deep understanding of my past lives as a Native American, even though the shaman in Mount Shasta told me I had lived a lifetime as a Shoshone Indian.

While I was working at Whole Foods, many people told me I should study with John Barnes, who invented the original style of Myofascial Release. When I discovered that I would need to know this technique at New Day Spa, I had to strategize and make tough choices. I quit working for Body Bliss and went back to Whole Foods full time, so that I could make $700 dollars for the three-day, level one training with John Barnes. I didn't need Continuing Education Units (CEUs) for my license in Arizona, but it was the "When in Rome…" thing to do in Sedona.

Learning Myofascial Release was extremely liberating, because it changed how I approached bodywork, even though I 'thought' I knew how from massage school. Instead of moving from head to toe, I began thinking in fascial planes! The physical therapists training me taught me how to use the power of observation to really see how the body has irregularities in lengths or in posture with my eyes. It was using eagle-like vision to notice the symmetry or asymmetry of a body.

When I arrived at the Poco Diablo resort for the training, I was already tired of my relationship with Paul. It took a lot of extra attention and focus to switch gears and learn this new skill. There were at least 500 people in the training and the hotel was flooded with massage folks and physical therapists. When it was all set up, it seemed like there were miles and miles of massage tables.

When John lectured, you could sense he was not just a pioneer and trailblazer, but a true Shaman. This is because he knows how animals heal in nature and had miraculous results in allowing stillness to heal them. I enjoyed receiving a "Buddha transmission" from John, because there was something he must have done to put this new healing power in my bones. I not only felt different after the conference, but I knew that my bodywork would not be the same because of him. This new certification got me the job at Sedona's New Day Spa, which originally felt intimidating.

Turquoise Scrubs and Self Worth
Sedona, Arizona 2014

While working at Whole Foods, I slowly transitioned by working at the New Day Spa one day a week and at Whole Foods three or four days a week. One afternoon while working at the Deli counter, I was feeling particularly uncomfortable with the way I was dressed in uniform and had a ton of self-sabotaging thoughts while taking sandwich orders. I never felt equal to the shoppers coming into the shop who were wealthy. However, that afternoon I was planning to work a shift at the spa.

What happened that day was an experience that boosted my self-esteem and confidence through my massage therapist persona. While transporting myself from Whole Foods to the New Day Spa. I realized that there was a transformation I made when changing from a black deli apron to the blue scrubs we wore at the Spa. I discovered my mood and thoughts changed from seeing myself as an unworthy slave to one of a doctor. It wasn't really my perception that brought this about, but rather the clients.

A client asked me about their health and what was best for them. I felt like I held a position of status in society. Yet it offered me the question, "Why would my self-esteem and self-worth be based on how others perceive me or what costume I wear?"

I noticed how my body felt more alive and responsive being seen as someone with wisdom. However, this would not be completely aligned with healing the fragments of non-wholeness in my self-belief. A client asked me one day, "Are there any Natives in Sedona?" In my ignorance and deep soul sadness, I laughed and abruptly said, "No!"

I explained that Sedona was all about capitalism and profit over the underlying meaning of the area itself. I said there had been Natives here at one time, but they left because of the development. I had not really made any connection to the Yavapai Tribe at that time and hadn't considered them as being in close proximity to Sedona, so I wasn't able to give my client that kind of reference.

The transition period away from Whole Foods was fairly short and I was eventually able to just focus on one job. Looking back now, I can't believe how much energy I had to massage seven people every shift! I also look back and see how much kinder I am to myself, with proper boundaries and ethical standards for my practice.

Tibetan Medicine Wheel Ceremony
Amitabha Stupa and Peace Park, Sedona 2014

It had been a long time since I created a medicine wheel. I wanted to invite people to the final Medicine Wheel ceremony, but was not well integrated into the community in Sedona and did not know many people. I managed to meet a few sound healers and invited them.

I also wanted to build a medicine wheel somewhere that I could easily reach for seven days. At the time, I had a shabby red bicycle to get me around town. I decided to hold the ceremony at the Tara Shrine in the Buddhist Amitabha Stupa and Peace Park in Sedona. A stone circle there was already positioned to align with the four directions. It was an experiment to see if I could integrate the energies of this site with the energies that, in past medicine wheels, included my medicine helpers native to the land in Ohio.

I made this wheel during the fall equinox, so it was pretty cool out. I did all my work in tandem with the tourists, who were allowed to enter the circle at any time. I prayed and energetically created the circle, moving the energy with my prayers and moving my body clockwise.

While setting crystals and tobacco around the circle, I learned that the wind blew strongly every time offerings were made to the four directions. Of course, the Tara shrine would be the center of the wheel, so I made offerings there too.

I had a subtle thought and wished that someone could come along on the seventh day to tell those at the ceremony a bit about the history of the Tara Shrine site and the Peace Park, but I didn't emphasize it through the prayers.

Each time I went to do my prayers in this circle, the stunning beauty of the Sedona red rocks filled my heart and soul. The wind spirits always presented me with the confidence that I needed to persevere. I could hear quails scurry around in the scrub oak bushes, making sounds that cats make. Living hermit-like for the several years I was in Sedona was unbearable most of the time. The assistance I received from the elementals and nature provided some emotional sustenance.

On the day of the final Medicine Wheel ceremony, I finished my shift at Whole Foods, I jumped on the junkie red bike and hightailed it up Andante Drive to the Peace Park. I had a tiny bit of time to go home to the Sacred Geometry house and when I went to the living room to look over the valley, I could see storm clouds coming into Sedona ready to pour rain, but over the Peace Park there was a clearing. I thought, "My medicine is working." The clouds had cleared over the medicine wheel and I could perform my ceremony.

As I hauled ass across Sedona on the red bike, I was nearly exhausted and late for my own ceremony. I had to have faith I would make it up the hill on Andante to meet Tim and Aaron. As I arrived, I saw a Tibetan monk standing in the wheel with another man, who was explaining in detail the origins of the Tara Shrine and the building process. Tim was standing with the men listening intently. For a moment, I confused myself into thinking that I had no place in this circle because the Tibetan monk was there.

I thought, "Who am I to conduct this ceremony? Who am I, because I am perhaps not as experienced as him?" I felt like I had to wait for them to leave before I could start the ceremony. I eavesdropped as much as possible to hear what they were saying. Then I remembered that I manifested the Tibetan monk from the very beginning, when I was setting the wheel!

Serpentbird
at the Peace Park Stupa
in Sedona

The White Unicorn Car
Eclipses, Ceremony, Trauma, and Death!
Solar and Lunar Eclipse Ceremonies - Sedona, Arizona 2015

While in Sedona, I made three medicine wheels on the land. The first was on the solar eclipse of September 13, 2015, and I built the medicine wheel in the saddle of the Airport Vortex. The vistas were so beautiful. I prayed and set my medicine wheel, then returned to pray for six days until the final ceremony on the seventh day. I did this while still working at Whole Foods and part time at Body Bliss. I had a difficult time reaching the ceremony sites, because I had no transportation. However, my will was strong enough to achieve what I needed to.

One day, I saw a small white card on the community bulletin board in Whole Foods, with a message written heavily in pencil. "1994 Subaru Legacy for sale driven by 90-year-old male who is retiring from driving. $400." I had no money saved but decided to use "the law of attraction" to draw in the funds. I pretended that I had the money and called the phone number on the card.

The old man and his daughter brought the car to Whole Foods so I could go on a test drive. I took it up Willow Drive and drove around a loop and back down onto 89A. I told them I had not saved the money yet, but I wanted this car. I decided it was going to be my 'white unicorn' car. They told me they needed it for about another month anyway. The most magical part was that I learned that the Subaru logo is a representation of the Pleiades Seven Sisters. This was confirmation for me that I was being cared for by the beings who originally wanted to help me find the lost knowledge about the medicine wheel.

At the airport vortex in Sedona, I returned each night, prayed with tobacco, and offered sage smudge. On the seventh and final day of prayer, I spread a large ring of cornmeal around the whole wheel, about 1000 feet. Since it was so large, I also drew a smaller wheel in the center.

I wanted everyone to understand what it was, and I knew that some of the people who would come might not understand how it worked. I was lucky that the forest service or the black masters would not disassemble the wheel.

As the official start time of the ceremony approached, the scene that I was intending to create felt bizarre. I tried to trust that friends were on their way, but I felt a deep empty place in my body of loneliness and worry and hoped that the Ascended Masters were working with me.

A man with his wife was taking photographs and he had a huge tripod. Then an elder couple approached. I was dressed in a white top and long white skirt. I sat on a little blanket in the red sands and began my inner self talk to remain in my center and allow the teachings of the wheel enmesh with me. The couple asked me in a harsh tone, "What are you doing?"

I said that I was conducting a ceremony that was going to begin soon. They both hovered at the edge of a line of yellow cornmeal. Their feet almost touched it, but they looked down at it in disgust. I saw a kind of mirror-type energy emerge between the wheel, their eyes, and my 'dragon vision.' It seemed like they wanted to cross the line and go off to a prime location to take photos of the vistas, but they could NOT cross it. I was in amazement as I watched them pack up their tripod and camera and move on. I laughed loudly in my brain at these stubborn, materialistic tourists.

Peace was not resonating with them, and that is why they couldn't enter the circle. However, many of the people who were drawn to the wheel suffered from trauma and did want healing. Jennifer VanZant, Tall Paul and Seth, Hummingbird (who sang and drummed), Jahni Coyote (who played didgeridoo), Brian Dennis, and some other folks were drawn in. One woman was already praying at the Airport Vortex, still recovering from her loss of a lover years ago.

Paul arrived with Seth who literally had a red neck with stitches and staples in his throat after he had tried to cut himself days before. I gaped at his neck and was horrified by the huge metal staples. Taking it all in, I could feel both sides of him, as equally powerful dark and light. I was in a position where my inner being felt unequipped to handle some people and their wounds, but I knew at the same time I was being presented with an opportunity to go to a new understanding and depth as a compassionate healer and teacher. I remember wondering how I got to a place where I was helping people with their traumas. After that ceremony, I referred to it as the "Trauma Wheel."

Seth, who was a member of the Salt River Indian Community, committed suicide in October 2015 by jumping from Midgley Bridge in Sedona. Looking back, I often think about whether I could have done more for him in the ceremony. As I said, I was overwhelmed with the image of the staples in his neck. It was my first time making his acquaintance and I was leading many people in the ritual that night. I do remember his sweet side, which came through when he said, "Good to meet you, Sister!" I believed Seth knew he was in a place of peace that night with his friend on Airport Vortex. After his death, Paul and I carried out a lot of prayer work to help him in the spirit world. You never know what challenges will come to you as a Priestess, but with each one of them, you must be wholly present and ready for anything.

The Priestess, the Eagle, and the Wolf
Spring Equinox Medicine Wheel Ceremony - Sedona, Arizona 2015

In the spring of 2015, I wanted to create a medicine wheel for the Equinox, so I scouted the land at the very top of Airport Mesa. I knew suspicious archaeological excavations were going on in the saddle of the Airport Vortex. That was where I wanted to have the ceremony, but there seemed to be white Christian-type folks in National Forest Service outfits digging there each day. They had shovels and rakes and found tiny red rocks that they held up into the sunlight to examine. This was where my sacred altar was. I felt horrified. I heard from my local friends that the forest service would dismantle a medicine wheel. Why? Does anyone know why? To this day I don't get it! Could it be an ongoing 'spiritual war' between Christians and Indigenous Peoples?

I discussed with my friend Brooke about doing a full seven-day ritual so she could learn how to build the vortex energy. I explained that it involved prayer and using the energy of our bodies to intensify the swirling vortex energy within the sacred area. For this ceremony, I wanted to learn more about drumming, so I borrowed an Elk hide drum from Joseph Greywolf. It had a deep bass sound that I really enjoyed. Brooke and I decided that we would focus on prayers around the water element. She learned a song that some women in South America wrote specifically for healing water. I had a difficult time keeping up with her, but she blazed the trail.

I buried and set the crystals I use for all my ceremonies in the soft sand before I instructed her. They always had to be buried because people take them. It was a challenge here because it was amidst scrub brush and cactus.

I marked the area around each crystal with stone circles, so that we could find the spots. One day, while I was instructing Brooke about what to do in the medicine wheel - how to pray, make tobacco offerings, and smudge with sage - something really strange happened. With each footstep I took in the fine white sands, I felt myself fighting an invisible force. The force was a strong wind that pressed against my body so hard it was most likely composed of land spirits, totem energies, and angelic or ancestral teachers. I could barely walk in front of Brooke because of this force.

It was then that I knew she needed a formal initiation into the practice of medicine wheel magic. I felt and understood the unusual forces within the wind, clairaudiently instructing me to put Brooke's footsteps before my own. I could NOT walk in front of her if I tried. Quite possibly, if my eyes had been attuned, I could have seen in my third eye who or what was putting me in my place. I invited Brooke to step in front of me. Inside the circle, her footprints were imprinted in the white sand, and then my own as I taught her the lessons of the circle.

There were many big 'aha' or unexpected awareness moments that came from this spring equinox ceremony. Thankfully, Brooke worked the energy of the wheel more than I did. I had just landed the job at the New Day Spa and had to attend spa training. She didn't hesitate to step into this new ritual by holding it steady for the entire seven days.

One of the biggest realizations I had was that women were going to be the leaders in my ceremonies, more than men. This was not to be exclusive, but to balance the energy on Earth. I came to understand that I needed to heal an aversion I had to developing relationships with female friends. This ceremony showed me the discomfort I felt when trying to find a way to connect to 'sisters,' since the connection I had to my younger sister Melissa always seemed to be in disrepair. Women's empowerment was a theme I knew I would always be promoting in the world, but this spring ceremony revealed the bigger cycle of time we were entering.

The next big 'aha' moment was when I called in the totem of the hawk. This is an energy medicine that I use representing messages. Brooke used sage and drew magical circles with smoke in the air at the east gate and I knew clearly that Eagle medicine should also be beckoned. I usually hesitated to use the eagle medicine, because it felt like I wasn't ready for this massive power yet. However, after this ceremony, I overlayed the totem energy of eagle with the hawk in all my ceremonies. I discovered that the totem of the eagle is an energy only some people carry in this lifetime. Brooke brought this energy to the ceremony, not me.

One night, while saying thank you prayers and making tobacco offerings in the south, I asked, "Who is here?" The angel Gabriel spoke to me telepathically. Wow! It started the kind of energetic presence he held; masculine, strong, assuring. We looked up into the stars and Brooke looked on her cell phone to find out more about what I was seeing in my mind's eye. I saw him in a dark blue cloak. We deciphered that this ceremony was to be kept in secret and hidden from plain sight. Of course, people would see us smudging and praying, but the physical objects would be somewhat hidden. On this night, we heard guidance from the wolf and Archangel Gabriel, so we Googled and discovered that our future work would soon be revealed to us.

At the time of Brooke's ritual initiation, I felt I would be called to do bigger work in the world than just work for a Spa. However, I kept wondering how this could be…would Brooke be teaching the medicine wheel? We are TEACHERS! On the seventh day, we invited a handful of people to come, including males, but there were just three females. When my friend Connie arrived, the three of us held prayer for a few hours. We invoked the center, then the east and then the south, where I channeled a meditation that was given to me the evening Gabriel made his visit.

While channeling, I felt Brooke and Connie were no longer closing their eyes or following along with me in a meditation. At first, I was disturbed and angry, but when I opened my eyes to see what they were seeing, I was awestruck! Above us in the west was the largest wolf shaped cloud any of us had seen. The wolf head was large, puffy, white, and had a heart-shaped eye. The cloud wasn't just large, it stretched out across the sky as big as a mountain! Connie kept repeating, "This is amazing, this is unbelievable!" I knew then that the prayers Brooke and I had put in for seven days culminated in the help of the forces of nature, elementals, cloud people, and ancestors. Although the ceremony was small, it was life changing for all of us.

Camping is Modern Shamanism
Forest Road 89B, Sedona, Arizona - Summer 2015

Soon after the ceremony with Brooke, I decided to move out of the Sacred Geometry House on Panorama Drive in Sedona where we met. I opted to try living out of my car and a tent on National Forest land at 89B off Hwy 89A. I lived rebelliously and contentedly by myself, in the desert of scrub and juniper for six months. This was a miracle, because I was supposed to move my tent site every 14 days, but I didn't. It was clear that my team of spirit guides protected me. Every morning around 8:00 am, a park ranger would come and check our vehicle tags to see how long we were using the sites. My spirit guides would touch my skin and wake me up before I could be counted. Many folks camping there commented how I always left just in the nick of time!

This was one of the best times of my life, because I was in blissfully close union with the desert land, the potent smells of the juniper trees, and the elements of sun, wind, and rain. I enjoyed seeing the sunset and sunrise each day. Sometimes our camp crew would huddle together to watch the sunset in the evenings. The orange ball of light would dance and shimmy over the purple mountain with creamy majesty until it melted over the hills.

Moving into my outdoor abode, my naive mind had not noted that we were about to enter Sedona's summer monsoon season. My 'Momma Turtle Tent' was sturdy and double walled, so I was able to camp outside even in the monsoon weather. A few times I stayed in my Subaru in the campground lot overnight because I couldn't make it to the tent in the downpours. The Subaru had a glass moon-roof with weakened rubber seals, so water leaked through. I had to use whatever towels I had in the car to soak up the rain. The stress of my poetry books being ruined in the boxes on the back seat was always a 'thing.' I consulted Richard, a local veteran, for advice on how to direct rain away from my tent. He told me to dig a small trough in the dirt around the tarp to direct the water. With this experience, I overcame my fear of the elements and storms to the point of creating rebellious strength.

One underlying tone in my psyche disrupted my peace ALL the time. Every night my thoughts of not making enough money to have a home of my own, or even whether I could ever have one, disturbed me. I kept wondering why my life was like this. Instead of doing anything to increase my income, I was giving others an opportunity to heal through my massage work. This wasn't balanced. I could not see a solution and didn't know anyone who could help me see it differently, especially since everyone around me was camping on the land to "get by."

Writing this memoir, I could see how my stories would be a gift to my community. I could see that I could change my story of worthiness by embracing other talents. For seven years, I focused on bodywork and massage, but then expanded into other ventures for revenue.

That summer I planned to get away from Sedona and move to Taos, New Mexico. I had dreams of 'parking in a different parking space.' Back then, I thought that moving to another place where there were more artists with a more bohemian lifestyle would be better for me. I wanted more love, more experiences of community working together. The dream indicated my soul was searching for a break from massage and being more of my true self as an artist. I always had a fascination with Earthships and sustainability, so now that my massage training had ended, I felt free to leave Sedona. I left without a formal ceremony to thank her. You will later read how this was SO PROBLEMATIC!

Marigold Life at the Hanuman Temple
Taos, New Mexico - Summer 2015

In August 2015, I sent an email to the Hanuman Temple in Taos asking about the Navaratri Festival. I got a response from the manager that I could come and live there during the festival. I couldn't get Earthships out of my mind. I wanted to be self-sufficient and save my human life from the future zombie apocalypse of 2020 that my higher self knew was coming. Back then, 2020 seemed very far away. I wanted to live among a community of like-minded souls that worked together to grow food and live in harmony with the land.

I lived at the Hanuman Temple for about four weeks. My goal was really to get an internship with Earthship Biotecture, founded by Michael Reynolds. However, I fell sick with a raging virus and my body was not strong enough to do the heavy manual labor required for pounding dirt into Earthship tires. Sadly, my dream of building Earthships waned.

I was very fortunate to have been at the Hanuman Temple during the month of September, because there were three major festivals going on at this time. I was able to live, once again rent free, in my tent, which was set up on what they called a camping pad. This was a raised bed of dirt, packed in a frame made of two-by-eights, located behind the Temple in a field on an organic permaculture farm, with a stunning view of tall and short grasses and flowers. Those four weeks were cold and rainy, but when the sun was shining the days were stunningly gorgeous.

Although I was not able to participate in the Earthship internship, I was able to experience a communal ecosystem over a four-week period. It was required by the manager that I go to sunrise Arti, a service of devotional chanting of the Hanuman Chalisa. I was expected to chant every morning at seven a.m. and do a daily chore for the temple or for the organic farm. There were many beautiful souls who sought out this temple as a place to drink a sacred nectar. I was surrounded by devotional spirits, who wanted to sincerely connect with the land and the people around them. Every morning after Arti, we drank homemade chai and sat out on the lawn. There was lunch and dinner each day, made with the same devotion as the prayers were chanted. The temple really felt like home to me very quickly and catered to all the senses with colors, spices, incense, and more.

Many East Indian families flocked to the temple kitchen to spend an entire Sunday sharing their culinary artistry. They would come to chant in the temple shrine after the American bohemian hippies like me finished the morning service. Every day at noon, we would be served the most mouth-watering prasad.

In the practice of Hinduism, prasad is a devotional offering made to God, typically consisting of food that is later shared among devotees. There were always a million conversations happening during lunch on the lawn gardens and in various places at the picnic tables. This was the heart fulfilling activity I needed in my life. I needed community and conversation, which I did not feel I received in Sedona.

After waking up day after day to sparkling morning grasses and fields of flowers like sunflowers, zinnias, and marigolds, you begin to feel whole again. There was fresh lettuce and many varieties of beans. By the third festival, I found myself in tears of joy, which simultaneously stained my face with a strange pain of separation. It felt like I was haunted by old beliefs that I didn't belong anywhere and no one liked me. Those beliefs still left me in a space of lack of inclusiveness and intimacy, which followed me on all my journeys.

Wherever I went, no matter how kindred the beings tended to be, my soul was never quite able to break through those beliefs. Finally in 2020, I settled into myself after committing to five more years of soul searching, healings, psychedelic mushroom journeys, and therapy sessions.

I was in awe of the beauty pouring out of this land and these newfound friends. There were people of all colors living in unity here. However, the lot in front of the temple carried a heavy vibration. I saw fights between couples who had spats with pocketknives and could feel the pressure of crime lurking all around me. However, it was this journey that provided the experience I needed to appreciate what Sedona had offered me.

Once the festivals ended, I knew I could no longer stay there. I phoned a friend of mine who worked at the New Day Spa back in Sedona. Luckily when I spoke to her, she explained that my boss might hire me back since someone had just quit. Jill said I could come back and work for her there, so I got in my little white Subaru and high-tailed it back.

Chasing "Tall Paul" and the Shaman Drum
Sedona, Arizona 2015

During this short hop back to Sedona, I realized it was time to buy my own Shaman drum. I went to the Trading Post store, where there was a wall displaying at least 40 drums. Tall Paul went with me and I spent $400 on a drum. This was the instrument my soul needed. I tested several deer and elk skin drums, but the one I liked was made from buffalo hide. It had a very deep bass sound and produced different sounds as I struck my mallet on various areas of the drum. There was much power in this act of owning the drum, and it felt a bit overwhelming. The drum was called "Dreaming the Tree Beings" and had two tiny little handprints that were naturally etched into the Buffalo Skin.

Up until then, I borrowed other people's instruments because I was always traveling and moving. Little did I know that day, but this drum would be with me for six years, until it finally split in the Sedona desert heat in 2020. My voice and lyric writing flowed like water, yet keeping a steady beat was difficult while singing.

At New Day Spa I became exhausted and burnt out again after doing seven massages a day, five days a week. Goddess what was I thinking? I was triggered by other people's energy, having heart palpitations and panic attacks. This is where the wounds from my mother and father were wanting to surface and be healed. The heart palpitations I was having were not small by any means. They clamored and resonated loudly until I thought I was going to die, but at the time I was still in denial about any wound healing I had to do.

I kept blaming my fatigue and burnout on the 'Coyote' medicine that seemed to come into the spa and whip around me from every direction like an evil ghost wind. Much later, when I was in my late 40s, I realized that what I thought were forces attacking me were actually unprocessed trauma and PTSD within my own heart. I tried to keep working at the New Day Spa, but it became obvious that I had to go back to Ohio and see my family. I had no idea when I could return to massaging people. Fear came to me daily, and I was so tired that I wondered whether I would ever massage again.

Death on Thanksgiving with Psychedelic Jesus
Sedona, Arizona on Forest Road 89B - November 2015

My tent was still set up in the desert off Forest Road 89B. It was cold and windy. I had been staying in town with an elderly couple and hadn't gone back to clean up the tent. When I did, the rangers had left a ticket on it, saying it had to be moved. I climbed inside with blankets and pillows just for the night. At sunset, I prayed with strong intent over some mushrooms. I cried because I was alone on Thanksgiving and very unhappy with the life I was living. The angels whispered in my ear, "It's time to go outside." I was afraid though, because I wasn't sure who was in camp, and my mind was attacking itself with thoughts of fear. I remember being on an unmarked footpath of fine white sand, near the creosote bushes and Yerba Santa plants. The bushes glowed in the sunset and swayed in the wind, breathtaking yet sparse and simple. That was how as the desert looked to me after spending so much time in this camp.

Then, a being of light that looked like me whipped around with the wind. She could have been my higher self. She came from the south and looked like a Grecian goddess, with a white robe and dark hair. Just then I felt my 3rd third eye crack open and Jesus was standing with me like a father. He was giving me direct orders and said, "There are only two choices, love or fear."

I remember feeling as ugly as a witch and rejected by a recent lover. I was wearing all black and on my knees at that point, feeling broken and alone without family or a partner. Then the eagle medicine flooded my mind and body, and I felt a channel of power come to my mind. I stared at one of the beautiful Juniper trees and pointed my hands in a prayerful, but knife-like shape in front of my face.

With the focus I had and the power that was coursing through me, I tried to get out of fear. Jesus was there being of service even though I didn't call him. He was the fatherly support I needed to continue my work as a healer. After a lot of tears and a regaining of stamina, I could barely remember how to power up my phone back at the tent. I really needed a friend or I thought I would die! I called Brooke, she came and picked me up, brought me to her trailer, and made me a plate of food. I was grateful for her company and every bite of food.

Death of the White Unicorn Car

I was in dire straits because my 1994 Subaru, which I believe was given to me by the Pleiadians, was dying. I wouldn't be able to drive the 17 miles from the spa in Sedona to Cottonwood where I lived. I kept taking the car to mechanics to try and save it, but knew I was running out of time.

I used to go to a park and sit watching the horses nearby, finding myself in my own world, staring out into a pasture. Once, afterwards, I did a mushroom journey near a creek and was told by Jesus to let go of my job. I really didn't want to because I had only recently started back there again!

At this time, my sister had just had her second baby. I knew I was in trouble because my body was burned out. I had no support, feeling despair on top of despair because my family couldn't support me in the emotional turmoil I was working through.

Going to see family did not ease my stress. I went to go live with my mom in Sebastian, Florida, where I knew no one. After staying in my mother's house, strange things happened when we drove up through Georgia and she stopped the car at a McDonalds with her dog. She was screaming because she kept getting lost and missed her exit a bunch of times. When we finally got to the McDonalds parking lot and she got out of the van, I began meditating.

My body was weak and tired around her. This made it easy for me to go into a trance. I asked the angels to show me what I needed to know and kept seeing a two-story stone house. The remembrance was minimal, but the feelings and image were stable enough in my 3rd eye that I knew it meant something.

My past life in Georgia in the 1800s carried one of the deepest pains I held from a previous lifetime to this current one. At this point in time, though, I did not understand the importance of remembering what happened between me and my mother in that past life. It was my Sanskar lodged in my sternum at my solar plexus chakra. I went to Cleveland after this upsetting time in my life. It was just after I turned 40, right around the time Prince the artist died.

Medicine Wheel Magic in Ohio
Medicine Women's Wheel in Columbus, Ohio - May 6, 2016

Fortunately, I was able to escape my mother's house and return to Columbus, where my friends were. My friend Amanda Preston hosted me for the entire time and I planned a huge gathering for women. I had time to pray on the land at Amanda's for the full seven days before the Medicine Wheel Ceremony. I carved time out for myself, took baths, made quinoa, and boiled dandelions. I sang melodies that came into my mind. One of them was an addictive tune called the Rainbow Medicine Song.

Rainbow Medicine Song

This is the Rainbow Medicine
This is the Rainbow Song
This is the Rainbow Medicine
Why don't you sing along?

Heyya hey Heeyyyah hey

This is the Rainbow Medicine
This is the rainbow tribe
This is the Rainbow Medicine
It is time to come alive!

Heya hey Heeeyaha hey.

This is the Rainbow Medicine
Red, Orange, Yellow Blue
This is the Rainbow Medicine
It is for me and you

Hey ya ha hey, Hey ya ha hey.

This medicine wheel ceremony was attended by 20 women. I had several activities planned, but the sharing circle was the most needed and most powerful. During the week, it was cloudy and we received a lot of rain, so I wondered if the weather would be clear for the ceremony. It was. I had to work in dreadfully grey-looking weather but went out each day in boots to pray and smudge with sage.

I asked Janaan Al Jahanni, a local Columbus belly dancer, to come and show us belly dance moves that were serpent-like. I felt this would help the women understand the wisdom of the serpent totem I use for the west direction. I have found in many of the medicine wheels that this dance and movement is the best way to move negative energy out from the body.

During the sharing circle, all the women sat on the ground. I was overwhelmed at how massive our gathering was. Such powerful women! There was plenty of anger, sadness, and loss among the stories these women shared. They felt safe in releasing all their sorrow and pain within the sacred circle. I found that during the ceremony, it was difficult for me to feel good in my body because their stories made me feel as heavy as stone. One woman's son held the deer antler we passed around as a 'talking stick' for about ten minutes. He was about eight years old and had a lot to say. We all waited and waited for him to pass it on. I thought it was hilarious.

After the circle was closed, I attempted to do clairvoyant readings and provide messages for the women, but it was overloading my energetic capacity.

Crossing Life's Canyons
Travels through Ohio, Colorado, and Arizona in a Shitty Volkswagen
September 2016

I left Ohio in my sister's silver VW Golf, sleeping in the back seat because I could not afford hotel accommodations. Pain in my knees would wake me up after four hours of sleep, interrupting my sleep cycle and leaving me feeling overwhelmed. The car constantly had problems. When I got to Colorado on the way to Arizona, the car's oil change light came on. At every turn, it seemed this car had another issue.

I decided I wanted to see the Grand Canyon before heading back into Arizona. I took my two carnelian stone rings off and looked down into the mouth of the canyon, then prayed and offered my gratitude for making it this far. I felt confused during this journey and asked myself, "Why me? Why THE WEST?"

I sat at the edge of the canyon and tried many times to offer the two rings and tobacco over the edge, but I was too attached. I realized that I had performed many ceremonies with these rings on and the energy in the rings had to be returned to the Earth. In my heart, I spoke to the land through prayer and said, humbly, "I guess I am married to the west, so here I am!"

Back To Sedona
October 2016

By October 2016, I was back in Sedona and working two jobs. I was giving massages at Namti Spa and serving breakfast to tourists at the Holiday Inn. This time in Sedona was mostly uneventful. I was more financially upside down than any other time I lived there, staying with friends and of course did more camping on the land.

This time I set my tent up on a small mountain, overlooking Forest Route 525. The whole mountain seemed to be covered in spiny cactus, Mormon tea bushes, juniper scrub and dense black rocks. However, one small area in the middle of the mountain had a bit of flat land and served as my oasis. It was covered in beautiful fine red sand with one massive juniper tree, which lent me and my tent some shelter from the September rains. The views of the sunset and the clean air gave me more sanity and value than my work or social life ever could.

During this time, the movement at Standing Rock Reservation was escalating toward a standoff. I was very sensitive to the collective consciousness of the times. I went out onto the Airport Vortex and used the gateways to work with Archangel Michael, to bring in energy, and to pray my way out of Sedona. I decided to use Facebook Live Video to make a prayer and a plea to have Sedona release me, so I could finally leave! I gave thanks and used tobacco to anchor and amplify my intention.

By January, I was finally able to leave and moved to Colorado. I prayed for a long time to find my soulmate and kept asking God where I should move to next. I wanted it to be his call because I didn't want to make any more mistakes or hard stops.

When I speak of my prayers to leave Sedona, people ask, "Why would you ask permission to leave a place?" My answer is that Sedona is a living, breathing being. She knows that I am a starseed and lightworker who is actively healing the thousands of people who come there from all over the world to heal themselves. Why would she want me to leave?

It is time that humanity awakens its consciousness to know that the Earth has living temples. These power spots and vortexes are available to help us accelerate our ascension process. I wanted to leave but had offered so much to the land and the people I was constantly overworked and burnt out. I felt that what I put into the area wasn't reciprocated equally from the community in Sedona. No matter how much I connected with people, I found that the attitude of the community was mostly focused on consumerism rather than connection.

"What is a Lightworker?"

My experience as a massage therapist gave me the versatility and ability to access everyday folk who don't often think about their spiritual connection or their connection to God. The mechanism of 'touch' often provides a key that opens conversations to higher thought. This then creates an opportunity to discuss trapped emotions, energy work, chakras, and the life of a soul. I found over time that my massage bodywork is not separate from energy work. People tell me that they can feel the 'energy' even when I'm not thinking about it. I must be careful to gauge myself as I don't use my personal energy, but use Reiki, or universal energy.

While in conversation on the massage table, many people have asked me, "What is a lightworker?" I am always surprised and then uncertain how to answer, because it's not something I need to think about. I tell them I feel called to assignments on the planet where I am most needed at the time and associate the number 144 with a 'lightworking' assignment.

These assignments are usually working with a soul group, as I mention in the "Soul Group Reunion" chapter. Other assignments are land healings, which now I mostly do alone. This type of assignment I mention in the chapter "Warrior of Knives and Skin." These assignments are soul callings from my own self as well as a collaboration with higher councils of light, who can see the broader vision of how and when the frequencies of the light grids on the planet can be altered and healed. I have a particular talent in being able to handle darker shadow work and ancestral work; I can clear past war energies which are dense and require my human energy field to clear them. Hence the name Lightworker.

Meditation with God for Direction

I meditated with God to ask where I should move next. I couldn't stand being in Sedona anymore, feeling alone and isolated like a hermit. After being there for three and a half years, my Serpentbird snakeskin was crawling, rather than shedding! Yet as I live out my karma and this completion lifetime, I knew I wouldn't be allowed to choose. I knew this decision was GOD'S DIRECTION ONLY and I would trust it. Many times, people ask me where I am from and where I am going. If you are from a third dimensional householder life, you may never understand the path of a healer, a starseed, or a galactic human.

When I daydreamed of moving somewhere else, I thought I deserved a lover, friend, partner, and soulmate. Much of the time I would ask in a sense, "Where is love?" Until my core wounds could be addressed, love from other humans would continue to be in a far-off galaxy.

March Mayhem in Phoenix
NeoTribal Gathering - March 18th, 2016

In the spring of 2016, I travelled to Phoenix, Arizona to find a new community. As I slept on my friend Andrew's couch, I heard a voice say "Colorado." Meanwhile, a big "Simpsons" cartoon cloud descended in my dreamtime, in the shape of the word Colorado. Finally, I received some answers.

During the spring, when the white Subaru was still working, I made a few video interviews for my YouTube channel with some exciting changemakers. One of them was Andrew Ecker, the owner of "Drumming Sounds." Much like me, Andrew was fired up about bringing people together in the community. In 2016, I attempted to help out at Andrew's NeoTribal festival.

Little did I know that weekend as I camped for two days over my birthday, past life junk would be surfacing. I ended up meeting some good folks, but ultimately inside I felt awful and did not know why. All the people I crossed paths with at the festival were folks I had past lives with in India. It disappointed me to feel so shattered and fragmented in my own heart, so much so that I couldn't enjoy where I was, in what should have been a fabulous, accepting community.

The weekend was filled with Native American elders and leaders participating in ceremony and prayer. There was drumming, dance, fires, coffee, healing tents, crafts, and speeches on preserving the planet and people. It was hotter than hell outside during this March weekend, which added to my irritability in handling my dark emotions.

I was irritated speaking with people I was hoping would become good friends. I spent most of the time sitting outside of prayer circles, drum circles, and other events I thought I wanted to participate in. I would go into my tent and lay down for naps in the intense heat then cry, because I felt people didn't care about me. This showed me years later how important it would be for me to learn about my eternal soul and how to find information on my past lives through advanced meditation.

Snow Owls of Breckenridge
Colorado, Winter 2016

In November I left Sedona in my sister's shitty silver car to move to Breckenridge, Colorado. The whole way I was very stressed out because the car obviously still had mechanical issues. Why were my cars/vehicles always broken? Could it be ancestral? My friend Lakai in Sedona said, "Yes, it is!" Isn't that atrocious, living your whole adult life with cursed vehicles that are haunted and controlled by your ancestral past? It would be years before I fully understood how deep the broken car issue was. I drove up the canyon to Flagstaff in winter. Then I crossed though the Coconino pine forest, then across and through to Colorado. It was stunningly beautiful, but much of the journey was cold. I was fearful that the car would not make it, because it always had a problem which caused me a lot of anxiety.

When I made it to Breckenridge, it was wintery as fuck! It sucked to drive the VW Golf up mountains without chains because of the ice on the roads. I had a job lined up at Blue Sage Day Spa, which also provided me with housing. Apparently, this gig would also haunt me because the people and the job were all tied to a past life. GOD! So, with absolutely no support, high up on a snowy mountain with total strangers, I had to manifest a new job and housing! Oh, and on top of all of this, my car was practically useless because it was smoking and purging black fumes from the gas tank or something.

I prayed and prayed. One morning I went outside with all my hats, scarves, gloves, boots, and such, and had barely walked a few feet when a hippy snowboarder girl in a small chevy sedan pulled over and picked me up. She had owl feathers tucked in her rear-view mirror. Yes, my friends, she was a snowboarding hippy-witch.

I asked her to take me to the yoga studio, which had great classes. We reached the building, and before I even grabbed the car door handle to get out, she gave me an owl feather. Damn! I just went through an initiation but didn't even understand the lesson. I was stressed out, which is why I was going to yoga class in the first place. After I thanked her for the owl feather, she told me to keep quiet about it, because it was illegal to have them in our possession. Then, an American bald eagle flying low enough that we could both see it flew directly over her car, which was unbelievable!

It was God's way of telling me I was on the right path and not to give up! At the time, I didn't think the Eagle appearing at that moment meant I should become a yoga teacher. My short time in Breckenridge was so bitter cold my nose hairs froze wherever I went. The clean air, sunshine, and beauty made up for the temperatures. I drank a lot of mocha latte and rode the free public busses everywhere. I also made myself go to Acroyoga classes. I made myself go because I desperately needed community outside of my regular job.

That winter it was necessary to wear *two* of everything. Two hats, two pairs of gloves, two sweaters, two layers of pants and sometimes a neck gator and a scarf, but I learned to enjoy the mystical air of Breckenridge. The air was so clean and crisp that it shocked my nose hairs. I got through it all by asking my guides to give me information on how to land a different job and to get housing quickly.

They told me to look for ads in the newspaper. In this day and age, that seems ridiculous, but sure enough, while having my favorite hot drink and looking through the paper, there it was in black and white. Beaver Run Spa. I landed the job, which also placed me in a strange dorm room with some odd females. The dorm room was toasty, though, and I had a nice bed. At the spa, I was able to use the saltwater pool and jacuzzi after I finished massaging people. I was in Pisces heaven.

That winter up in the dorm, I had time to myself to realize that I could be working on my psychic abilities. I found a Reiki Master course online that helped me brush up on my knowledge and get a certificate. Then I did free distance healing and Reiki in trade for reviews from friends I had made in the past.

In mid-January or February, my friend Shawna connected me with an easy-going guy named Brad, who lived in Boulder. He was willing to have me temporarily stay with him for free until I found housing. My sister's car, the VW Golf, was inoperable, but I had a free 100-mile tow from AAA. I rode with the tow guy to Boulder and we took the damn thing to a VW mechanic there. A kind man bought it for scrap, so I was car-less, but ended up with $500 bucks that I really needed for this next chapter.

That night I was in the parking lot at the VW mechanics. It was icy cold, and I was drawing animal totem cards for the upcoming chapter of life. I drew the hummingbird and other positive omens, which helped me relax a little. I was sitting inside the office shop, feeling relieved, hungry, cold, tired, delirious, and sick to my stomach all at the same time. I sat at the counter with my whole body slumped over and tried to order an Uber.

Yet again, I was living on blind faith and trusting my friend Shawna's recommendation. Having never met my new roommate Brad, it was a bit daunting, but my inner strength was holding me together. The Uber driver delivered me to a huge complex of condos that night. When I called Brad, he said he would be back in about a half hour and told me where to find the key. When I opened the door and walked in, it looked and smelled like a bachelor pad. Apparently, he was going to remodel it. After I looked around, I felt alone and full of despair. Then I cried.

That winter, my solar plexus chakra was weak. My self-esteem was challenged. My Tarot cards kept me going, though, because they kept predicting partnership. I kept pulling the Two of Cups card, which indicated my Twin Flame, Brandon, who would soon enter my life. Sure enough, after I landed a job with Elements Massage, I met him. When I first saw him in his cute 'skateboard shoes' and long curly orange hair, my heart melted. Out of nowhere, God spoke in my ear and told me that Brandon was a spoiled brat! I could see that being the case but was attracted to him anyway.

Why did God send me to Colorado? A psychic named Nicole said I was there to heal my inner child. She also assured me that this character, Brandon, would be my friend for life! I didn't take that message lightly, especially since I did not know a single person in Boulder.

Healing Abandonment Issues
Boulder, Colorado - Spring 2016

Brandon was my twin flame. He triggered multiple layers of buried feelings within me, including my father issues of abandonment, low self-esteem, and lack of self-worth. There were times when Brandon didn't show up to my apartment when I asked him to. With each minute that went by, my heart raced in fear. Eventually I tried using EFT tapping techniques with affirmations for self-love. I also started buying myself a dozen roses once a week to assist my self-love practice.

Once, I sat in a beautiful park by a tree and could not stop crying, because I thought the world was so cruel to have brought me a man who was unavailable and could not love me back. I knew that he was mirroring my dad program and asked the Pleiadians for a healing mantra for my heart. I couldn't stop crying since I couldn't bear to think that my twin flame didn't love me back. They told me to say, "In the infinity where I am, I am whole and complete." As I tapped my heart, I can say that it did not stop me from crying, but it did shift the beliefs I had toward myself. I felt like the cell structure of my body changed as I decided to reprogram it.

Later I learned that my reality would not change from manifesting true partners until I cleared energy around my most painful experiences. What I mean here is that it is nice to say affirmations, but you can NOT move forward in your life experience until you FULLY feel the old energy and physically move it out completely. In other words, my experience of my dad not meeting up with me when I wanted him to was not a feeling I had let go of yet. Therefore, the pattern was repeated with Brandon, because the law of attraction was just giving me the mirror image of what was stored in my body.

Thunderbird Drive
Boulder, Colorado - March 18, 2016

It was in Boulder where I stabilized myself in terms of housing for a year. I used the money I earned from the spa in Breckenridge and rented an apartment. I prayed on my birthday, March 18th, 2017, for a big breakthrough. I rode my bicycle from the apartment building at Brad's and set out with Google Maps to find the "Nest" apartments on Thunderbird Drive. Yes, Serpentbird and Nest…hmmm. I was getting the picture. When I looked up into the blue sky, a beautiful white and brown hawk flew above my head. His presence was an answered prayer.

The bird stayed with me for over two minutes, circling and circling right over me and my blue bike. Without hesitation, I yelled out to him that this was the best birthday present ever! Tears sprung from my eyes and stung as I watched him circling above. I was about to turn the wrong way, when suddenly I realized there was a bicycle bridge leading over the highway.

I headed toward the bridge. Just then I saw the hawk again. He flew over the bicycle bridge, over the Foothills Parkway, and continued guiding me by hovering and circling over the Nest apartments. It was like God was directing this sweet Hawk, and he was telling me, "Please rent your apartment here!" It was incredible.

Boulder Healing, Memoir Begins
Boulder, Colorado - Spring 2017

Boulder was my goldmine that year, because I finally had a home and a pretty well-paying job at the same time. The year ended with a bang, like a Thunderbird crashing bolts of creativity and breakthroughs into me. One of these was discovering the Boulder Psychic Institute. I remember being at the center the day president Trump was sworn in. The looks on people's faces waiting in line for their healing sessions were totally wrinkled with frowns. The room felt heavy and thick with frustration.

I had just moved to Boulder and could barely stand on my own two feet. I sat in a long line of wooden chairs with other young Boulder folks. I was called forward and received a healing session. Later, I received a psychic reading with a male and a female psychic who read my energy field with their eyes closed. One woman told me to write this memoir. She said, "You know you have been asked to do this for a long time, but you are not listening." She added, "You know it won't take much time, just write in your free time when you are off work." I thought to myself, "Ah, another impossible thing!" Yet her voice and concern were strong. She said I was 'mirroring' her own issues and she needed to do it as well. She said she also saw me writing a book about the Akashic Records.

The man who was giving me a reading told me, regarding the book, that I had not slowed down enough to really process what I had discovered on my journey to become a healer. His voice was deep, but soft and kind. Every time I went home at night I would think, "Oh jeez, I need to write this." His voice returned to me in soft echoes with the same kindness and his fatherly advice would rush back to me. I could then stop and focus on writing my memoir, because his feelings came through in the reading. His 'care' is what made me 'care,' instead of running away from myself. I still had a hard time disciplining myself for writing, which is why this has taken me several years. For many of those years, I did NOT feel that my story really mattered.

Through writing my story, I realized that I did not believe in myself. What I know now is that this was a deep-seated feeling in my core, but my mission and message to the world has since been honed and refined. It is also a huge responsibility to have a large mission and hold the vision to leave an indelible mark upon the world. I created the idea for Serpentbird in 2009 but couldn't quit my day job and make Serpentbird a full-time endeavor for many reasons.

I always wanted to have my own company and run my website as an art and environmental online magazine with a team of people. However, all my journeys to resolve inner belief in myself had to be taken first. I now feel that these dreams are starting to come true, since the time I set an intention for Serpentbird back in 2009. It is also useful and important to have start-up money and technological tools to make all these beautiful things happen. That takes being grounded, having an apartment or house, and a marketing budget. During these journeys to finalize my karma, I realized that none of that could be possible.

All the Elements
Elements Massage - Boulder, Colorado 2017-2018

Living in the Nest Apartments, my huge apartment felt like a palace fit for a Queen and provided a big opportunity to heal my body. My friend Laura Belg helped me heal on a deep level by teaching me how to do a 90-day parasite cleanse with diatomaceous earth. This cleanse saved my life because I was sick every two weeks and didn't know why. I rode my bike to work five days a week, massaging four or five bodies per shift. I then biked four miles home through the dark every night for a whole year.

Looking back, I can barely believe I did it. I biked, then did the bodywork with clients, and drank the diatomaceous earth, which was a chalky tasting 'potion.' 90 days later, I was free of intestinal parasites. I had been sick with this condition for years. She read my blood in her biolab under a powerful microscope at the beginning and end of the cleanse. After drinking the mixture for three months, I was completely healed.

I found that working at Elements Massage was a fulfilling role and I put a lot of heart and soul into the people I was working with. Times with the crew were always an interesting mix of laughs and smiles. I felt like I was home because this crew was centered in their hearts. I couldn't seem to make friends in the larger community of Boulder but guessed it would just take time to find them.

In addition to the physical challenges I faced that year, I served a few clients who were handicapped and in wheelchairs. One was a man who had some form of mental challenge but worked at the nearby Whole Foods Market. I saw him just after taking a massage class called "Shoulder Rehab," where I learned to fiercely pull up on the collar bone to release pressure on the brachial nerves.

When this man first came to me, he had bad tremors while on my massage table and his arm hurt a lot from fetching metal shopping carts all day. His forward head posture and his arm were extremely disfigured. I was able to try the "collar bone" move on him, which stopped the tremors in less than a minute. He seemed relieved after the treatment and went back to work that day fetching and shoving carts. It seemed clear that God had given me some strange new knowledge and made sure that I put it into action immediately.

Love Triangle with Brandon
Boulder, Colorado 2017

The secret love triangle I created while chasing Brandon was during a difficult time in my life. He was already in a relationship with a woman and they were just about to have a child. Earlier that year, I convinced him to come over to my apartment to trade massages and one day when he came, I kissed him, even though I knew he wasn't available. That perfect Pisces kiss was more healing and satisfying than I imagined.

Soon afterward there was a thunderstorm outside, which I was convinced was brought on by our ancient power. All the ancient Spirits seemed to be acting in concert with our passion. My heart opened wide, and my sexual energies and desire overcame me. I felt drunk for at least three days.

The fucked-up romance continued every few weeks when he came over as well as while we worked our jobs at Elements Massage. Brandon stayed with his partner beyond that year, but he was miserable because they fought continuously. I felt that I was supposed to be supportive while he went through it. As the days passed, I wished I could have found someone else in Boulder to fall for. Yet I was mysteriously and very magnetically drawn to Brandon. Later I realized it was because I was following a pattern of energy that was linked to my father, so I could learn a lesson around healing my abandonment issues.

I tried to be "just" a good friend to Brandon, but day and night I longed for his unique touch. One day, God even delivered a message to me that "He made him a Pisces healer." Oh yeah, a Pisces healer on drugs! UUUGH! I thought I was supposed to heal him, since he was my Twin Flame. It turns out I was reliving a pattern that was actually carried out by my mom and dad.

Thinking of Brandon, I could barely focus most of the time. His curly long red hair, beautiful hands, and soft skin were on my mind non-stop. I had a huge apartment and went to bed ALONE crying every night. Three years later, Brandon became more drawn to me. We remained good friends through massage and other "benefits," but I knew through meditation we would not form a partnership.

The Akashic Portal
My Private Healing Room - Boulder, 2017-18

I used the extra room in my apartment to practice my medicine wheel inside rather than outdoors. In July 2017, I took a specific class on the Akashic Records, based on Linda Howe's method. It consists of a Pathway Prayer, using intention and your legal name as a 'prayer key' to begin channeling the information. As my teacher in Lafayette, Colorado, said, "Just keep practicing."

The truth I discovered was that no one could "teach me" the method of reading the Akashic Records, because I AM the Akashic Record. It was my perseverance and consistent practice of using the pathway prayer and meditating with friends and clients that honed this ability. I spent at least 30 days consistently working on my own records, sometimes using others to be my guinea pigs. I spent my extra free time doing a lot of free healings for people whose soul records I knew I could get into. What I learned about the Akashic Records and the medicine wheel healings is that we can heal the environment and our planet through the cells of our bodies. I heard that phrase all the time when I first started learning about healing arts. "Heal yourself and you heal the planet." I did not believe this until I went deeper and deeper into the unhealed aspects of my inner being.

I practiced doing Akashic readings on the phone and sometimes at Elements Massage as well. I started a company called "Healing That Empowers," which failed to be profitable because of my lack of sufficient marketing. I did feel proud of myself for spending a lot of my extra time helping people on the phone and going to another level with my psychic abilities.

Touching Hands in Multidimensional Space

Akash Akal Ether, Soul, Time, Space!
I carve my pathways of light.
I trace my Karma backwards and forwards
in gold loops of light and dark writings.
A scribe knows the mystery,
if she allows breath to open remembrance.

Colors of chakras appear,
swell and sphere,
circulate and peer
through veils of history as she gasps from the horrors.

Dead cells burn off as I writhe and wring out the torture
by turning on the ground
as my undulating goddess snake, sifting and churning,
burning off emotions that were never fully moved.

Only to return my crystalline body
back to sanity.
Back to the temple of purity.
Experiences of Trauma decorate multiple timelines.
The Scribe and The Record Keeper now touch hands!
From now and from Egypt
Completing the feelings never truly felt. Redeeming from soul groups.
Boundaries never drawn in the ancient sands.
How could they?

As the Priests and the colonizers bound and cut my hands?

Pyramid structures and Temples we thought were storehouses of love
were sometimes dark rooms of torture.
Trauma and healers disguised in pleasure seeking halls.

Dark halls painted with Gods on pillars,
I unlock my muscles neck, jaw, heart, and intestines from sin.
Through the timelines, through the lifetimes,
I call back to me now.
Purity please.

I plead not guilty.
I was a victim many times over to perpetrators
such as Pharaohs, Redcoats, Spanish and French Colonizers.
How victorious through the din.
Many times as a man and now woman!

In this life a record keeper, sitting beneath the Tree of Life
where blood has illuminated the story.
Ahh the story!
I crush my hands till they go to pins and needles at night.
What did I do, signing away the future of humanity?
Signing slaves into custody for my own life to be spared.
And was it worth that much?

For the Magna Carta was not great,
and the Egyptian Temples were not holy, sovereign, or fair.
Back and forth, around and around,
we souls dive into the planet seeking every experience possible.
They take turns being the victim, being perpetrator again and again.

Yet the Goddess of Hatshepsut and the Serpentbird return,
to touch their hands within the circle of completion.

The medicine wheel by grace amends,
with its crystals that hum with her divine lost,
and now returned teachings.
Let the fires of grace burn, Let the fires of grace burn.
The holy grail has now been returned.

Serpentbird's Transformational Healing
Colorado 2017

Serpentbird is a master of white light who feels most at home with shamanism. During a solo mushroom journey on the top of a mountain near Morrison in Colorado, I discovered that I was an ancient healer shaman in Hawaii. A shaman is a healer who is a bridge between the visible world and the invisible world through the axis mundi, or the world tree.

Through ritual and powerful ceremonial tools, I enter a trance to experience ecstatic states that override the mundane world. I then enter a frequency where I work with benevolent ancestors of the land I am working with, or the ancestors of my clients.

In general, my healing arts can be conducted in person or over video or phone. I do not know in which lifetime I acquired the skill for distance healing, but I suspect it was when I lived in Tibet. In fact, distance healing seems to come effortlessly to me and is effective for both parties. This means through the benevolent power of the cosmos I receive healing light downloads at the same time my client does.

Healings for a "Starseed" or "Lightworker" is usually very different in style and depth because that soul has had many incarnations and holds a deeper understanding of subtle energy. It is usually more fun for me as well because the information can be delivered easily with the help of angels or spirit animals.

Some modalities I use are aura healing with color, life purpose reading, channeling, Akashic soul healing, trauma release through somatic re-experiencing, healing with Archangels and cosmic beings, and Chakra clearing with channeled breathing techniques.

Medicinal plant healings can be experienced on the body with tobacco, sage smoke, Palo Santo, and essential oils that dissolve cellular memory. Crystal healings on the body incorporating medicine songs with vocals, shakers, and drumming are some of my favorite sessions to perform.

I don't often use traditional Reiki, but I can. I prefer to use the "Change Your Aura, Change Your Life" method by Barbara Y. Martin. This method invites the client to become more of an active participant in removing the root causes of their energy blockages. What is useful about working with Serpentbird is that I can blend any and all modalities at will. I do this by receiving a 'transmission' that is built through an invocation prayer with tobacco at the beginning of each session. The transmission can be up to two hours long. The aspect of ceremony is not separated from the work because it is a co-creation between the higher self of the client and many ancestor beings that I work with.

My massage therapy practice can be a gateway for skeptical clients that can then be used to access the realm of the unseen when they are open to new levels of awareness. Many times, Akashic Records that need to be reviewed by a client can be more easily accessed by observing body cues during massage as a way to gain information. This method is helpful when working with those who are unfamiliar with a spiritual path.

The Girl with the Celtic Heart Tattoo
Boulder, Colorado 2017

I learned a powerful skill while closely observing the body language of a female client at Elements Massage. She complained she was having issues with her shoulder, coming from behind her scapula. As she was laying there, I saw that she had an unusual and beautiful tattoo on her back, right over her heart chakra.

She told me that she and her mom both have the same Celtic knot symbol in the same spot! I found this intriguing and it led me to believe that it was related to her Akashic Soul Record. Toward the end of the session, her body was writhing and churning on the table. As I was using deep tissue techniques under her scapula bone, she was having a powerful kundalini awakening.

I told her in the gentlest way possible that I suspected her issue had more to do with her heart than her scapula and rhomboids. I did not want to 'steal' her as a personal client from the business, but she said she would be moving soon. I gave her my number and said we could do a private session around her issues.

I set up my massage room in my apartment the night before her appointment and prayed for her. That night I had wild dreams where her ancestors were 'getting hold of me.' Her Grandmother ancestor was frantically running through a basement saying, "She is going to find out!"

The sunrise had already begun before I opened my eyes. I rolled out of bed and realized that whatever happened when she came would be interesting. However, I did not know how I would help her reproduce the same kundalini awakening sensations she had the week before during her massage.

Pressure Drop for Television
Thunderbird Drive, Boulder, Colorado 2017

In February of 2017, I felt much more cosmic pressure on me. My guides told me to apply at Gaia TV, which was only three 3 miles down the road from where I lived. My guides communicated through my daytime meditation with visions in my third eye. They wanted me to make some sample video sketches to send to Gaia. I thought they wanted me to work 'for' Gaia, but looking back, maybe they wanted me to be 'on' Gaia. During that time, I was struggling with horrible self-esteem issues from not feeling loved or wanted by my Twin Flame guy.

It took forever for me to rebuild enough courage to get in front of the camera again and make my video interview for Gaia, but they sent me an email saying I didn't have enough experience in the television or film world to work for them. I spent a few weeks feeling discouraged and depressed and felt their assessment of me not having enough experience was incorrect.

While meditating in the Akashic Records, my spirit team showed me how to move forward. **On my birthday, March 18, 2017, I created a psychedelic YouTube web series called *Serpentbird Activation*.** You might ask, "What is a psychedelic TV show?" Seeing is believing, so I recommend going to my Serpentbird Activation channel on YouTube and taking a look.

The Red Dragonfly Car Challenge
Thunderbird Drive, Boulder Colorado - March 2018

In a brief 24-hour period, three of my Piscean friends spoke to me separately and another friend lovingly warned me I was about to take a quantum leap. I didn't believe it at first. I often forget that I am a "Starseed."

I was losing my mind in the flurry of excitement from my TV show and feeling the pain of losing my beautiful apartment. I was losing it because I was guided to move to Denver by my Spirit team. To successfully leave the apartment and move, I had to bite the bullet and buy a new car. This was the challenge.

However, there were confirmation signs I was on the right track. Out of nowhere, a new car smell wafted through my apartment. There was no explanation of how that was possible, but it happened. I had to show my good credit track record to a dealer and buy a car ASAP!

One morning, a friend drove me all the way to a car dealership in Longmont, near Boulder. I was exhausted from all the biking and bodywork I had been doing, so that morning I could barely see straight. When we arrived at the lot we drove by a Red Soul with a black top. I knew that was going to be my car because I could almost feel the angels pointing it out to me.

Walking out the door with the keys, I was worried about what the responsibility of owning a car would bring. For reassurance, heaven made sure that when I turned the key for the very first time, the clock showed 4:44 on the vehicle console. Amen and hallelujah! I drove off into the sunset, heading back to Boulder in my own car.

When I arrived at the apartment parking lot, I realized I didn't have my parking pass with me, so I went in and got it. Like four minutes later, some girl was trying to boot my car! My brand-new car I'd just driven into the apartment lot! I screamed at her, told her I lived there, and showed her the parking pass! It was then that I figured I was really supposed to get the fuck out and move to Denver!

PSYCH! Now my guides wanted me to jump timelines and go to Santa Fe, New Mexico. Instead of listening to what they were really saying, I went to the Santa Fe Art District in Denver. This led me through three years of ultimate chaos, confusion, and frequent bouts of homelessness.

I parked my new "Red Dragonfly" on Klamath Street near the gallery hop on Friday night. Following Google maps, I found the Public TV station named Denver Open Media. When I arrived there, for some reason my egoic mind came up with some pretty pompous thoughts.

For once, my higher self was telling me to flaunt what I had, since most of the time I'm so humble. In this case, meeting new people with no knowledge of my previous background in film and television, I decided to get straight to the point. I walked through the front glass doors and went straight to the membership table, where the young interns were. They explained a bit about memberships, then I said, "I just want to publish my work on this station and have my OWN show." They told me to go upstairs and talk to Jesse, who told me that if I paid a hundred dollars to be a member, I could put my show on their channels. He asked me a bit about the story I was going to submit, which I had already put on YouTube.

When he listened to my story and heard what I was saying, I felt well received. After he told me all I had to do was pay the fee and they would air the show, I started crying. I was happy and felt a sense of freedom because I saved myself the agony of working as a slave to Gaia TV. Most importantly, I could tell my story. I was ecstatic and overwhelmed with mixed emotions. I walked back down the stairs and out onto the street, where I breathed a sigh of relief and got some fresh air.

Tobacco Prayer in the Parking Garage
Denver, Colorado - March 2018

When I moved to Denver, I put all my stuff in a storage bin in the River North Art District (RiNo) downtown. I had already lined up a job at Massage Envy. It felt like a downgrade of job choices, but there was more to learn about accepting this new experience aside from the company reputation. It turned out I was right. The team of therapists held a mixed bag of good and bad vibes. The main issue, yet again, was that even though I had found a job, I had nowhere to live except in my brand-new car.

While I was on third shift at Massage Envy, out of extreme fear I took out my tobacco pouch and yelled, "Send the runners now!" I meant, "Send in a spirit team NOW!" I was in a parking garage, asking out loud to manifest a place to live. I stopped my tears and went up the elevator to the breakroom.

A physically strong woman who had a subtly sweet demeanor said, "I haven't met you yet. How is it going here at Massage Envy?" I said, "Well, it's okay." Later, I was embarrassed because I was so upset and was being an ungrateful snob about the job, even after saying gratitude prayers. She looked me directly in the eyes and asked, "What's wrong?" I told her, "I don't have a place to live yet." Without hesitation she said, "Oh, is that all?" Knowing nothing about me, she said with a little Texas twang, "Well, you can come live with me!" I looked at her cockeyed and smiled. It was a miracle. My prayer was answered in two minutes!

Moving in with Celest, her son Jason, and their two little dogs, I felt relieved. But I sensed my inner child was feeling like a stranger in a strange land. As I was getting to know Celest, she told me she felt it was important to help women. I felt so loved and cared for that something in me changed. It was like a hole in my heart was getting filled in. Even though I was an adult, my inner child was still hurting and the nurturing Celest brought me was a blessing. After years of helping others, it was a refreshing payback.

Serpentbird DeFractivization EP3
Fast Forward, Television...(continued from p.165)
Colorado Springs, Colorado 2018

I lived in Celest's spare closet-room in Denver for about six months. I felt pretty depressed that I was working at Massage Envy and not "going places." I was very grateful to Celest for the room, but it was always a bit unsettling knowing that I was in a bedroom that was just a bus stop to somewhere else. To where? I was always thinking, "UHHHH, JUST SOMEWHERE BETTER."

I had recently been to a few hypnosis sessions and saw myself trapped in a lower underworld trying to find the way out. Slowly I cleared the depression, and a new fire emerged in my soul. Underneath a pile of underwear, pantyhose, and crumpled clothing, I went into Pisces-mode and began to daydream about how to film my third episode of Serpentbird Activation.

I had heard about a statewide ballot measure called Proposition 112 advocated by Colorado Risings' online posts. The measure would keep new fracking wells dramatically farther away from homes and schools, expanding the distance from a 500-foot minimum to 2,500 feet, the biggest statewide setback requirement in the country. The change would threaten the industry's existence. Proposition 112's half-mile setback would also apply to drinking water sources, rivers, playgrounds and gathering spots like amphitheaters.

After getting in touch with Colorado Rising, I attended a meeting to train with them on how to collect signatures for their petitions. I knew that this clipboard with the petition sheets were going to be seen on my TV show, which I hoped would help their campaign.

I was renting a small aluminum-lined Cube Smart storage unit far across town in the RiNo Art District. I went there on and off for two months and slowly began rearranging all my belongings into a sexy-plush 5x5 foot movie set. I loaded the set with Colorado Rising posters, and "Serpentbird Props" to look like Serpentbird's "top secret" basement "lair" office. I enjoyed making a faux bottle of fracking fluid in a glass jar marked with an "X" for Radioactive. I found ways to use a bag of Chipotle Chips as sarcastic slapstick.

The main challenge I enjoyed in producing this show was that I always filmed in one long take. I didn't have a personal computer to edit the footage, so it was a fun challenge to do it this way. The "one take" method made it very difficult because I planned a cathartic dialogue in which I spoke on the "Red Anarchy Phone" prop and performed poems with drumming.

The final day I made it to the storage unit to shoot the third episode, I felt some heavy pressure around me. I had a gorgeous long red-haired wig, turquoise jewelry, and face paint with me. I was excited about painting my face and becoming "The Serpentbird." However, when I painted my face, I could tell that the ancestors were concerned about my presentation, especially because I painted an oil well on my face. I persevered through the heavy pressure and recorded many takes since I wanted it to air on community TV. After completing the videos in RiNo, I kept my wig and face paint on and drove my car to the Santa Fe Art District. I walked up and down Santa Fe Drive and Klamath Avenue on the First Friday Art Walk collecting signatures, which wasn't easy. I could see that the rage coming from my soul penetrated through the layers of eyeshadow and the large acrylic STAR painted on my third eye. I was excited about the show until God told me NOT to air it because I might get shot and killed by oil tycoons.

You can view Serpentbird DeFractivization EP3 on my Serpentbird Activation YouTube Channel.

Hot Spring Junkie in Silent Wishing Water
Colorado healing soaks 2018 - 2024

Let her Speak of Water
Water will speak
if you can listen so deep
Mama Wa
is the program and the poet
Water wisdom will tell you about
every life you have lived.
You will swim in the same waters
that the worlds' saints drank.
As you may try to honor her with a song,
and the moon is high....
she will say, "No, my child, you only need to
LISTEN TO ME.
BE STILL, BE SILENT
AND LISTEN TO ME."

Oftentimes in 2018, I would drive up Hot Sulphur Springs in Granby. There was a small campground next to this cute family resort of twenty-one mineral water pools, so I would car camp in a space overnight. The town is at 7,600' elevation, so temperatures changed dramatically between day and night. I frequently checked the temperature on my phone to see how cold it would be, so I would know how many layers I should wear and how many blankets I'd need. Many times, the daytime temperature would be 40 degrees, dropping to 25 at night with snow and wind. Other times it would go from 30 degrees to -7 in the blink of an eye. It excited me to wake up with a cold nose and see the trees with puffy white snow all over them. I knew that once it was 8:00 a.m. I could run into the resort and start my soaking adventure.

I discovered over the three years of being a committed "hot spring junkie," that it was increasingly difficult to make a visit to these sacred waters without taking foam earplugs. I didn't want to listen to other people complaining about their lives while they were relaxing. More importantly, I just wanted to enjoy the little chipmunks and hummingbirds that roamed the hills. I wanted to watch as the majestic clouds formed and sailed through the skies on the winds.

Feeling the silence and being silent in gratitude while in the water gave me a solemn feeling. I realized I was the only human starseed holding this as a place of sacred beauty that should not be disturbed by the vibrations of the spoken word.

Who can hear their own heartbeat here? All I could hear was people complaining and gossiping when entering and exiting a mineral pool. While I was there to restore my skin and nervous system back into balance, human mouths were mansplaining and tainting the precious waters. I dodged the drama whenever and however I could. WATER HAS MEMORY AND CAN BE PROGRAMMED. The least we can do is SHUT UP!

The fascinating part is you can soak up on a hill overlooking the valley and the Colorado River and watch all the "elementals" play with each other. You can visibly see what an ecosystem does in a shorter span of time than in other places. In the town of Hot Sulphur Springs, I've watched the elemental beings create four seasons, like magic shows every time I've visited.

I often wonder why the UTE Indians, who held these lands as their sacred healing vessels, are not the ones safeguarding the land and water anymore. I could feel the presence of several male UTE guides when I visited there.

Sitting at the edge of the Colorado River running between the campground and the hot springs, one of the guides worked with me and helped answer my life questions.

Fast forward to 2024. While in Denver, I decided to visit my least favorite hot spring called Indian Hot Springs. It was only my least favorite because it was more chlorinated than other springs in Colorado. I also was more triggered by the pain of the unhealed traumas of the Indian war energies remaining there.

I packed up my swimsuit, towels, and the new brochures for Akashic Healing, hoping there would be a possibility to strike up a partnership with the spa. I took a brief stop at the visitor center in Idaho Springs and bought a hand carved Elk Whistle necklace. When I arrived at Indian Hot Springs, it was "spring break" and the prices to soak there were out of this world. I had a conversation with a woman at the front desk about perhaps giving me a discount since I am a healer and a Colorado resident. After much disappointment, I decided not to pay and went to my car to "Blow the Whistle."

I performed the only rebel act of "Land Back" I knew by using my writing power. My Google Review and photographs of the signage were my weapons of choice. I logged into my business account and outlined the price gouging parameters of this corporate farce. It was clear that using the original logos of an Indian Chief on their signage would be enough to lure people to this charming place. The owners would clearly continue undermining and outpricing the value of the individuals who are native to this land. In my inner vision I see a time when those who were the original stewards have their lands and water there returned.

Autumn Medicine Wheel
Washington Park - Denver, Colorado 2018

When I was living with Celest in the apartment on Birch Street, I received some dreamtime visions with me leading a ceremony of about 30 people in a circle. I thought the ancients were telling me to make a Medicine Wheel Ceremony, so I studied maps of the area and decided Washington Park would be the easiest route through traffic to be able to complete a seven-day prayer practice on the land.

I invited people to attend through Facebook. Twenty people said they wanted to come, yet on my seventh day of doing rituals, NO ONE CAME. I still walked around the circle and did my prayers but felt like a dog with its tail between its legs. After finishing the ceremony alone and dug up the crystals from the earth, I cried walking to my car. What I had to learn was that spirit wanted me to write my book and get it done without other activities distracting me.

Dark Night of the Soul
Mom healing crisis in Sebastian, Florida - August 2018

One day while I was on shift at Massage Envy in Denver, I felt multiple shocks in my heart. I had so many heart palpitations, it turned into an "official" healing crisis. I went to the break room, lay down on the extra massage table and fearfully tried to figure out what to do next. I called my mother because that seemed like the only logical answer. As soon as we spoke, my nervous system ramped down, as though I had taken my foot off an accelerator and my 'car' was running at normal speed. I could feel cords from my body running to hers and back.

I was like, "Fuck no." I really didn't want to see her but asked if I could come to Florida to rest. She reminded me that we don't normally get along and that I would have to be nice. I said, "Yes I know, I understand." So she agreed I could come visit.

The samskara was so painful I had to quit work suddenly without any notice. As if my life couldn't get any more intense and be worse on my body, I had to move out of Celest's apartment. I just knew it was time. It took me a week to simply get out of bed because my body felt heavy, like concrete. I watched YouTube videos on the "Dark Night of the Soul" that helped me understand what I was facing.

I loaded things until my Kia was packed to the gills. When I was finally packed up and turned the key, it was exactly 9:11 on the clock. I paused in disbelief. Really? This number? I was like, "Should I stay, or should I go?"

While feeling overwhelmed by my cellular healing process, I couldn't make levelheaded decisions. I realized later that the purpose of me going to see my mother in person was to learn to stand my ground, stomp my foot, and show her where my boundaries were. After attempting to explain that she kept me as a slave in a past life, she laughed at me like an evil witch. She scoffed at the idea that I had any inherent wisdom over the history of my soul.

My mother kept all the normal pictures of my sister, her beautiful storybook that told of a 'normal' life with her husband and kids, with my one picture on the end table near the couch. I told her I needed to take this picture down. She asked why and I told her it was because she had loads of pictures hung of Mel and only one of me. I took this picture because I wanted to be done with her and the legacy of the family ousting the 'black sheep.' It was an awful picture of me after college, when my hair was short and my eyes showed that I was visibly carrying a variety of PTSDs.

I never thought I would be learning these kinds of lessons in my 40s. When I was a young girl, it didn't occur to me that I should stand up and speak when enough is enough. My guides were helping me with recurring number signs of 108 that meant I WAS DONE WITH HER, FOREVER.

It was perplexing and haunting at first to feel that I would no longer have a mother figure in my life. Yet I understood on an eerie cosmic level the message that was being transmitted to me. This separation had to happen on a physical level so I could be an individual in my own right. Standing in front of her, saying the words, and stomping my feet was my way of disconnecting my physical body and completing with her.

PART FOUR: BEAR-ING THE INSIDE

New Mexico Land Repayment
Santa Fe, New Mexico 2018

Even in my late 20s, I knew I needed to move to New Mexico, but never knew why until the winter of 2018. After the horrendous meltdown with my mother in Florida, I was called to go to Santa Fe. I thought I was going there to find a soulmate, a job, or a new start. What I found was the lost fragment of my soul.

I drove up through Florida and Georgia, headed to Nashville, Tennessee thinking I was on an enjoyable quest, but no. Maybe I would see some cool rock shows. Nope. This was more work to find myself. I froze in my new car at night from the high winds in Nashville because I could not afford to waste money on hotels. As I hit the gas pedal across Interstate 40 West, 2000 miles from Florida, I began to see signs everywhere that either had the words Wolf or Art on them. I figured my guides wanted me to apply at Meow Wolf Company.

Journey to Find My Heart
Santa Fe, New Mexico - Winter 2018

While job hunting in Santa Fe, Serpentbird hit her face on the pavement many times. I camped in my car in frigid November temperatures outside of rest stops. I was deathly afraid of cops, who were plentiful around the city. When I arrived, my guides were seriously upset because it was not safe for me to live in my car. I saw the number 911 often and finally resorted to checking myself into the "CASA FAMILIA" homeless shelter. This experience was confining because evening curfews were instituted. However, the experience showed me what blind spots I still had in playing a financial victim role in society. I practiced believing in myself and giving myself mental boundaries so I would not take on other people's poverty consciousness. I was at the shelter over Thanksgiving and Christmas, which actually turned out to be worthwhile. I got more rest, because I wasn't working at a spa all the time.

To restore my soul, many times I went to Hyde Park on the south side of Santa Fe. One day, I sat about a quarter of the way up the hill on the right side. After deeply breathing in the clean mountain air, I felt like marching further up to the peak. It became evident that a spirit had strongly grabbed ahold of my right arm.

I knew a force had been messing with my right arm for the last few months. However, now there was a different male spirit-force who held me. As I climbed, I heard a team of beings tell me to go to a power spot. I thought silently, yet telepathically, "Ummm, the power spot?"

I saw a beautiful clearing that made a perfect circle and knew this was where my benevolent spirit guides wanted me. The day was sunny, clear, and lovely with snow still on the ground, but it was not too cold.

I was convinced by the invisible native Spirit Team to dance a dance that I had not known in this current body life. However, my cells remembered and I felt all the rebel angst appear from the rejection I had experienced in the town. My feelings were charged and ready for a 'dance or die' kind of release.

I spun one way and double stomped my feet, and then spun the opposite way and double stomped. I wondered if I was doing it right, but at the same time I let go of the idea of what I was creating and let my Spirit Team dance through me. They told me telepathically they were Tesuque ancestors, and I could feel their joy in this collaboration.

After making a few circles and flailing my arms in the air, my spirit team led me to a spot where I could enact a full-on annihilation of a ghost spirit through its heart. The man who was originally bound to me had been with me in the Sundance rites in two lifetimes. I don't know why the spirit was attached, but this Spirit Team knew exactly what was happening.

After killing the energy and separating from it, they had me step up onto a small volcanic rock away from the scene. They took about two minutes to open a portal in the sky. Then they escorted the being to another place or dimension, far away from my auric field.

I was relieved that the heinous energy-crime was over, and wondered more about how a spirit could have remained connected to me for two lifetimes. I have yet to found out.

The experience with this team was not finished, but now that I was free of the spirit, I was asked to climb the second peak at Hyde Park. Feeling invigorated with an awakened new warrior vibe, I still felt the main male guide pulling my right wrist and arm. I was asked to climb straight up the mountain. I thought, "WHAT? Bushwhack through cactus and shrub brush?"

The long winding trail was obviously not a part of this quest. I looked up at the mountain, the pine trees and spiky cactuses in the snow, then I looked down at my Columbia boots. **My spirit team told me very loud and clear, to "carve my own path."** I was trying to fit into something, which was the Meow Wolf Company. You see, for years I have banged my head severely into walls only to find that as a Starseed or Jedi, the only way out is 'in' and by following that practice, to stand out from the herd.

So, bushwhacking it was! I climbed further and further up the side of the mountain, over the shale and around the cacti. I was breathing hard along the way, but once I reached the top, I found a place with a lot of trees where I could stop and rest for a while. I reached a tree and rested, then kept going, rested at another tree, and so on until my foot stumbled on a rock. I looked down to see that I had stumbled right into a sacred Medicine Wheel.

This was hilarious. I spent at least three hours up there asking what my next steps should be. As I looked over the stunning view of the valley with the majesty of its purple mountains, I felt three or four Hopi spirits come toward me to give me telepathic information. I knew they arrived because they announced themselves as HoPi! The sound syllables were emphasized differently than I would normally say. I was told more about my upcoming meeting with a soul mate. I kept asking, "What do I do next?"

The Pleiadians chimed in, "Go on TV." I told them mentally how it's usually too difficult to do that. I asked, "What else?" And they replied, "Radio then. Start the Starseed Radio Network!"

I did a Google search and found there was already a Starseed Radio and several other similar projects with that name. They told me to carve my own path. Again, I was trying to 'fit into' something rather than trust myself.

Car Life in Rose Punk Glasses
2018, 2019, 2020

I left the homeless shelter in Santa Fe, New Mexico and returned to Longmont, Colorado in January. I didn't find a massage or art job in Santa Fe and really did NOT want to live there anyway.

The years 2018 and 2019 were very chaotic and mentally confusing for me. I was glad I had somewhere to live during the coldest part of winter. I practiced massage therapy in Boulder and got back to working on my memoir.

By late February, I had to leave the cozy basement room I rented in Longmont because the family I stayed with was going through a healing crisis. I was guided to go back to Denver AGAIN! I lived in my car because there were no roommate options. I should mention that even with all the spa hopping, my bank account didn't have enough funds to put down a deposit on an apartment. The main reason for my misfortune was because I had a karmic debt and land contract that I had not completed in Santa Fe. Because of that, I had difficulty finding housing.

That summer, I 'spa hopped' so many times it is difficult to remember where I was at any point. It was like swinging tree to tree from exotic and frightening heights. I lived on two different planets, working at a spa up in Estes Park in the Rocky Mountains and at another spa in Denver. At Estes Park, which was way up the mountain, I lived in my car in parking lots and road pull-offs. Sleeping next to the Big Thompson River put me into a deep healing sleep and I felt very safe and nurtured next to the majestic river. In the mornings, I visited a coffee shop where I could write, took breaks in their backyard with tall green grass, and dipped my bare feet in the river. I listened to the rippling sounds of the water as it dappled against the many-colored stones. I stared at the small flakes of fool's gold that settled on my feet in the cool water, making my skin glisten in the sunlight.

I joined the local recreation center in Estes Park so that I could do my stretching and have access to their huge whirlpool. I had the fortitude to make it through a few months of massaging at the Spa in the Rockies. It was beautiful to wake up in a variety of areas with elk and moose roaming around, sometimes causing traffic jams in town. I worked on this memoir in coffee shops on my mornings off.

On my days off, I drove down to Longmont to shop at Natural Grocers, or to sleep near McIntosh Lake. This lake also put me into deep trance and dream-filled states at night. My time in the mountains was simple and beautiful but being homeless really tainted my 'rose-punk' glasses.

I spent an enormous amount of energy trying to protect myself and my car all the time. I felt the cops might see me at any moment, especially at night, and ask me what I was doing, which frightened me.

I lived in a RED KIA SOUL! Funny how I somehow had a cloak of invisibility that blended into both rural and urban landscapes in a car that is painted red. Car living taught me to be on high alert, keeping my space in the car neat and tight and to be resourceful, of course. I saw things that others would not normally see, like what other folks do to survive in the urban landscape. On Google, I searched for parks that were open 24 hours. Isn't that silly? Does Mother Nature say to itself, "Oh, I'm closed after sunset?" I sorted out and cherished sacred hot springs, lakes, and rivers with more intensity than ever before. It no longer became an afterthought to think, "Where is that great freeway exit that leads me to the Roaring Fork River in Glenwood Springs, Colorado?"

Living in my car allowed a lot of freedom for me. During the 2019/2020 car living challenge, I roamed between Boulder and Denver, Golden and Colorado Springs and Manitou Springs. I used every minute of this challenge to feel free. The truth is, perhaps we are never free until we free ourselves from all the lessons we learn along the way. I had a Planet Fitness Gym membership, so my vehicle and the gym were my home until COVID hit in March 2020.

I started doing small pastel chalk drawings of different areas to reawaken my artistic talents. This helped me have a better outlook on where I was headed in life, but I quickly learned I couldn't make much of a living on Etsy from chalk drawings, at least while I was doing the car life thing.

Mountain Deer Medicine Screams
On the phone in Boulder, Colorado 2019

During the tail end of winter, I made a phone call to a Cherokee medicine woman in Sedona for advice on my path. I told her that I was financing my car and was confused about what to do. I felt called to change careers, but somehow could not. She screamed at me, asking, "Why are you working at a massage joint when you aren't done healing yourself?" I sought advice from a gentle Mountain Deer, but what I got was a hard reality check that shook me to the core.

I could no longer ignore the piles of shit that had gone unattended. I thought to myself that nothing was 'good enough' for Mountain Deer. I realized later that I wasn't digging deep enough into my childhood wounds. I had already tried to, but apparently there was more. I was already feeling down and couldn't handle someone chastising me, yet if Mountain Deer had not been there for me, I would not have been there for myself in the long term.

White Priestess Initiation
Ceremony with the Pleiadians in Golden, Colorado - Summer Solstice 2019

I bonded with a sister Starseed named Skye Rae Dawning during a few art parties in Boulder. By April of 2019 we were meeting and sharing life stories together. The call to learn more about her got stronger the more we met up. It became clear one night, by what she shared with me over dinner, that she thrives on communing with nature, the Goddess, and Ceremonies. I understood that her passion and desire to help others was much more than most folks held. I also knew that she was part of the Rainbow Warrior prophecy and had to be a part of the Bird Tribes.

By the summer solstice, the time was right for us to host a ceremony. I was instructed by the Pleiadians to do my first large Priestess Initiation Gathering. The energy of it was to celebrate women who have been healers, to give them community and spiritual sustenance.

I chose a public park near the base of Lookout Mountain in Golden, because the land was very green and had an area large enough for a big gathering in a circle. There were stunning views of mountains and valleys for 360 degrees around us. Skye and I met up at the site and prayed on the land. She commented frequently on how the magpies sang and spoke to her. We also met up at her home and I taught her my Rainbow Medicine Song.

This gave more time for Skye to connect with her mom and daughter, which made me feel like I was a part of their witchy-magical family. The Medicine Wheel would be different this time because I had left the soul fragment of my Mescalero Apache male warrior self behind. This fragment, being very masculine in nature, had been useful in the drive to get things done.

I was now able to bring in direct transmissions from the Pleiadians, who guided me all the way through the Ceremony. On the night before the first of seven days of prayers and blessings, I asked mentally about driving to Golden. What I heard was, "Wait until tomorrow." The next morning, I found at least seven big saucer cloud formations cloaking Pleiadian ships. WOW! There was my salute! I felt honored but overwhelmed at the same time. I always wondered if there were really ships under those clouds, yet the cloud shapes were typical of what other UFO fanatics say cloak them.

When I began my seven-day rites on the land, I was working at a spa in downtown Denver that was particularly difficult. There was always drama, and my massage work was not well received at this place. I prayed on the land using tobacco with the intention of bringing forward my most empowered and embodied self. By the second or third day of the ritual, I had been given clear signs that my job would be ending at the spa. It was a relief, but the reality of bills needing to be paid was in my thoughts. However, the point I want to emphasize is that what I intended and prayed for was answered.

I had to tell myself that the value of what I received from bonding with nature on the land and working deep within myself was worth more than what I could have made in dollars at the spa.

I decided to give all my attention to the Medicine Wheel ritual and to writing this memoir during the remaining five days leading up to the Ceremony with the Sisterhood. Living in both worlds was apparently not possible for me to develop a rich and potent ceremony.

That week in Golden, as I prayed and listened to the land, the ancients and nature spirits gave me melodies and inspired words for three new songs. It is important to understand that these songs are now permanently installed as song-lines because the songs came from the land before they came into my heart.

I found it easy to write songs as instructions for helping the women step into their empowerment. I was open to hearing the joyful songs that the land was feeling! Skye and I met up again on a day when rain swept in and out of the area. I had Skye practice laying out a crystal grid to initiate her, but later realized that wasn't necessary. I had a drawing pad, and we sketched out the alignment of the five-pointed star grid that the Pleiadians told me to use.

As we laid the grid and began to meditate with each unique crystal being, I heard clairaudient messages and noticed which totem energies would be coming into each power spot. I got information that Owl Medicine would play a big role. We would have a specific 'Owl Round' of ritual dance that would help the women clear their bodies by spinning counterclockwise, then clockwise. I was told a spirit wind would come with the Owl to move out their stagnant energy.

The Pleiadians told me to use five crystals in this wheel, not the usual four directions. This wheel was all about developing intuitive powers, freedom, creativity, and of course magic. I was also told to buy new crystals to help us develop intuition. Blue was a theme. When I went to the crystal store in Boulder, I picked out six stones so we could have a center stone: Lapis Lazuli, Hawk's Eye, Peruvian opal, Lepidolite, Ocean Jasper, Shiva Lingam, and a Rose Quartz.

While practicing laying our crystal grid with Skye, I discovered that she was a reincarnation of a Plains Indian, a native medicine man who trained with the Hopi in a past life. She was highly trained to work with Thunderbeings and was initiated in Snake Dance. It was clear that she was one of the Rainbow Warrior tribe because of her ancient knowledge, ceremonial spirit, and skills.

Just when it turned 4 p.m. and the ceremony was about to start, we saw a handsome man riding a lawnmower with a spiraling seed-spreading contraption on the front of it. He drove around and around as I was at my car getting changed into a pristine white Egyptian-like gown. I knew what was happening, with the threat of all the crystal altars getting tossed around.

I had to proceed with peace and calm, remembering that the Medicine Wheel taught me in the past not to be attached to outcomes. I could feel my blood heating under my skin, but used my mind to affirm that the ceremony would continue even if the crystals were not in place when he was finished. I approached him in my flowing gown and shell headdress. He seemed amused and curious. I told him I had set out crystals in the field and that I was having a gathering in a bit. He said with a smile, "Okay, I'm almost done here."

After he was finished, miraculously, not even one of the stones upholding the crystals had been knocked out of place! All five stone pedestals were where I had placed them, with each small crystal still sitting on top.

On our ceremony day, because of impending rain I set up our instruments and tea in the roofed pavilion. The women gradually arrived. I had them gather near the picnic table so they could talk and finish getting themselves ready. It was exciting for me to see them all dressed in white outfits for the ceremony.

The first ritual we performed was one where we cleared the women before they entered the circle. Usually, I focus on using a lot of sage and smoke for clearing, but this time we decided to use feathers and a song. I had written a few songs that I could sing with the drum as the women stood in a line facing the sunset. It was magical to see all of them standing proudly amidst the strikingly green grass in the golden sunlight.

Skye met each woman with a powerful and welcoming presence. One by one, she jumped and fiercely scraped their auric fields with her Owl feathers and organic dance moves. Then she painted designs with white dots on their faces. Lastly, she hugged each woman with immense gratitude for their presence in the ceremony. Many women stood in awe of her. Others were almost literally blown over by the wind spirits that were called in with my drumming. I spun in circles as I sang, repeating the songs until everyone was greeted.

Be Here Sister!
Be Here Sister Sistar, sistar, sistar
Come Together This is it!
We walked through fire
to find this place.
With our power together
We will find grace!
La la la la la la la
Let us open our heart sound
To the temple eternal
Out of time and space
Rise up sistar, Higher, higher!

During the ceremony, the Ancients and Thunderbeings put on such a show that most likely we wouldn't have been able to capture it on video. There were eight sisters in total: Barbara Ross, Barbara Dells, Cynthia, Serpentbird, Skye, Deb, Aspen, and Jaimie. I was guided to have the women wear all white dresses to help with a reset for their empowerment and to bring in the summer season.

We opened the ceremony with several prayers and songs to call in the seven directions, honoring mother earth and the season. Skye sang some songs as we sat in the middle with the other women sitting in a circle around us. An altar of stones and tobacco offerings was the centerpiece. I introduced the Pleiadians and relayed the information that they had given us throughout the preparation week.

Then I discussed the rules of the ceremony. We had the women come in closer and placed our hands onto the back of each other's hearts. Skye then sang the AMA WADO water song. We placed a large tin foil pan of water on the center altar and I sprinkled pink salt in the pan to help with our Spiritual purification.

After that, we did a gratitude round and the women introduced themselves. We discussed how they were in service to themselves and to the world at large and set an intention for what they would get out of the ceremony. A Yoni energy round was led by Skye to help us ground our energy with mother earth. This round consisted of yogic stretches and breathing for restoring the root chakra.

For the Owl round, I had the women spin and dance counterclockwise on the land emulating birds in flight. Everyone had their own time and space to spread their wings and twirl to clear themselves of any stagnant energy.

I led the Dreamtime round, where we had everyone lie down on blankets for visions of what they could receive from spirits to help them manifest the healing intention they had set for themselves earlier in the ceremony. Skye and I played instruments while I sang the Dreamtime Song.

Dreamtime Song
Strawberry Moon
you helped us find our roots
in the dreamtime

Summertime
under Pachamama shoots
medicine roots in the nighttime

Silly time Strawberry Moon
you make our dreams come true
and our hearts shine

Mamma Moon
you make our dreams come true
in the new time, all the time

When the stars come out
the ancients shout
INSPIRATION Medicine
In the dreamtime.

The Pleiadians gave me inspiration in my inner vision while I was car camping next to a park in Golden, Colorado. They very clearly showed me a ritual where the women would receive, in a group, a laying on of hands. I could see all of us kneeling with one knee up and one on the ground, in two rows that wove in and out. Then one woman would lay across the bent knees. I knew this would be too difficult for us to do over an extended time, so I decided we could sit in two rows with our legs outstretched and a blanket over the top of our knees. I had some small lapis lazuli pieces for the women to receive for the initiation. After the initiation, they would complete the ceremony by re-gifting the lapis stones back to the land.

Near the end of the ceremony, an unmarked steel grey/black military helicopter loudly buzzed over as we performed the Temple Tunnel Initiation. Skye was receiving healing and dreamily said "**IT'S OK TO BE POWERFUL!!**" I remarked that it wouldn't be a Serpentbird ceremony without one of those! Hahahaha!

I believe the joyous spinning we did in the Owl Round is what called in the Thunderbirds. As I looked around, watching all the ladies, everyone had a smile and look of bliss on their face. As we finished the Temple Initiation, heavy downpours began. We ran to the awnings where the picnic table was and tried to keep the musical instruments dry.

Prior to the American Indian Religious Freedom Act of 1978, dance and all native ceremonies were banned. This included Inipi or Sweat Lodges, Medicine Wheels, and Powwows. It is my belief that part of my mission is to 'dance channel' the dances that are remembered by my own DNA and the imprints that are stored on the land. It is a truth of mine to say that I still hesitate to dance in front of people because I feel it holds an old trauma from past lives, perhaps from trying to hide my faith from the colonizers.

Dance is a main component that the Hopi use to call in the rain spirits to water their crops. It may seem like a stretch of imagination to some, but I know that this is the power that our bodies, hearts, and minds have always had for healing our land and people. We do not need technological instruments or cloud seeding to control our weather. Mother Nature is the only one who should be controlling and creating weather.

Healing in groups rather than one on one may seem like people don't receive the individual attention they need, but the way I design my ceremonies, different types of rounds weave together that provide for group as well as individual attention. Even my Dreamtime sequence, although administered to the group as a whole, gives each person's psyche a chance to review their own process and come out of the session with their own medicinal healing tools or messages.

The fulfillment I receive when holding space as a Priestess is profound. A full range of emotions from crying to laughing and sharing each other's stories is held in the short time of being with each other.

During the initiation, I swear that my main Spirit guide shouted very clearly that I should visit Ojai, California. Looking back on that event, I am still skeptical and hard on myself for not inquiring further about whether that was really my guide or not. I didn't second guess the guidance, and off I went, since I had already given up my spa gig in downtown Denver.

Talking River Water Remembers
Boulder, Colorado 2020

About a year later I was up in Boulder, Colorado, meditating by a small stream where I had spent a lot of contemplation time. The stream was telling me that the "seeds" from the Priestess Initiation Ceremony were planted in the molecules and atoms of the water. The storms that passed over our ceremony were carried here to Boulder. The water remembered every emotion, good, bad, or indifferent. I was in tears by the end of my meditation, sitting on a small rock by the creek. I was overwhelmed with the power of my calling, as a priestess who has the power to transform all consciousness and life on this planet.

California Journey
July 2019

Going to California meant that I traveled the entire United States of America, from sea to shining sea, in my red Kia Soul over the last two years. I went to California without really knowing whether I was moving there or if I was just on a journey to visit. I knew this would be another journey, but again, I would lose myself in it.

Holy Waters of Zion
Zion National Forest - Utah, Summer 2019

I decided to visit Zion National Forest to take a 'time out' for myself. The reason this story is important is because of the connection I made with the Virgin River. I received life-changing downloads while there. The Virgin River is a beautiful river that winds through Colorado, Utah, and Nevada for 162 miles.

I visited the park and watched a movie playing at the visitor center, learning that the entire formation of the park was cut and shaped by the river itself. My first night in Utah, I camped in the back of my car by a church. I was afraid that people or cops might see me camped there, but at least felt somewhat safe by the church.

Throughout my travels, I often car camped at churches during the night and realized that they are unoccupied most of the time. This is one of the most unutilized resources of America that I see, churches that only operate on Sunday. Why not house the homeless? Large ashram-style environments and permaculture gardens could be implemented in these unoccupied buildings.

I was car camped just outside of the town of Springdale and woke the next day starving and tired from driving. I went to a local grocery and bought a sack of potatoes, used their microwave, and discovered the art of mayonnaise, green salsa, and potatoes as low budget survival. It was July and Utah was sweltering hot during the day.

Afterwards, parking inside the main gate of the National Forest, I heard my male Spirit guide say, "WEAR A SKIRT." I thought, "Uh, okay!" I knew that NOT following the ancestor guidance may have consequences. I put on my white skirt with ruffles, a white top, and my sun hat. I grabbed my pen and my little journal and proceeded to the restrooms.

I headed down to the Virgin River to pray. I got out the small handful of mushrooms that I had and gave thanks to the spirits who were helping me. Then I asked the plant medicine, "How many do I need to ingest?" When I received my answer, I chewed them and took a swig of water from my water bottle.

I sat there for a while and received a message while I was on the toilet. Brandon did not respect me and that disrespect was my lesson. I could see the beginning of a thread of information about the divine feminine as my pen squiggled over the lined pages of my journal during my psychedelic high.

Energy work is not limited by time or place, and the ladies room of Zion National Park proved to be my sanctuary for the release of stuck emotions.

Onward I went, wandering with my Spirit guide, my pen, and my journal. I was on my way along a forest path when I saw a female park ranger with beautiful waist-length wavy hair, wearing khaki pants and blouse with a large, brimmed ranger hat. I had the realization that this woman of wisdom looked awfully restricted by the patriarchal costume she had on. I saw clearly, with the aid of psychedelic mushrooms, that people from across the globe come here, and THIS is what they see? A woman park ranger, dressed as a very masculine male? What I saw on this psychedelic vision was that she could easily be dressed in a long skirt with some fancy turquoise for God sakes! In my opinion this would assist women in embodying their true feminine power.

My next step on the journey took me to the visitor center shop, where I was guided to buy a sew-on patch from the Zion Forever Foundation, committed to creating lifelong stewardship of the land.

In the afternoon I finally made it back to the waters of the Virgin River. Before getting into the water, I wrote some poetry that came through. That morning, prior to this experience, I rode the tram and heard a native man say, "If you listen to the land, you can hear our songs." I had some doubts about whether this was true, but sure enough the waters began to say, "Weyhey ya ho weyhey yah hey nay weyhey ya ho wey hey ya hey nay."

After I waded into the Virgin River, I asked her, shouting out loud, "What is your real name? She said, "Heyamanayaheya." She also told me there were bathing and cleansing rituals I should know of, and my body started flowing through some beautiful ceremonial movements.

Healing Deception
Los Angeles, California - Summer 2019

In the summer of 2019, my spirit guides told me to visit Ojai, California. The lesson of this trip was seeing my own self-deception. Sometimes, I listen to spirits who may not always have my best interest at heart. One of my mentors, John, told me that guides are 'me,' so I ultimately have to follow what 'I' am saying. It is important to note it in this memoir because I frequently need to remind myself to take charge of my own decisions.

I honor the co-creation with the larger perspective of life so much that I often surrender to any forces that seem helpful. At times in life, I believe in "Letting go and letting God," but at times I can't see the larger tapestry and it gets me into trouble. There are times when this principle was required of me so I would learn a lesson on trusting that there is a bigger picture for me to see. Being "Serpentbird" is about cycles of fast change, expansion, and evolution.

While in Hollywood, I car camped one night near a park. I had a vivid sexual dream that told me to write down my creative ideas for films. Looking back now, I see how I still did not have a strong belief in myself and my ability to succeed there.

Ecuadorian Hapé Ceremony
Matilija Hot Springs Ecotopia Ecovillage in Ojai, California - Summer 2019

I wanted to find a hot spring after living in my car in the fringes of the hills of California. Through new connections online, I found out about an upcoming Hapé (sacred tobacco) ceremony with the Huni Kuin family from Ecuador at Ecotopia, an Ecovillage on Chumash territory in Matilija Canyon, Ojai, California.

For this ceremony I dressed in a silky turquoise outfit appropriate for a bohemian California party. The Shamans had traveled by boat for four days from their island in Ecuador to get to the mainland before traveling to the USA. They were dressed in Aya beads and feathers. We went up in lines of two to each shaman. When I reached the front, the shaman had a beaded deer antler loaded with Hapé and shot it up my left nostril. They had already debriefed me that we can't tell the shamans *not* to dose us. When he went for my right nostril, I bowed down on my knees and held up my right hand to stop them from blasting me. Luckily, he eased up on the dosage. The plant medicine stopped the pain I had on the left side of my brain from an old concussion.

It felt somewhat inappropriate in my mind to be bowing before the male shamans. I felt like Queen Hatshepsut did, wanting to be the center of the ceremony. As the sun was setting, I walked to the hot spring pools where everyone was soaking nude. I could see the stars shining over the entire valley and the Matilija Watershed.

While roaming the hills of Ojai and swimming in her waters, my curiosity led me to search on Google Maps for retreat centers where I could car camp. I had a profound realization, finding that none of the retreat centers were dedicated to Goddesses. Most of them were named after male Christian or male Buddhist historical figures. It made me wonder where a woman could feel safe to retreat, heal, and grow. Soon after this mission in Ojai, I realized yet again I would be returning to Colorado.

Pisces Cycles, Collapsed Timelines
Denver, Colorado - Fall 2019

I kept getting number signs, 108, 808, 555, 1241. I thought this was a sign to leave town when I had just gotten back to Colorado. What the HELL? The question I struggle to answer is what needs completing – is it within myself on the inner dimension, or does my external world need to change?

Once I started work at a massage company in Denver, I finally felt a bit more stable. But by October, I was already having numerous anxiety and panic attacks while working at the spa. I would shake and tremble while attempting to massage and heal people. AGAIN!

I decided to do a Green Candle Ritual with Brandon, on the new moon just before Halloween. I asked God to present to me the right people and situations for my growth. Within 48 hours, a female client who came in for a massage struck up a 'spiritual' conversation with me. She recommended I go to Greg McHugh for therapy. I did not feel I needed additional therapy because I was paying for quantum healing sessions with another healer, who performed emotion code sessions. But then my quantum healer fired me as a client and recommended therapy!

During this chapter of my life, I was again surprised at what I didn't know. I called Greg and he was able to see me on Halloween Day. During his intake process, Greg explained in detail that he usually had to do "Spirit Releasement" before he could do hypnotherapy and past life sessions. Sure enough, after six sessions we had cleared my auric field of my whole family line of Ancestors.

After only a few sessions, we were able to access my prior lifetime with the Abel family in Georgia. It turned out that both my dad and Irwin, his brother, were responsible for holding me captive then. The broken car theme in my current life was between me and my mother, who was controlling me by holding me captive in the basement in that lifetime.

The realizations and clearings I had in Greg's office were so effective that I would often leave the office in a soup of newly broken junk DNA and cellular memory. My body felt weak after the sessions, but my inner self felt triumphant. After the cells detoxed, I felt lighter and lighter. I used some capsules of home-grown powdered psychedelics made by my 'medicine man' in Denver. The capsules absorbed and decomposed the cellular waste for faster recovery after the sessions.

My biggest surprise was discovering that 30 of my ancestors from my Jewish family lineage were all attached to me. Where many healers had tried to assist me, Greg was the therapist to drastically alter my life-path as a healer. His fatherly presence was also needed and appreciated at the time I found him because I was living in my car through the early winter and didn't know how I would make enough money to get indoors again. It was partially because the ancestral clearing and healing work we did was so intense that my body felt weak. He was sure that I would pull through.

The insight I gained was that all the energy work people do through Akashic Records, Reiki, Sound healing or Crystal healing, can many times be only a temporary feel-good fix. To be able to help a client along their life path, we need much more depth. This is why for my healing sessions I use the "Change Your Aura, Change Your Life" color system, blended with my own "Egyptian Reiki." The Aura healing system I use includes speaking affirmations on how to ask specific color frequencies to move stuck emotions, or manifest better life situations.

As a society, we have not resolved the heinous acts of our ancestors and their contracts with dark entities. Through prayer, hypnosis, regression techniques, and breath work, I was able to feel my way through a heavy darkness that spanned many generations. Some of the feelings were connected to the fear of lack of money. After the ancestors crossed to the other side, I was able to feel my 'own' feelings and not theirs.

Greg and I debated whether I was responsible for healing this family or not, because I consider myself a wounded healer. The psychic I consulted with in Los Angeles said that I was responsible. She said a child born into our family could do it, but she didn't think it would be likely.

It is important to know that after my trip to California and upon returning to Denver, I pretty much lived out of my car and a storage bin for all of October and November. I froze in minus eight-degree weather. I knew it was minus eight, because my Red Kia would tell me. I slept every night with two pairs of everything on and drank hot chocolate at gas stations in the mornings as soon as they were open.

No matter how hard I looked, I could not find an affordable room for rent or even a roommate. Finally, I had to 'Hack the Matrix.' I rented an office space that was $325 a month so I would not FREEZE TO DEATH. I equipped this office space with my massage table and all kinds of art supplies. I could see clients in the space in that building, but really what I should have done was just focus on my writing. I was still 'supposed to' be in Santa Fe for a big lesson, which is why I felt that nothing seemed to be working out for me in Denver.

Looking back, it is possible I was not in a good place to be administering healing, but financially I had no other choice. Then on top of that, how the hell was I even able to adjust my body to the cellular changes that occurred after each session I had with my therapist Greg? I know I used a lot of essential oils and mushroom compounds to remove the junk DNA, but that would not explain how I managed this lifestyle while living in my car on the streets at night. It is really horrifying to think about. I hope people can appreciate my strength in this adversity.

My overall thought about Colorado is that it is an amazing place to be a healer, and to heal thyself. I found great teachers and qualified practitioners of the healing arts. Colorado's rivers and extraordinary power places like The Garden of The Gods contain immense beauty to help heal the deepest soul wounds. The presence of ancient tribes such as the UTE are here, if you are willing to be quiet and listen to them.

Sedona Soul Mission, Soul Group Reunion
King Ramseys II Dynasty
Denver to Sedona, April to November 2020

I spent an eight-month stint in Sedona during the pandemic. It was a terrific place to be at that time, because Sedona can offer refuge for the spiritual seeker. The sun has a deep influence on the mood of people and took the edge off the world stage, keeping me in the Sedona bubble. While reconnecting with the powers of Sedona, I enjoyed ice cream sunsets and even some rainbows up at the Peace Park on Andante. However, this trip was NOT all sunshine and rainbows.

During the pandemic in 2020, we were all trying to figure out what this PLANDEMIC was about. I myself didn't believe that the virus was more threatening than the flu. I preferred using plants such as Artemisia Ludoviciana or Lakota Sage as my herbal defense. I was blessed to find it in bloom when I arrived, I could fill my nose with the heavenly scent of sage. I also felt honored that Sedona would call me back at this time.

At first, I wasn't aware that I had been predestined to fulfill a group soul mission. When I began working the spa and meeting this group, it was revealed that we had known each other in Egypt.

When My Legs Were Crossed
Hathor Temple in Egypt, Sedona 2020

When I returned to Sedona, some interesting synchronistic events brought me to an area of town I had not visited in six years. At a stream near Oak Cliffs Drive, I saw a healer who I had gone to before to help me heal an Egyptian timeline.

I thought I had already discovered and healed myself after that one session, but it was now apparent that I didn't. My spirit guides told me to work with her again. I discovered that my body was still holding the memory of being raped. I knew this because when I worked with Thea, on her healing table overlooking a beautiful resort below, my body re-experienced some oral sex positions and I felt the remnants of my neck being stepped on and twisted until I finally died. The somatic re-experience was painful. Thea used the holy names of many masters to administer her grace healing with prayer. As she called the angels in, I could see huge wall sized purple and violet flames consuming me, burning off the pain and anguish.

While working with this elder healer woman who I had a deep respect for, something triggered me about her style of healing. While I was writhing and twisting in pain on the Tesla biomagnetic mat, I was using my hands to pull energy out of my etheric body. Thea told me to just rest and that the masters were there lifting it off. I said, "Uh, OK." She told me I was used to doing things myself, but to just be still. Then, when the story of what was happening presented itself, I said, "I'm just trying to get the story!"

I was a scribe many times in Egypt, so this was important to me. She told me not to worry and that the story didn't matter. This whole experience was there to trigger me. From then on, even though I respect her, I made up my mind that the story *does* matter. I thought with a fierce triggered passion, "How else do we learn?" Yes, moving the energy out of my cells and auric field matters very much.

In Egypt's Hathor Temple, I was used and abused, raped by gangs of people. The temples in Egypt are not what people think they were. Some of them were used as sites for torture rather than for paying homage to the Gods and Goddesses.

One day while working at a spa in Sedona to save money to move to Santa Fe, I noticed my body was unconsciously doing something very strange. I was in my Red Kia Soul when I glanced down below the steering wheel and saw that my toes were pointed in toward each other. Not only were my toes turning inward, they were also bracing to hold my yoni tightly closed to hold off men from raping me. I wondered how long it would take for this samskara to clear!

I had no idea that this "problem" would resurface from 2020 and even until now as I am completing this memoir in 2024. This rape trauma also stems from my life as Queen Hatshepsut in the 15th century BC. These samskara imprints in my body have come from 3500 years ago. The imprint also comes with a dark hole vacuum, which is my victim mentality and my fear of feeling unsafe.

In 2020, however, I thought about how I could clear it without endless visits to my healer friend Thea. The fact was, I still had the program running in my subtle body. I was fiercely determined to find a healing modality I could use to remove every last drop of it. Now in 2024 I can tell you that it takes "feel to heal" presence and EVERY tool you can find to heal rape trauma. Pranayama breathwork, yoga, hypnosis, vagus nerve reset, crystals, and drawing "angry at men" pictures have helped me.

During the six months working at this spa, I saw more women than I ever had before, with permanently bowed ankles that were guarding against rape trauma. I could see through observation that this was very sad for them. They were hardly conscious of the permanent change their ankles and feet had taken as a result of guarding themselves. In addition to seeing the women with the "problem," the "problem" for me was whether or not I should tell them the real reason they found me that day for a massage.

One day at the spa, I worked with a woman who complained of having chronic low back pain. I could see that she had pelvic torsion, so I recommended working on her psoas muscle from the anterior side. When I uncovered her ankles, I saw she had a blue lotus tattoo, which symbolizes the sun in Egypt because the flowers reopen at dawn. Her ankles were very visibly and permanently deformed, so that her feet naturally rolled inward. My clairaudient sense told me that this trauma was from her father in this life as well as her past life in Egypt.

I decided that I would not have a conversation about what her low back pain was really stemming from. I wanted to keep my massage therapist position. At night I tossed and turned knowing that I could have helped her more, if I was working in a private practice of my own. However, when I put in my notice of leaving the spa, I asked for an "exit interview" with the spa owner. I informed him of what types of clients I was dealing with and that he should consider giving the women coming to the spa referrals to private therapists in town, who specialize in healing sexual trauma cases.

By the law of attraction, if you have a type of energy in your subtle body, a subconscious program, then you will continue to attract similar experiences. Our goal as healers, I feel, is to help people 'see the unseen,' so clients can become conscious of it. It was after I worked this six-month period that I decided my next book will be a workbook about the Akashic Records and healing Trauma.

It was evident to me, from working at the spa, that rape is still a very prevalent act that many women keep to themselves knowingly, or unknowingly. If I could change the spa industry, I would make it known to the client what is actually going on with them is unresolved rape trauma. My past life rape trauma wounds are *still* unraveling.

Warriors of Knives and Skin
Santa Fe, New Mexico -1800s to 2021

The Red Soul
I am a Red Soul,
with a collection of complex timelines as Indigenous.
My hands are dirty to this day,
with the red soil of America in the1800s.
My blood is still running
down into the dry valley beneath Sun Mountain.
They took my son and left me for dead.
I died starving with my knives.
In the secret society I was sworn into,
I danced for power and earned
Buffalo Headdresses and Earrings
before we went out to kill.
The accouterments however
were a display of vanity.
There was never any sleep when you…
"Got knives."

Just a few weeks before I moved to Santa Fe, New Mexico, I saw videos of an event on my newsfeed. It was Indigenous Peoples Day 2020, and hundreds of people were gathered around The Soldiers Monument in Santa Fe Plaza. The monument was torn down by 50 people using ropes and chains to bring it down. The Obelisk had this phrase etched in marble, "To the heroes who have fallen in various battles with *savage* Indians in the Territory of New Mexico." Decades ago, a man chiseled away the word *savage*. The tearing away of the old world piqued my curiosity of my upcoming land mission and ignited the flame in my rebel heart. When the 20-foot obelisk was knocked down by activists, I felt them pave the way for me to further heal the land.

Thanks to my friend Paul's advice, I rented a studio apartment and landed a spa job in Santa Fe before throwing myself into the mission. This put me in a better position than when I tried to complete this land-healing mission in 2018 and ended up at the homeless shelter. Living on Zia Road on "Tewa Land" in Santa Fe was invigorating but lonely. The Zia is a well-known symbol of the Sun in New Mexico. It also represents the Medicine

Wheel, according to the Zia people. I was amazed that I was living here on Zia Road, it was an honor.

It was important to have a quiet apartment space that allowed me to digest the lessons of these journeys. While I lived in my car on and off for two years, I was lucky to have the strength and energy needed to write and work on this memoir once a week.

My therapist Greg McHugh told me we could continue working on my past lives via video chat without me physically moving to Santa Fe. There is *no* way I would have understood the history of this area without moving there and immersing myself in the Akashic field of the land.

When I went hiking near the Old Santa Fe Trail on the wagon trade routes, my anger exploded on the path. Many times, as I stepped out of my car, huge gusts of DIVINE WIND blew me over. My entire body would become paralyzed for 20 to 40 minutes at a time. I thought that this must be an energy upgrade. Could it be that my ANGELS were protecting me from harm "out there?" My body went into a sort of paralyzed state every time I got close to the old wagon routes. My muscles were very weak with pain and soreness, so I'd have to climb into the hatchback to lie down.

I would lay there half-paralyzed for at least 20 minutes. Once the waves of fatigue settled, I could get out of the vehicle and walk in a sort of drunken stupor towards the trails. I approached the beautiful Pink Rhodonite rocks in this drunken state but immediately had to energy puke and spit near them because the pain was overwhelming.

Many times, people suggested walking the Atalaya Trail but each time I tried to go there I erupted into rage. I judged people wearing masks as they walked by me, while I would not wear one. Protecting myself from Coronavirus in the wild of nature seemed ridiculous. "Well," my ego would say, "These rich white people, who do they think they are?" I tried to approach the trail, but my body would not go! I tried to hike that trail at least three times in three months. It was my soul speaking to 'them' from a past life feeling all 'red' and native again, defending 'our' territory.

My friend Lakai and I did some remote healing trades for a few weeks because I had no idea what was happening to me. However, when we first tried to connect on the phone, our calls dropped for no reason. I realized that my team of spirit guides wanted me to get information on my past life in Santa Fe on my own. I was frustrated, but leaned into the energy in the Akashic Record of the past dimension. This deepened my trust in my Akashic Team. After I found a way to re-experience the trauma and did some of the work of re-membering on my own, I was able to work with Lakai again.

My guides told me to "dance the records" so I developed a 'dance it out' technique. This way I wasn't using my mental or even psychic abilities to recover the lost information. I simply had to let my body tell me the story through interpretive dance. I knew that I was going to have to learn to access the records daily to get through this pain. I set an intention to use my purple yoga mat as a centering place where I could meet my Akashic Team.

I started trusting my body in how it remembered my lifetime as a native person. I remembered wearing a furry Buffalo hide, with its head on top of mine. I danced as though I was showing off to the people in a circle around me, doing a deranged ceremonial act of dancing with a knife.

After making a few more phone calls to Lakai, we uncovered more pieces of the puzzle. He reported that he could see clearly through his third eye that I was a Skinwalker in a secret society. I was in shock learning what I did in that lifetime. This explains why I had to physically move to Santa Fe and explains why I felt so much anger every time I walked the Santa Fe Trail. I was initiated into the secret group and sworn in with a small, white-handled knife. I swore to be a part of a gang of killers who defended the land against foreign settlers.

The hills near what is now St. John's College and the Atalaya Mountain trail is most likely where I died. I found out by doing more research online that it was an Indian burial ground, but there are no markings of the graveyard at the college!

Psychics always told me I was a warrior in a past life, but now I understood on a new level. Ahhh. Yes, a warrior! It was important for my soul to re-experience what it meant to kill people - most likely hundreds of people such as the Spanish settlers. This hunt and kill lifestyle came with a horrific final retribution. I spent the last three years of my life, from 2018 to 2021, hunting down the Santa Fe part of this mystery.

The story of my Warrior past was now unleashed. Even though it was finally revealed, the emotion and disconnection from the tribe of my origin still feels severed. This story marks a clear distinction for me that I defended our lands in war or peace. The difference between then and now is that the Warrior life was my commitment to kill because it was the will of the tribe of Skinwalkers. I died feeling shame and defeat. My heart was broken by the settlers stealing the land. I was tied with rope at my neck and around my appendages. Then I was burned by fire. I was stabbed in the back of my heart. I died while fighting to live in each breath, while blood spilled up through my body and out of my mouth. I choked in my spit and blood. A rope was still fastened to my neck. I died with a knife in my hand. I would not let it go, because this was 'our' land.

It is possible that I was a somewhat normal man from the Acoma Pueblo, just south of Albuquerque. However, on my way to Santa Fe, I encountered interference. In my past life, I was intrigued by the Skinwalker clan and coerced to join. I became like a deranged animal and carried my knives everywhere day and night. I know this because my hands 'showed' me things when I was driving around town, or when I tried to sleep at night. My hands held the knives tightly under my pillow. I continued to crush my hands at night, making them numb out. Most of the time we carried two knives because there were so many Spanish and French invaders coming to colonize us. It's still hard for me to believe that they were coming here to claim the land and remove anything in their way. I went *everywhere* with my knives.

My desire to create peace in this lifetime has been cultivated through my prayers and my relationship with the Ascended masters. My ability to transmute my hate toward 'rich white folk' of this area is not easy because my "Red Soul" remembers it being my land and won't forgive.

My guides told me to continue to bless people as I saw them on Sun Mountain trail, which terrified me at first.

My guides and higher self-made it known to me that the roles of artist, healer, and filmmaker are all part of a bigger picture. It was not until I was here in New Mexico that I processed fully that my mission on the planet is to be a teacher, to help people transform and heal their traumas. Ahhh, Wolf life.

Now that I have re-experienced the heinous acts of violence I performed on the land, I realize that killing people only caused me to have to repeat the remembrance. I had cut through the cell memory that bound me to this area of Santa Fe and to the trails where the wagons crossed through our country. On the Old Santa Fe Trail, many people come here to visit and experience a rich history. Yet few really conceive the sacrifices that were made and the blood that still stains these hills. There is whitewashing of the history here, and some say you need to go to a university to learn about it because there was so much blood spilled in the plaza that you won't hear about it in high school classes. Now that I know how I had hurt myself by hurting others, I will never do that by my own hands again.

I had a dream that if I didn't return *one last time* to the trail, I would still be tethered to this land. I would have to drive back again from Colorado. This is how heinous my war crimes were, that even after six months of healing myself and this land, there was one more assignment. I had several psychic friends warn me that I would need to perform an intense "witchy" ceremony to sever the connection!

As I drove to The Old Santa Fe trail in my "Red Soul," Subaru killers were running me off the road! I raised my fist and clasped my fingers down, as though the knife handle was still in my hand. As I drove the road my ethereal knife was wrapped tight inside my sweating palms. The war was far from over because it was still happening in another dimension and would continue until I found a way to end the contract with demonic ghosts who were still policing and apprehending me with rope. I was on trial and trying to hide in covered wagons. Inter-dimensional DEATH was so thick, I could feel it in the air in Santa Fe, New Mexico.

I blasted shamanic music tracks on Spotify that a fellow healer, Tim Norton made, so I would get pumped. I parked my car *one last time* at the side of the trail. The sky was clear and blue with no clouds. I took a burrito and my coffee with me to the trail and decided to take a small paring knife with me. I took a bag of rose petals and my shell and sage for the final ceremony. I went deep under some cedars to pray. I scraped my hand with the knife to draw a bit of blood to offer on the land. I then buried the knife and rubbed dirt on my hands to wipe off any of the last DNA that I needed to get rid of. I stood up and put rose petals over the knife, then smudged with sage. I yelled loudly into the sky, for forgiveness of all my wrongdoings in any timeline near Sun Mountain Trail and in Santa Fe.

The ancient ancestral winds blew in and clouds began to form. The trees moved with the wind and wafted pine pollen into my nose. The cactuses were blooming with succulent red flowers. More ancestors swirled in as I asked for the timelines from the 1800s and back, then the 1800s and forward would be forgiven. My hands to the sky could feel the moisture building as the elementals merged into Thunderbeings. The Thunderbirds cleansed the whole land, earth, and sky, soaking me in my prayers. I knew my work was done and returned to the car, finally I could leave in PEACE.

Rebuilding Trust in Community
Boulder, Colorado - June 2021

Brandon kept inviting me to return to Colorful, Colorado because he had an apartment there and said he missed me. I loaded up the Red Kia Soul to capacity once more, boxing up my expensive paint brushes, easel, clothes, shoes, and bikes. Originally I resisted the move, because I felt it would be too toxic to re-enter a sexual relationship with him and I was being prompted by my card readings to only have a platonic friendship.

I wanted my apartment to serve as a stable place to finish this book, but made phone calls to Brandon and arranged to stay with him. I knew that it might not be a stable situation, but I had to take the risk because nothing else was supporting me in New Mexico.

My suspicion was correct about our relationship. We traded massages again and he was right back into trying to hustle me into sexual union. I shared what I could with him because he was my twin flame, but everything I did made me sigh with grief. This tension led to arguing night after night for three months, I so finally bailed to the back of my car and lonely sunsets. It became clear through his actions and words: I was a guest and not a girlfriend.

These lonely, soul crushing challenges further unearthed beliefs that felt like broken shards in my navel. Rooting in the Boulder community was not something that came naturally. After being an Ohio native and having a Tribe there as the buzzword states, I was craving a chance to see if I could really trust this place to feel like home.

For my own self-realization, my money beliefs, and for the purpose of this book's mission, I set out on a quest for juicy waters to fill my lonely grail. I re-loaded the Red Kia Soul to again live out of my car.

The cycle of homelessness continued. My mental and physical stamina were beyond challenged. I kept using the Boulder Creative Housing Boards and messaged over 25 different co-housing communities through Facebook. What resulted was one rejection after another. My age apparently was now a problem. Co-housing at 20 and co-housing at 45 is a different ballgame.

In the summer evenings, I would go to the park and do the Qigong horse stance for 20 minutes stating loudly to the universe, "I BELONG." I held my hands tightly around my gut and warmed my belly. I went to ecstatic dances to meet new people even though I was malnourished, butt-tired, and grumpy.

I went dancing and persevered through hippie flavored Boulder-strong body odor and all, and found my authentic relating skills had to be built through immense feelings of "not belonging." The facilitators sent us on a partner-to-partner trip around the room at The Riverside.

Each of my words of grief hit the air as though the air was made of panels of glass. The grief would exit from my lips and create layered matrices of fear. I sustained my will to one day feel like a taproot could grow from my womb down to my yoni and connect further down into the core crystal temple, below the Boulder Flatirons. "Ah," I sighed, "One day."

As I played authentic relating games with complete strangers, I felt my feelings deeply. My womb became the looking glass mirror through which I needed to see how much rocky soil lived within my bodily temple. There in the pit of my womb, I sought solid rock. I felt that I was okay, because no matter what, I know GOD. What I knew to be a healthy, free spirit with talents, success, and integrity was crumbling before each new face I met.

The foundation of me had no foundation. Pedestals had no pedestals. I was an abandoned Temple, a Queen with no throne, a Tree with no roots. A gypsy soul without a community. Could I ever trust that my emotions would be seen and cared for in Boulder, Colorado until I died? In these authentic relating games, I was not fully trusting that it could be a possibility in the times we are living in.

When the time came for me to get serious about finding roommates in the city, I went through many more tests of faith. Having faith and trust was something that had to be created within myself. It is not something you just speak about. I began using the Facebook creative housing board to find a place.

I soon realized after setting alerts and writing private messages that this was quite a crapshoot. Who would want to live with a woman in her late 40s who spent most of her time living a highly unpredictable shamanic existence? Two different friends who lived in Sedona gave me a similar solution. It came down to praying to my ancestors and lighting a candle with all my heart and soul. There was no way that my income from giving massage therapy was going to afford me an apartment. There were many interviews with potential roommates in Boulder. Each time I set out on the path, I relearned how to speak more confidently about myself. People on the message boards said that you have to 'sell yourself' as a roommate.

These days you can hardly light any kind of fire outside, because of the risk of starting wildfires on the planet. My candle magic prayer was done in the Red Soul at dusk outside the 24hr fitness gym. I stared intently with my eyes while I flicked the Bic lighter to light the three wicks on the orange candle. I prayed to my ancestors with a sense of wonder and stated my intentions out loud.

After drinking a can of Pepsi, I drove through Boulder to Gunbarrel to meet a couple who wanted to give me an in-person interview for their room. They gave me a tour of the condo, and sure enough I would have my own room with a door and my own bathroom with a bathtub. My interview with the new roommates was heavily focused on the topic of mushrooms. There were many varieties of magic mushrooms and Sacred Tobacco plants in the apartment. They wanted to be sure I was okay with that and wouldn't tell the landlord about it. I was fine with it all.

Red Dragonfly Girl
Autumn Equinox Medicine Wheel - Boulder, Colorado 2021

Thousands of Red Dragonflies created a flying parade above the sun-kissed lush grass. The first day I started the medicine wheel rituals, the sun was shining sweetly into my soul. It took eight full days to understand what I was benevolently being initiated into. I could hardly believe that after so many turbulent times, I was letting my feet drink in this holy land called a medicine wheel once again. My roomies said they would come on the seventh day, but I told them perhaps not to, since they had a 48-hour stomach bug. On the morning of the seventh day, however, they said they wanted to come. I was feeling like "Holy shit, this medicine is potent." I set down some green stones on newspapers so I could find them in the grass and began my initial prayers with tobacco. Each morning, I went into the field and did my prayer rounds. It was a bit difficult to focus while construction crews were working on one of the apartment buildings behind me.

I made the medicine wheel invisible, except for my tobacco trails. Each morning, I called in my totem beings and directions. I had no idea that my prayers calling in a soulmate partner would mean completely releasing my Twin Flame, but by the second day of prayers, my lover Brandon, who I had known for five years, found another woman to take my place. The release of my Twin Soul also meant that I had healed a significant amount of trauma within.

I created and spoke gratitude prayers aloud to the presence of the divine, regarding what I learned from the relationship. Then two Blue Herons swooned above my head. When I saw the omen, I fell to my knees and cried with my whole body. I was upset, but I knew I had my warning. It was over, since he wouldn't be on this Red Road to my soul mission.

On the fourth day, I sat outside and prayed in the center for clarity about some personal development. I received a lot of healing from each totem, including a new healing technique called "Cobra Breath." On the seventh day of the ritual, my new roommates and one other friend came, making four of us. I felt that was very symbolic of grounding and a good foundation was being set by the wheel. I felt my throat chakra highly activated by the Wolf Totem. The message that came through was that I held back too much of my teachings, creativity, and emotions. It hurt me to keep my creativity inside.

On the 8th day, September 23rd, I had the whole day off from work to process on a deeper level what had happened during the seven days. I went to a park with enormous trees to receive a final transmission of all that I had missed. I set out on a mission to get coffee at a place I had never been. I ordered my usual mocha and a BLT sandwich. I stuffed the sandwich full of psychedelic mushrooms in the hopes of a successful outcome, but was not really convinced anything special would happen. I spent hours and hours with large oak trees and sycamores. My belly rumbled and I was officially "tripping." I took out my journal and pen and dialogued with my higher self and the cosmos on topics ranging from Egypt to Mayan Cosmology.

Then, a Dragon Gate flew open from within the Earth space I was occupying. The Dragons told me I was about to be a changed woman. The download made me remember the thousands of Red Dragonflies that I saw on the first day of my prayer ritual. They imparted that my survival issues would be solved if I focused on my lower three chakras and really began living on earth from my inherent power.

Red Dragonfly Initiation
Hour of Power
Thousands of red dragonflies
flew above the green summer grass.
Priestess Root Chakra initiation began.
Warrior defending the sacredness from M.A.N.
Masculine, Attack, Never-ending.

On day one of my Medicine Wheel ritual, the Red Dragonflies initiated me to bring me a firm foundation infused with abundance and luck, signifying I was about go through an alchemical change I had not felt in a long time.

By the seventh day, my ritual should have been done but I was guided to complete one more day of integration out in Nature. The Dragon Gate beneath the Earth opened. My Kundalini energy was intense as I walked amongst the big old trees at Thompson Park.

Trees wider than my arms could hug and rich with tapestries of twisting textures and knots helped bring me the peace I needed to complete the energy transmission from the cosmos and up from the Dragon Gate.

I climbed inside the Red Soul, closed the doors and windows tight like a drum, and began purging my lower three chakras with screams and guttural sounds. I had so much pain and grief exiting my root that I squeezed my legs and screamed like I was having a baby. I felt my womb full of grief from lack of respect from partners who have unrealized insight into my vessel's worth and potential to birth a baby. Again, lack of respect for the sacred, one of my soul's themes.

I called Brandon and said, "I hope you fuck that girl like it doesn't even matter." I told him this because he has a way with women, using this power as a drug. Like all his other drugs, the vagina was just another drug.

My mind continued tripping on Mushroom Medicine. I realized that MY MEDICINE WHEEL does matter. It has Serpentbird Power and now Red Dragonfly Power, strangely more fierce than I had known before.

The Healer's Nightmare
Marshall Fire - Boulder and Broomfield, Colorado 2022

On December 30th, 2021, 115 mile an hour winds ravaged through Broomfield and Boulder. The wind sparked a grass fire that burned 500 or more homes within 20 minutes. Tens of thousands of people were evacuated in Boulder County, many of them were my clients.

That Christmas, I was alone at my apartment in bed with COVID. My roommates were out of town. I went to my medicine wheel prayer spot and cried to the ancestors to bring rain and snow to where it was needed. Then, 12 hours after the fire had spread, there was a snowstorm. I felt through my bones what some call the "End Times." I could hear the voices of terror of the fire victims and animals crying through my veins and hurtling through my psychic blood. Hours later, I learned that the homes had burned down and many of my massage clients from Broomfield were traumatized without acknowledging that they were.

If all this wasn't enough, I went to my massage job on Christmas Day and New Year's Day feeling sad and angry and most of all, without the love of a family of my own. I could barely touch people and didn't have the emotional fortitude to support anyone else's misfortune from the loss of their homes.

Two weeks after the Marshall fire happened, my body suffered its own trauma. I laid down on top of my hands, letting my body inform me that I had enough! My boss asked why I couldn't just take a few weeks off and come back to work? I told her, "When I lay on my hands, it means NO!" My soul was tapped out. There was no way for me to move forward in Colorado now. I had no money to pay rent and had reached a stalemate.

One, Four, Four, Embrace!
Journeys through Oregon and California - January 30th, 2022

I was called to go through an initiatory fire and be a Phoenix-Bird once again. I needed the energy of the mother ocean to rebirth myself and handle my immense plutonian midlife crisis. I was happy to leave the drama of Boulder, and start again, but how? Visiting these places made me feel like the Starseed alien I was.

I continued to feel invisible and unworthy. With all my depressed feelings, I had to find ways to befriend the sea as my guide on this journey. Many times, I stopped in seaside towns. Seeing a cove of rocks, I'd park my car and find more 11:11s appearing. What I know now is that I was being called to integrate and heal from the trauma of the fire in Broomfield and unite my lost soul parts from many timelines.

As I drove Highway 1 along the California coast, I felt like an idiot! I had done this at least three times before. Was I being forced by the ancestors to try to fit into the Hollywood machine, only to be spit out on my ass again? Hollywood would tell me I didn't have enough experience, just like it always had. I knew I was a storyteller, but how could I break into something I'd always been rejected from?

I had to create my own destiny, and this was it. How do I leave this book with a proper ending? I had to go deeper into myself. I dipped myself into the reflective mirrored presence of the Mother Ocean in California, steeped in mysteries and the deep dark unknown.

Leg and Shimmer

The next leg, The Fool's dance, Recreating who I am.
My creative sands slide through my healing hands and witching times.
The tides of heartbreak cry within my sacral belly.

Underneath the ancient stars, I speak Hawaiian light language
and sing myself a lullaby to soothe my new self.
As I cruise in the red Kia Soul my soul feels weak,
as I am a stranger in this vast sea of Angels who are strangers.

Blessings would come if I stopped worrying
about not being good enough for the Hollywood machine.
Oh, how I love the sunrise cream peach sky
and the smell of piss on Hollywood cement this morning.

My dreamtime is visited by ancestors
who encourage me toward empowered leadership.
I woke up in Chico with the sun shining out the back of the coop
in swirled orange and pink skies.

The cream sky melts my bitterness and Colorado misfortune.
I spent lonely nights with the lover on my mind,
no longer holding my heart and body close. I drink the marmalade sunrise.

The ancestors promise me California mornings will be disco and hot mochas
Hot crea-tiv-ity!
Talks about the New Earth and her voice shaking through mine.

Will we have time to save her? Wouldn't it be lovely to save her?

I Am the United States of Medicine

The land is sacred, I am sacred, I am scared!
I am the land, the land is holy, I am the land, I am scared!
Sacred I am, scarred I am
with paved parking lots,
spilled motor oil and tarred feathers.
I am the United States.

I am lonely, I am homeless,
I am home,
scarred by the scars of the landscape,
scarred by parking lots full of tar and feathers.

The golden eagle in the tree.
The soccer field.
The angled parking lot with sleeping homeless,
I am homeless here.

The encampment of tents in the corner of the field.
I am in the holy land that was perfect.
I am not perfect.

I am a medicine woman
remembering my womb
of the past colonizers
who raped me and ravaged THIS LAND!

I am sacred, I am scared.
I am holy.
I pray for this land and remember that if I had not seen
this tarred and feathered parking lot,
the Golden Eagle and his holy tree would not be sacred with me.
I am home. I am homeless.

I pray with my tobacco in gratitude
that home is everywhere within my heart,
this land is my land,
this land is YOUR land.
Remember?

Traveling and being a bohemian rebel pushes me to embrace what it means to be a "144," one of the 144,000 beings of light. (These 144,000 Jews are "sealed," which means they have the special protection of God. They are kept safe from the divine judgments and from the wrath of the Antichrist. They can freely perform their mission during the tribulation.)

I am embracing the 'boho' life instead of calling myself homeless and retraining my brain to leave the critical, self-hating voice behind.

From deep within my core, I had to call the 'voice of love,' which is my true self. Choosing to hear myself say it is all right: you are here as a medicine woman, making a blessing everywhere you are, embracing the voice of not belonging, or no community, to a voice that speaks. Everywhere you go, you are home, and all these people are your community.

I am undoing the threat of accusation of the rich or modern folks who ask me where I live, or why am I here. I am listening to my inner guide, who wants to go on pilgrimage to my old ancestral lands. I am letting go of hearing their loud judgements of my disorganized appearance and embracing and honoring my love of the land, earth, and sky.

When I was in Southern California, living in my car near Columbia Park in Torrance, I felt a lot of fear right before the sun went down. I would make prayer request calls to Agape International, with trained prayer practitioners. I had the opportunity to have phone calls with three potent and powerful women. Each call contained a missing piece of what I needed to find within myself. One woman prayed for me and told me that wherever I was, it was a blessing and there was a reason why I was in that spot, that the ground there is holy! Everywhere I go, God is there! I just cried and cried into tissues in my car and then stuffed them into the small bins inside the door handles.

I knew that calling these healers was what I needed for my healing process. After each call with Agape, I fell asleep with more peace and serenity. New levels of self-love were achieved with my perception of how I am living as a bohemian soul. Instead of accepting outer judgements about my way of life, I can accept what my soul has chosen in this life. Finally, I integrated my inner critical voices and learned how to honor where I was to find peace of mind.

Shoshone Ancestors Beckoning
Mission Viejo, San Juan Capistrano, California

The strangeness of the times, the mythic calls, and the Holy Grail beckoned me. At night while sleeping in my car, an ancestor whispered clearly and sternly, "Mission Viejo." I thought, "WTF? Who are you?"

For a week, I ignored the call but noticed the names "Mission Viejo" and "San Juan Capistrano" with more feeling and curiosity. I realized that perhaps the stern instruction was valid. In fact, this was a caring ancestor guide.

I had two days off from my massage gig, and left Manhattan Beach at 4:00 a.m. I dashed over unfamiliar blood-stained freeways through the dark to avoid rising gas prices and the usual daytime Cali traffic. I arrived at Planet Fitness in Laguna Niguel just after 5:00 a.m. I took a short nap in the back of the Red Dragonfly and prayed with tobacco among beautiful eucalyptus trees, giving thanks for all that the day would bring.

I went inside Planet Fitness and took a shower. The water spoke to me, and I heard the ancestors tell me to open a portal for them before I went to the museum at the old Spanish Mission. All these encoded messages were coming to my awareness, but I found it hard to believe that I was able to tap into my clairvoyance because I was so exhausted from driving. My equilibrium was hardly functioning, but the ancestors were lifting me up with their energy.

When I got to Laguna Beach, the view was so breath-taking along Hwy 1, I parked by the roadside and drew a small circle in the air with my finger. Apparently, that was all I needed to do, to allow the ancestors to pass through from the Ocean gate and come with me to the Spanish Mission.

What I learned from this mission was that my time here on Earth feels seemingly insignificant and invisible to humans. The etheric and mystical land healing that I can perform with my mind is the whole point. My soul is seeking wholeness, so the calling of it must be 'complete' with the land, the ancestors, and holy historical grounds. The ancestors of this Starseed know that it is important for me to recognize my soul history, that I was a part of a community, a tribe, an indigenous nation with a culture of dance, ceremony, and song.

Adventurer on the Path of Nine

Integration of Ancestry, Hermosa Beach, California - Summer 2022

The Abel family sold me on the concept that ALL of my ancestors were Jewish. To their knowledge, it may be so. However, as the Starseed Soul Serpentbird, it seems impossible that my soul has always been solely Jewish. Why would I be drawn so many times to New Mexico, Arizona, and now California?

As my path in California unfolded, my ancestors guided me and asked me to perform land healings to raise the energy in a few places. While working with my friend Lakai on my ancestor healings, he confirmed that I do in fact have DNA of the natives of Turtle Island. Lakai and I had a two and a half hour Zoom call while I laid down in the back of my Kia Soul, "The Red Dragonfly." He set up an elaborate altar in his home and connected our two worlds energetically for the purpose of healing ancestors from my Shoshone lineage. We traveled to an ancestral homeland in Nevada and cleared a big blockage on the land there.

As I slept that evening, I dreamed that I was in a town like Hermosa, but it was an ancient version of Hermosa. The feeling was that I had newly arrived, yet as the dream sequence played on, I saw the ancient past.

In the past, the town seemed to allow a large green tidal wave to come and let the river sweep everyone downstream. As I finally succumbed to the tidal wave and get swept downstream, the water flowed below its normal levels. Then I saw large native carvings like arrows reveal themselves to me. I stared at the rock walls on either side of the river and saw arrows, circles, and lines, much like primitive art.

As I woke up on Valley Drive in Hermosa Beach, my heart compelled me to see the larger pattern and my purpose in this life. It was a passion to know THE WORLD! The world beneath the matrix of corporate structure, and to resurrect myself by accepting that I was here to help Mother Earth birth in her ascension. "What does this mean?" you might ask. By performing ancestral and land healings, I was lifting heavy energies of war and the rape of indigenous women of ancient pasts. Working with Lakai frequently, we were repairing the grids of Earth by healing the ancestors of pain and trauma.

I must accept my mission as a peaceful warrior healing herself. My loving self must not create a single judgment or label such as bohemian, hippie, or wanderer lost, but a pilgrim and a midwife and child of the sacred who wants to preserve the depth of humanity.

Galactic 911 and the Red Fire Trucks

Apparently, when there is a toxic pile-up of current and past life timelines, you get physical warnings in this dimension. The Galactic Council informed me that there was a "Galactic Emergency." With the help of my higher self through my deep beach meditations, the "lost brother," and my ancestor guides, I slowly began to unravel many of the messages. In a span of a month, I saw fucking red fire trucks everywhere I went! I even found a matchbox toy Hot Wheels fire truck on the surf near Hermosa Beach at sunset. Here I was, being the executive "record keeper," taking the fires of timelines and shrinking the timelines into matchbox size fires, until they were no more! My Facebook posts that month were about my 'days at the office' with ocean views to live for.

In the Akashic Records, there were many more Egyptian timelines that needed to be cleared. One night, actually three in the morning, the ancestors whispered one potent name: Ramses the III. I sighed a deep breath and rolled over in the cab of my Kia Soul where I slept. I opened YouTube and immediately found the hidden secret of why I was at the spa in Sedona in 2020.

It turned out that a group of priestesses had taken the venom from serpents and poisoned King Ramses III. We poisoned him because we were kept as servants to three main men and were trained to serve them with various sex acts. Ramses had built the Temple walls so high that we had no contact with people on the outside.

Each day at "the office," I realized how my enlightenment was entangled and dependent on the enlightenment of the whole. I had to go through the fiery timeliness for the freedom of the collective. I had to call friends, who were seemingly on their own path now, and ask them to channel and 'complete' with me. My friend Kim and I were able to find out that the men oppressing the priestesses thought that by tying and raping us standing up, they thought they could gain psychic powers. We laughed about how it seemed very silly now that anyone could gain psychic powers from the root chakra!

Blind Hebrew Girl Draws with Fire!
Revisiting the Records with Crow

For six months, I meditated almost every day at the ocean. Whenever I meditated on the sand, I had a sense that Roman soldiers were coming to arrest me. However, I could not get deep enough into my soul records to get more of the story. After several attempts in about a month, I stared into the ocean waves and asked out loud, "What am I letting go of?" The answer came from a male guide who was so close to me it was like he was brushing against my right hip. He said to me in a deep voice, "Marc." Just then, as though for comic-cosmic relief, I saw a large crow walking along the shore. The reason this was funny is because the universe sent me an animal spirit - Marc's name when I met him was "Crow." Everyone who played music in Columbus knew his name was Crow.

I really didn't want to let him go because we had remained friends since we divorced over ten years before. I came to accept that it was the story between us that I was transmuting.

After reaching out to him in Boston, we had a two hour zoom call while I sat in my car in Los Angeles and my phone battery almost died. After reading the Pathway Prayer to open the records, I explained to him that I wanted to forgive him for any animosity or anger that our relationship took on. We both received a lot of peace and healing through my asking for forgiveness.

Finally, after two hours of being in a deep trance, I discovered why we were not able to stay together as a couple. As Marc and I meditated in the energy of the Akashic Records, I uncovered all my anger and resentment that broke our bond of marriage.

In my past life in Pompeii, the temple was called ISIS. I was a blind woman who was employed by the state as a seer and healer. I would heal *everyone* with the Hebrew alphabet letters. The feeling I got in the records is that my heart was pure, and I would not hold back my gift of healing to suit the specific cultural or religious affiliation of a person. I freely went around healing *everyone*.

I would do a sort of etheric holy fire reiki with the Hebrew letters. I was so powerful as a blind healer that the Roman soldiers wanted what I had for themselves. I was tricked into believing that I would be helping my family by going to the bell tower to see the priest.

I met "Marc" in the bell tower, my twin-flame partner from multiple timelines. He said some incantations and tricked me through a ceremony. There was a cauldron of hot water in the bell tower, which overlooked Rome and the fires of Pompeii. I had lost my home through these fires, as well as the Isis Temple where I lived and worked under contract. I was forced to leave the temple because I practiced monotheism.

Marc told me that a powerful scepter for writing was located at the bottom of the pot. The hypnotic incantations coerced my ancient being to put my beautiful, healing hands inside the vessel of hot water. My hands were scalded and burned as I reached into the cauldron for the writing instrument.

Somehow in this meeting with the priest, the Romans wanted Marc and I to conceive a baby boy. Their evil plan was to disable my hands but force me to have a child with my abilities so that they could use the child as a healer within their jurisdiction. They would no longer have the 'problem' of a Jew who was healing in the temples. After my long phone session with Marc, I realized that I had more power as a healer than I previously understood. I was an ancient blind healer who used the mystical power of the Sefirot to heal people without discrimination.

In an attempt of the evil Roman soldiers to take my baby, I had a miscarriage. I was heartbroken. The boy we conceived was actually Marc's dad in this lifetime.

The anger and resentment I felt toward Marc kept rearing its ugly head in every medicine wheel ceremony we did in Ohio, especially at our wedding. Finally, I knew where this anger was coming from! I wanted my true healing power back and my FREEDOM.

Unexpectedly, during this purge of cellular memory, I discovered new Goddess worship. I needed more than the healers and psychics who were helping me, I needed the fierce and fiery flames of the Goddess. I consulted with my psychic friend Erin, and she told me that these

Goddesses wanted to help me. I never realized until she said it that they were around me already. All I needed to do was start chanting their holy names.

After that, while near the sea, I found myself surrounded in a Sea of Holy Fires! Then I heard a spirit guide tell me to chant the name Durga. I had not worked with Durga in this lifetime, so I consulted YouTube to learn about her before using her mantras. At first, I was intimidated by her, because she is so dark and fierce, but when my guides affirmed that I should chant her name, I did so. The flames came and enveloped me by the sea, transmuting all the deep dark everything into ecstasy!

Nana's Sacred Cacao Ceremony
and Yoni Downloads, Central Los Angeles

A massive gathering happened one night in an unassuming small yard in central Los Angeles. Nana Marina Cruz brought her sacred Cacao from Guatemala and held a fire circle. This was my first experience seeing a wheel of flowers, candles, and cigars being transformed into a ring of fire dedicated to the ancestors. There were at least 60 people gathered in this urban yard, praying, drumming, and drinking the sacred cacao. I went to the altar later in the ceremony, after Nana had walked the circle many times. I put my hands on the Earth, and they felt so loved and nurtured they felt glued to the ground. I had nowhere to go, nothing to do, but felt held.

During the next three days, as I was walking in Hermosa Beach, I felt the cacao and the Grandmothers who make the cacao in Guatemala healing my womb and telling me to preserve this sacred space. I kept feeling my belly and noticing the shape of this 'holy vessel' as a chalice. I was seeing more clearly how sacred it is and the voices of the grandmothers were telling me not to allow it to get muddy or tainted with careless or unconscious sex. Ah, the frustration of being a priestess, holding such purity and waiting for the pure love of another.

Windwalker's Medicine Wheel
Joshua Tree, California - Summer 2022

I was working at Massage Revolution in California when I began seeing galactic guides in my sleep, who showed me clear impressions of Joshua

Tree and the desert. I had just come back from the ANIWA gathering of shamans in Big Bear, which was supposed to be about the Rainbow Warrior Prophecy. I am saying 'supposed' to be, because the level of consciousness to unite all of us was certainly not elevated enough to carry this prophecy forward between the generations.

I felt that it was very polarized between the people who really cared for humanity and those who just wanted to look 'glam' and party. For me, working at the festival was one challenge after another. I felt that God was punctuating the emphasis of our water crisis to me. While working as the 'dish tank girl' and wrangling dishes in the kitchen, the water pump for the entire mountain broke!

I sacrificed my precious time to be at the ANIWA festival with Shamans from around the world over to people who couldn't 'hear' me. I spent my days explaining to dirty hippies and glam girls from Silicon Valley that we didn't have water to do the dishes with. That meant there was also no water to drink or any water in the bathrooms for two of the days I was working. No one wanted to believe the words coming out of my mouth. I suffered extreme fatigue there, while getting multiple psychic attacks from other spirits.

When I finally had enough of California, I drove through the desert toward Joshua Tree, not knowing what would happen. I scoured the internet and found a medicine man who was willing to meet with me. I told him that everything in California seemed to be wrapping up for me, but I wanted to make sure. I began to have dreams from the ancestors about returning to Colorado, but still, I wanted to be certain because I was having a lot of bad luck.

When I met Windwalker, I was exhausted from living in the car and traveling constantly. He was very kind and generous to me while I was struggling to have any energy to talk, or even breathe! I knew then that he had a compassionate heart and a deep wisdom about the cycles of life.

He took me on a tour of his medicine wheel with many spirit animals and talked a bit about how he built this enormous medicine wheel on the property. It was on his private land, which made it a sacred space to do healing work.

After he gave me a brief tour, we went to the Tipi to pray and get clarity. Windwalker smudged me with sage and smoke and then journeyed for me with his drum. I could see myself laying in a bed of tall grass, but I was in a creek full of water. We both felt a swift presence of wind come into the Tipi as if a man had entered. When the drum journey ended, he told me that a young warrior Arapaho guide with a red bandana was with us. He said that the water I was seeing in the vision meant that I was still cleansing. I was very relieved because I feel more at home in Colorado than in California.

Rainbows, Witch Wounds, and Magic!
From the Shores of California to Colorado 2022-2023

Even though I am a lightworker and psychic, many times I do not know the next fork in the road. I have to surrender to the 'void' and wait for the ancestors to speak in my dreams. My completion lifetime is one where completion with twin flames from other timelines is necessary for rapid growth.

When I returned to Colorado in the fall of 2022, I had no idea what to do with my life. I had no community, had outgrown old friends, and kept seeing signs and synchronicities to go to yoga classes. During those weeks, I worked at a dumb corporate massage job and prayed with my tobacco as usual. I asked my guides for more help, since I had no clue what was next for me.

After work one day, I went outside and it was sunny but had rained and the hood of my car was still wet. I planned to go to a fundraiser at the Yoga Center of Denver that evening. As I hopped into the driver's seat and turned on the engine, I noticed a large black crow feather glistening on the red silky wet hood of my Kia Soul. I was surprised and baffled about how it magically jumped into my vision. Of course, being a Serpentbird, I quickly scooped it off the hood of my car and put it in an envelope. Then I headed out to a community dance night at the yoga studio. As I walked through the halls, I kept seeing signs with the question. "So, do you want to be a yoga teacher?" I thought to myself, "Yes! I kind of do!"

During the month or two when I worked at the corporate gig, I car camped near a pretty lake in Littleton, Colorado at night. The lake reflected beautiful sunrises and sunsets, while I surrendered and tried to figure out what to do. I had warning dreams from Spirit that I would get three parking infractions if I didn't move my ass! I wondered why the warning came up suddenly and what I was 'suddenly' supposed to know what to do with the warning! Additionally, I kept waking up at 4:11 on the dot night after night, which kept me tossing and turning.

That week, I felt an interesting warm presence all around me, which I recognized was from old Tibetan spirits. They felt like the smell of incense, the enchanting scent of bliss! There was also a team of angelic ancestors by my side, helping me. They tested me by energetically cutting me off from contacting other healers and psychics for help in solving this mystery. When I called someone or messaged them online, I would not get a response.

I finally committed to getting myself grounded, so I meditated intently by tall trees. It was like having a serious karmic meeting with a team of beings I couldn't see but could feel. I also felt the prayers that my hands made in other Tibetan lifetimes pouring through, so I made the mudra shapes as if I was holding the sacred Tibetan bell and Dorje. I asked the guides questions about different yoga centers and trainings. "Is it Jeff?" I asked. "No, the other one," they answered. "What other one?" I asked.

While I was stumped again, I aggressively searched online for any Hatha Yoga trainings in Denver. I called a woman who was kind of bitchy and said she wasn't teaching anymore, but if there was anyone I should study with, it was Dan. So, there it was. I found him! I looked up his school online, filled out a questionnaire, then called him.

One of my witchy sisters confirmed later that indeed a team of Red Robed Tibetans helped me transition to a new chapter in my life of becoming a spiritual teacher. She said they had been in her kitchen for days and no one said a word. Once we were able to hop on a video call, she exclaimed, "Now they are all talking!"

Within days of meditating and meeting Dan, I put my last $3,000 down for a yoga teacher training course, while still living in my car. The first time we spoke, which I thought was "the first time we spoke," he mentioned the "NOW" moment. Then he asked, "How are we going to get along during this course?" I frowned with my eyebrows, pushing them together and driving two more lines of pain between my eyes.

While we were on the phone, all of a sudden my voice got crazy loud. We screamed at each other about our qualifications. When I met him at the church, I parked my car exactly at 11:11. Damn, another twin flame!

I now understand that twin flames are a quickening for growth and there are many twin souls for me to experience. This energy between us was enticing, yet violent, tempest, and raw! In a way, it was romantic because I could feel a passion for my own liberation. This romance was an illusion in our twin-soul purposes but would not become a divine union in the realm of physical earthly love.

I only had about three days to battle my logical mind versus what the ancestors were asking of me. At first, I wondered why the ancestors are asking me to work with Dan and not study at another yoga studio in town. I had to focus on what they told me in meditation, that "this was the guy" and to trust their advice.

I was nervous about handing over my last three grand to Dan, but when the day came for me to drive over to the church where the classes were held, I stepped outside after my work shift and a giant rainbow covered the sky. I ran around the parking lot shooting a million photos so that I would be able to remember it. It formed a big arc over my red car and after I saw this confirmation, I felt at peace with my decision. My drive down Broadway to the church felt like I was starring in my own movie and joyriding into my next soul mission. However, this required yet ANOTHER fire of initiation.

During the Yoga Teacher Training, my body naturally went through a detox from doing the yoga postures. The samskaras I was purging from my cell memory felt like 10 trash trucks full of concrete weights, wrapped tightly in the 'weightless' flights of my soul that transmigrated from timeline to timeline.

Two lifetimes with Dan slowly surfaced from my chakras as we twisted through the asanas and I unraveled the mysteries. These were traumas from a witch life in Salem, Massachusetts, and a life when we were both males in the sixth Han Dynasty, during China's war with Tibet. I was not able to recover much of that story in pictures or words, but my body continued showing me the stories. I know that "Dan" killed me by the sword in my throat. Our unfinished rivalry explains why we were screaming at each other over the phone. It also revealed why I had so much animosity toward him.

During the three-month training, my higher wisdom alerted me that what I was experiencing wasn't something I would be able to share with his students. I had to bite my tongue and hold the secret of our past lives, otherwise the students would have developed animosity towards him. The secret that I knew and he did not was that I suffered from his hands in both of those past lives. I wanted him to understand that I already had magic and that my magic could not be taken from me.

I saw through the veils and felt the death, the loss, the rape, and more death! To know that I was a warrior of swords and a kung fu fighter should not have surprised me, but it did. One morning, my guides alerted me to bring flowers to the yoga studio after I discovered more of the past trauma.

I was able to create beauty out of the deaths by arranging the flowers in the studio where he happened to be teaching a very focused lesson on peace that day. I showed up early and installed my medicine wheel crystals around the room. I thought to myself, "Does he realize he is sitting inside the magic he once thought he could steal from me?"

This man was a hunter of witches, a rapist, and a stealer of magic. I told the truth and was hanged because of it. Now I saw the pattern of being killed twice by his hands at my throat. It was clear as I listened to the women in the yoga class that many of them had issues speaking up or speaking at all in front of the class. This made me sad, but it told me I must let my voice be LOUD! Let all women's voices be LOUD. I was thinking all of this while Lilith was raging through my astrology chart during this transit!

Through this yoga training, I expected to learn Hatha Yoga and become a teacher. However, it was more about the dynamic between myself and a man who had killed me in two lifetimes IN MY THROAT! I learned how to hold a secret, which every Shaman must know how to do in order to be a Shaman. I had to transmute a karma, which in my opinion should have been paid for by Dan, but in many ways was paid by me.

The fact is that in this life it is important to continue my Shamanic work and feel very at home within my soul. Revisiting Dan's soul helped me see the intersection and different vibrations between yoga and ritual based practices, which felt more organic and connected to the earth and animals than the clean yoga vibe.

I often felt my body oscillate between being a yogic nun persona and a witch filled with rage after being tied to a stake and burned alive. Some days, it felt more at home for me to hang out in the witchy zone. And you must remember that throughout the entire training, I couldn't afford a place to live and was car-camping every day around the neighborhood.

There were some nights during the last month of classes, where the temperatures were minus seven degrees with snow and winds. I had to buy insulation and make what I called heating bricks, to reflect heat back to me. At night I lined the windows of the Kia with the bricks. One week before the graduation, I finally landed an apartment studio of my own. Students often ask me, "Lori, how did you finish the Yoga Teacher Training while living in your car?" Often, they wouldn't wait for me to answer and didn't "get" that I had already been living in my car for the entire year of 2022, which commenced after the Marshall Fire. What a fucking journey.

If it were not for the tall trees of Cherry Creek and my consistent gratitude prayer rituals, I would have died once again!

I learned from this experience that I need to share my magic and not keep it all to myself in isolation. I need to fiercely pursue my creativity, because apparently, it's sad to say, not everyone has 'magic.' Magic is an energy that requires many lifetimes to master.

It takes a Wild Woman's Heart
to Heal the Hearts of Men

You must create it and attune to the ancestors that are willing to make the energy that is sparked with MAGIC!

Many questions can be formed around healing the hearts of men and creating a peace filled world. Most of the time, I think it's difficult to help men heal and I am better off spending my time helping women heal. I am exhausted from my story of love, which often ends in violence and hate. What will it take to change "my" story? A love of the sacred and the love of a woman's heart being sacred should be enough to heal the planet. I believe that men will have to listen more carefully to women and eliminate the old patterns of domination, divide, and conquer.

I am not saying that all women are good, pure, or true. I have known many women who are divisive and mean. What I am speaking of is the woman of the rose, the woman who remembers that softness is the greatest weapon against jealousy, envy, and hatred.

It is the light blue river water that cuts through rock to make beautiful canyons of many colors that harmonize with the shining sun. It is the woman who remembers that her divinity is made strong by being the calm in the storm. It is revering the essence of the feminine, which is the only vessel that leads us to a path of peace on Earth.

It is my soul mission to uphold feminine ideals in order to carve this path. As I mentioned in earlier chapters, having a Venus in Pisces in my astrology chart confirms this as well.

Warrior Priestess Returns 800 Years Later
Coyote Lightning War, Colorado Springs - 2024

In 2024, while working in Denver, I heard the 'drum call.' I banged the sound out on the wooden table in the break room as I heard it from the ethers.

I was called back to my role as Shaman and asked by the ancestors to return to the land. This mission would involve "earth magic" much as it did when I was on the Santa Fe Trail.

While working in Denver, I felt the pull to go to Colorado Springs for a metaphysical conference. When I decided to go, I pulled up to a Ross clothing store to buy a sweater. When I walked back to my car, I saw a huge 'wizard staff' of driftwood lying underneath a Toyota Camry parked next to me. I was stunned and wondered how it got there. I thought it must be *mine* and put it in my car. Later I would discover from a "Shaman-Wizard" that this staff of wisdom spans throughout many grid lines of the planet. I have been told that because I have lived many lives as a Shaman, I have certain access codes for the nodes and vortexes on Earth.

When I attended the conference, I felt welcomed and accepted by other lightworkers and healers. On a break for lunch, though, I felt my body getting heavy and weak. We were going through a Chiron in Aries transit, so I knew my 'warrior' spirit was being reactivated. During this transit, I felt my whole body burn in different areas, from my liver and other organs to my chakras spontaneously activating. While on this mission, I felt my solar plexus fire lighting up the most, which helped give me the energy I needed to make the 60-mile car trips frequently.

This activation of my warrior priestess archetype was so potent that I felt the weakness of my 'yellow' solar plexus was allowing my inner masculine to become stable. I had experiences of it being strong and then going dim again. The ancient medicine from the land of Colorado Springs and the movements of the stars were making a permanent change in my body temple.

I went outside the library in between speakers because my body was releasing waves of grief and pain. When I meditated by a tree and then opened my eyes, I gazed at the dragon line of mountains in front of me. My inner vision filled with the color turquoise, and I thought to myself, "Oh, my abundance is here in Colorado Springs." It was then I knew I was ready to leave Denver as soon as possible.

A man named Sean was at the conference. We had met five years ago after I connected with him on social media. He leads a group called "Sacred Earth Circle," so I went every Sunday morning for a few months. As the months went on, I discovered we had shared many lifetimes together. My guides told me that we have been fighting for a thousand years!

After moving everything out of my apartment, I met a Shaman-Wizard friend who guided me on a hike up Red Mountain. When I took the bus through Manitou towards the Manitou Incline, I felt my stomach begin to rumble with sickness and grief. The rumbling continued as we hiked. When the wizard helped me reach the actual entrance to the trail, I realized how out of shape my body was. I kept hiking even though it was challenging.

We reached a place in the forest where I asked to stop and process what was coming through for me. I could no longer hike or stand upright. On the side of a hill, the wizard put a long scarf on the ground and propped my hip and legs up with flat rocks. I laid on the scarf and smelled the warm earth coming up through the soil, filling my nostrils with life!

I closed my eyes and began calling back parts of my soul, while the ancestors spoke to me. I held my hands behind my head and did a vagus nerve reset. Then I changed the placements with one hand behind my neck and the other on my belly. My third eye dialed wide open and I could feel green and turquoise frequencies illuminating the veils. I saw piles of bones of the ancestors and saw black smoke over another taller mountain, as if there were guns leaving trails of smoke in the sky. I saw the pile of bones through my third eye, but beyond that there was another layer of reality I could not yet describe.

The Wizard guided me through the Akashic Record frequencies and helped me decipher the message I received from the Ancestors, that Coyote Lightning was an event. While lying in the soil, stones, and pine needles, I realized that my body had been severely damaged. My forehead felt like a rock had severely broken my skull. I felt grief and loss, with the themes of 'lost' and 'escape' resurfacing in my shadow. The wizard periodically checked in on me as she sat nearby, to see how I was feeling.

I felt pain and ecstasy as I allowed myself to heal and connect with the vibration of the akashic record downloading the ancestral calling. I could hear the **war cry** *"Hawwoooliiiilliiii Hawwwlilililili!"*

The Wizard said, "Yes, it is a vibration from the valley as well as a connection in Wyoming." We shared some beautiful moments being silent and staring over the valley towards Pikes Peak. We ate pine pollen balls that were soft and dripping from the pinecones around us. This further activated our inner vision, clearing a path through the brain stem to the pineal gland.

She took me on a second hike the next week so we could reach the summit of Red Mountain. I was nervous that I wouldn't make it all the way up to

7,375 feet. I breathed, hiked, drank water, took breaks, breathed, hiked, drank water. At one point along the winding path, I felt my wrists being shaken and bound behind my back. When we were almost to the top, we reached a pass through the pine forest that had steep stone steps. It was here that my vision got very blurry. I felt like I had vertigo and needed to lay down.

The Wizard was anxious to reach the summit saying, "I feel that we have an opportunity for clairvoyance once we reach the top." I was able to rest for a bit in a juggernaut of rocks that made a grand staircase with its boulders and steep climb. My guides told me I was bludgeoned to death with rocks! My assumption is that I was a warrior priestess sacrificed by the Arapaho priest. I know that I was killed by the Arapaho priest because my guides were dropping me lines about the tragedy even as I was moving out of my apartment. I had to piece together bits of the story from what I heard clairaudiently as well as from how my body and chakras responded. The juggernaut of rocks seemed to be a place where an altar could have been placed 800 years ago, because these rocks looked like they may have had more of an ordered arrangement in ancient times.

It is important to note, one time when I read the Akashic Records for a dear friend I saw an Incan priestess being covered with cloth. Her skull was severed and broken with a rock, then sacrificed by a priest. The feelings I experienced reclaiming my past life on Red Mountain felt very similar to that.

When we reached the summit, we witnessed two turkey vultures circling above us and when we gathered on one side, a red-tailed hawk flew near us. I made a crystal medicine wheel for myself to meditate in. When I looked over, the Wizard had passed out on the ground with a sacred object in her hand. She looked so beautiful! I could see her younger self and her dragon persona as well. I didn't ask her what her sacred object was, but she told me later that after seeing the red-tailed hawk, her prayer was answered.

As a priestess who had her head shattered into bits on a mountain by an Arapaho priest during a sacrifice, upon my return 800 years later my thought is, "Isn't it time to pass the 'stick' of leadership to women?"

Even though Sean killed me, I knew I had to forgive him. In the coming weeks, I found a way to collaborate with him in his Sacred Earth Circle meetings. I met him at a local coffee shop and we planned a healing ceremony for the group. As I began heading out the door, I leaned into his "cinnamon beard" and kissed him very lightly on the cheek. When I kissed Sean, the spell of karma was broken. It is clear to me now that no matter what karmic burdens we create in past lives, we must heal with love. One thousand years of fighting is now sealed with a kiss…

Healing my Divine Feminine
and the divide between men and women 2024

How the heck did this happen? With my warrior archetype and the dysfunctional nature of my family of origin combined with this day and age we are living in, I am guilty of being stuck in "giver" mode. I am not saying that I don't want or need a divine masculine counterpart. However, my past life rape trauma went so deep that my body still has its primal defenses up like a 24/7 Seven Eleven. Most recently while out on a date with myself at a music venue, a female bartender asked if I wanted my water glass refilled. I quickly said, "No, it's okay, I'll get it myself," as there was a bright orange 5-gallon jug on the shelf in the corner of the bar. I was just trying to take the load off her, but why? Why can't I receive? It should be so simple. Many of the women who come across my massage table are literally frozen in this trauma response as well. I am there coaching them to release it with their jaw and silent primal screams at the massage studio.

Anyway…here I am ten years or more after my marriage, still single, still being a warrior at war. But the other side of the coin now is that most single men in 2024 seem perfectly content in their own world. My dog, my motorcycle, my house, my job, my everything - and still asking women "to do" for them.

Serpentbird the Artist
The Rebel-ution

Now that I am entering another phase of my ascension, it is clearer that my career as a massage therapist will come to an end. I have empowered myself to fully step into teacher mode. I realize I can't allow my dreams and talents to be wasted. I already acquired skills in filmmaking and need to use my storytelling abilities to transform the world on a bigger scale with a bigger vision and message. I look to be more playful, heal my heart, and travel with a focus on my vision, which is to tell stories and make movies about how we can heal ourselves, because only then can we heal the planet.

I am only just beginning to work with the spirit realm of the ancestors here in Santa Fe, New Mexico, to find solutions to the water crisis on our earth. When God intervened in my last serious video project, He made sure that my messages to the world would focus on "what to do" instead of "what NOT to do."

I was on hiatus from producing videos for a few years, so I could receive messages from the realm of spirituality and magic before the realm of third dimensional reality. The gift I am bringing is the gift of the Thunderbirds, a group of elemental beings that bring the rain. The Thunderbeings know how to harness elemental magic through intent, a pure heart, and a will to feed the people to call the rains. As a native Tewa man in Santa Fe told me, "When there is no corn, there are no people." The way to create this magic is to believe and to dance upon Mother Earth with respect and great pride. I am being asked to help us reawaken to the power within our hearts, restoring it to create this magic. The medicine wheel ceremonies are intended to reclaim the value of respect in the hearts of people.

There are practical solutions for our Earth. It could be in the strength of our environmental lawyers and environmental groups. One such solution I see is to instigate more legal actions using "environmental personhood" as a means for respecting and protecting nature. For example, in the summer of 2019, the Yurok tribe in northern California gave the Klamath River personhood status, which gives it legal rights just like a human. What that means is that when a river is damaged by a toxic pollutant, a cause of action can be brought against the polluter to protect the river.

The Serpentbird Rainbow Warriors are part of the Rebel-ution!

What is a Sacred Voice?

What is Sacred?
Is it knowledge? Is it a degree?
Is it a buffalo? Is it lightning?
Is it a womb? Is it a woman spelling her decree?
It IS the ones who remember the sacred tree.

It must be wisdom from akash, ether, and the space in between
sacred codes, sacred blood
trust in truth from the sacral fire
code will be code
but divinity burns brighter!
Sacred birth comes from the
deepest, widest,
visceral primal scream!
womb of wisdom
must let go, to be free.
Sacred wisdom
burns with passion
to be held gentler than you can hold
the smallest of insects without crushing spirit.
Sacred must be clean and pure.
All the purification of fires burning through all the ego selves.

Unlearning must be sacred as patriarchy has destroyed what is pure.
By entangling words and structures,
by piracy and "ownership" of earth's resources.

In the spoken word
Is a voice sacred in its confident tune?
or in its tremble and traumatic releasing?
Sacred voice emits truth that beautifies
since vibration creates an invisible landscape that every rock and tree,
who will outlive me will inherit.

Sacred voice that can channel the ancestral calling
and sing it into songs of earth. Songlines.
Songlines will live in my footsteps.
I know the sacred when I hear the grandmothers and grandfathers
that I didn't think cared for me or even knew me,
The invitation to sit and remember with the chiefs and warriors of the past.
The invitation has come

from every pyramid and every portal on the earth,
Yes, I have lived many lives.
I know this is fact as I've listened to the voices of the Earth
Calling me. Calling me. Calling me.
I answer.
I am the sacred voice of Thunderbeings.
Inside of every molecule of water for all time,
I am a sacred voice.

Crow and Serpentbird on the Jazz Stage at ComFest in Columbus, Ohio – 2010

Truth Serum backstage at ComFest

PART FIVE: THE CENTER POINT

Join the Rainbow Warrior Tribe!
www.serpentbird.com

Owning land and keeping land would be a viable option for us. I envision making a permanent Serpentbird Medicine Wheel, if you are willing and able to support this by co-investing in the purchase of a land trust in Colorado. It will solidify the ongoing knowledge of this healing modality for the next seven generations and beyond. (Contact me for more info!)

Please remember that your story and your journey matters. God and I had predetermined I would not have a boring life this time around. I want to bless your path to enlightenment. May my story of initiation make your journey easier, lighter, and freer for you than it was for me.

You are invited to join my Facebook group "Serpentbird Rainbow Warrior Tribe." Learn how the medicine wheel works by attending a Serpentbird medicine wheel ceremony, or speak with me personally about priestess initiations, the seven-day immersion private training, goddess to goddess. My soul brother, SadaNam, leads ceremonies in Ohio and at festivals. Melanie Gnosa, who was part of the original Serpentbird Seven, is a Medicine Wheel Practitioner. Each of us can be contacted for trainings and ceremonies.

My ideal vision is to train as many people as I can, in alignment with peace and love, to understand how to do crystal grid work, to successfully keep the ley lines of the Earth working and harmonized enough to balance the weather, and to keep the rain cycles in balance. I believe this is what the original prophecy foretells.

I look forward to holding public book talks, speaking on and hosting podcast and television shows, and whatever else it takes to spread my message and heal our Earth. I will see you in book two and beyond. Please remember that "Serpentbird" is ONE WORD.

May infinite blessings of love and peace flow with you, on your journey to Awakening.

Love, Serpentbird

Glossary of Terms

Akasha - One of the five elements of nature. Refers to the sky or ether. The primordial substance that holds all the functions of the entire cosmos in place. According to Sadhguru, this is the fundamental element where the other four elements (earth, air, water, and fire) play upon. Sky or Ether. Other interpretations say that the records we access through our bodies, are stored in the waters within our bodies. This water holds the memory of all life.

Akashic Records - The Akashic Records are a body of wisdom and insight that reveal an individual's essence, expression and potential. Every thought, action, emotion and experience that has ever occurred in time has a recorded memory. The Akashic Records practice is an ability to access this information from your past, present and future. The ability to be a "Records" practitioner is a learned skill that requires high level meditation, and the ability of clairaudience, clairsentience and other -clairs.

Blue Star Kachina - Saquasoha - The Hopi, "the people of peace," foretell of a time of great purification. The Blue Star Kachina is a Hopi revelation about the coming of the end of a civilization on Earth. The prophecy describes a heavenly being called the Blue Star whose arrival on Earth will signal the beginning of the end of times.

Completion - Completion is an act of intentionally closing out a cycle of one's own or with others. This can be done in relationships with a process of forgiving oneself and the other person and clearing cords and karmic contracts.

Divine Feminine - A power or force that is dynamic. This power can be earth shaking "Shakti," which has the power to create the world or emanate softer subtle energy. The divine feminine can draw its power by the principle of receptivity and stillness. This then can foster the qualities of nurturing and develop one's intuition.

Gridworker - A being who has made an intent to share and build the energetic grid of light around the Earth through prayer, blessing ceremonies, crystal gridding, and medicine ceremony. Gridworkers use the power of power places and energetic nodes like vortexes to harness the energy of the sun and serve as a bridge for the ancients or extra-terrestrials to maintain the integrity of a portal.

High Priestess - One who receives revelatory visions through the practice of ritual and meditative stillness. She receives through the feminine principle of receptivity. This is known as intuition. She holds the vision for all humanity and upholds the truth.

Intuition - The way of feeling and trusting what is highest and best in our dense Earth-based reality.

Karma - Law of action. What you sow, you shall reap. The karma created in all timelines is imprinted within the cells of the body.

Lightworker - A being who has made an intent to help those in lower density programming be lifted by their unique gifts, such as motivational public speaking, visionary art, healing arts, music and more.

Magic - An extraordinary power influenced by a supernatural force. A mode of being that induces transformation.

Matriarchal Society - A matriarchal society is one where inheritance and succession are traced through the female line. Women hold a high status and are often the ones who make important decisions regarding family and community affairs.

Pleiadians - Also known as the seven sisters. The Pleiadians are emissaries of light from the Pleiades star cluster, which emanates from the star Alcyone. The Pleiadians encouraged me to write this memoir.

Record Keeper - One who has been a scribe and holds vast and deep knowledge and wisdom of planet earth and even other dimensions. Stones, crystals, humans, animals, and bodies of water all keep records of history. Whales, dolphins, horses, and turtles appear in creation stories as storing the records of the history of our planet Earth.

Rematriation - To restore sacred relationships between Indigenous people and their ancestral land. Honoring our matrilineal societies and lineages ways of tending to the land, in opposition of patriarchal violence and dynamics. LAND BACK!

Sadhguru - My personal guru from India. I still practice Shakti Chalana Kriya pranayama as he had taught me in 2000. Sadhguru is the founder of Isha Yoga. He is a mystic and poet, whose mission is to help humanity realize its ultimate potential within.

Samskara - Mental impressions, recollections, or psychological imprints. A knot of energy in a chakra that has accumulated throughout many lifetimes. This knot, or wound is often "triggered" when set off by an emotional trauma of a similar past life experience or physical connection to a relative with a shared past.

Shaman - A person who acts as an intermediary, going between natural and supernatural worlds. It is the oldest form of healing known to man.

Shamanka - Female shamans or shamankas are found among the Tungus people; the Buriats, Yakuts, Ostyaks, and the Kamchdals. The place of the shaman was usually held by especially gifted elder women. They are invokers, healers, herbalists, oracles and diviners, ecstatic dancers, shapeshifters, shamanic journeyers, and priestesses of the ancestors.

Songlines - Where melodic resonance describes the land and memory code.

Starseed - Some starseeds are volunteers coming "back from the future" to heighten the vibration of the Earth in order to help humanity. Awakener. Wayshower.

Trauma and PTSD - The emotional response to a shocking event that causes someone to be so overwhelmed that it impairs the ability to function. It could be from severe abuse, or of physical or psychological torment. PTSD is often caused by a stack of events that pile up energetically in the body and mind.

Witch - Term was used as an accusation where a woman was bewitching someone or casting spells to control them. In Salem, Massachusetts, they were viewed as evil, rounded up, and burned alive at the stake.

Yavapai - The Yavapai Native land in Sedona Arizona is where Serpentbird received the vision for this book. The spirits of the land told her to use the Medicine Wheel on her journey to heal her completion lifetime.

Zia - The Zia "Red Sun" is the symbol on the state flag of New Mexico. It is a sacred symbol representing the Medicine Wheel for the Zia people. The Zia symbol is a sun with four lines of rays emanating out of four sides. According to the Zia Pueblo, the number four is a sacred number to the Zia, representing the four cardinal directions, the four seasons of the year, the four stages of life, and the four sacred obligations one must develop: a strong body, a clear mind, a pure spirit, and a devotion to the welfare of others.

Lori Meditating
at the top of Bell Rock
in Sedona

Land Back

Land Back is a movement that seeks to reclaim Indigenous lands. The decolonization movement is not complete without land restitution for Indigenous people. Land Back requires that settlers work to repair the harm colonialism has done and continues to inflict on Indigenous people by returning control over ancestral territories back to its stewards, allowing them to begin restoring their connection to ancestral lands in meaningful ways. By transferring power and wealth back to Indigenous people, land restitution including the water, natural resources, and infrastructure on the land supports Indigenous sovereignty. The Land Back movement ultimately secures an Indigenous futurity that requires self-determination, environmental sustainability, and economic justice.

Acknowledgements and Gratitude

Rainbow Warrior Serpentbird people are the very best lightworkers in the world!

There is a directory for members on my personal website www.serpentbird.com. You are welcome to contact me directly at serpentbirdtribe@gmail.com for further information if you can't find these people on the internet.

Ohio Ground Crew
Amanda Rae Preston - Priestess Rae
Amy Shepherd
Bryan Jellick
Catie Beals
Dan and Sarah Binder
Frank Tennyson
James Goodwin
Janaan Al Jahanni
John Harrison
Krista Kitty
Laurel Hobden
Laura Belg
Laurel Hobden
Nicole Karras
Robert Eves
Zoe Boyalos

Ohio's Serpentbird 7
Lori M. Abel - Serpentbird
Alx Everett - SadaNam Singh
Dawn Thompson, Dawn of the New Era
Marcello Antifonario - Crow
Melanie Gnosa, Priestess and Licensed Minister
Michael Alan Cundiff, Truth Serum
Nick Schultz - Fire Skin

Colorado Ground Crew
Barbara M. Ross
Bradley Schoendorf
Brandon Kimball, Earth Heart Temple
Celest McGonagill
Cynthia Rose
Dave Weil
David Elliot, Emaho Energy Arts
Deb Augenbaugh
Derik Eselius
Gabriel A. Sol
Greg McHugh
Jesse Lockwood
Katrina Blair, Turtle Lake Refuge
Miekell Cottonwood
Prabhusukh Singh
Skye Rae Dawning

Arizona Ground Crew
Andrew Ecker, Drumming Sounds
Beau Dunavant, Gypsy Build
Brooke Wiggs
David Hart
Hosh Hsaio
Illup Gravengaard
Nico
Paul O'Malley
Peter Alan Gersten, Top of Bell Rock Club (TBRC)
Shelly Wells

New Mexico Ground Crew
Bear and Rainbow Robbins
Gregorio Gigante, Sovereign Santa Fe

California Crew
Abe Daniels - Windwalker
Dianna Carmel
Hector Garcia aka Puma
   -Ceremonialist and Sound Healer, Uniting the ways of the Eagle and Condor
Hobbit
Karina Saunier
Jaraneh Nova Music
Robert Ball Jr.

Michigan Crew
Trevor Reinhart - Lionheart
Susan Daves

Ode to the Teachers
Ayanvalideha, Cherokee Minister & Ceremonialist of the Ancient Ways
Greywolf Rick, Curator of the Sacred
Firedancer, Medicine Wheel Teacher
Greg McHugh, CHT
Grandfather Martin Gashweseoma, Hopi Elder, 3rd Mesa,
    Guardian of Prophecy Rock
Jaggi Vasudev Sadguru
Jaimie Sams
John F. Barnes, PT
John Harrison
Jose Arguelles
Nancy Mathews, Sedona School of Massage
Nate Butryn
Prabusukh Singh, Ph.D.

Also, thank you to:
Agape International Prayer Practitioners
Nice people
Sacred Tobacco
Spirits and things
Coffee shops with Wi-Fi

Crow and Serpentbird
backstage at ComFest
in Columbus, Ohio - 2010

ABOUT THE AUTHOR

Lori Michelle Abel is a spoken word poet and artist from Novelty, Ohio. She is a "curator of the sacred." Her mission with *Rainbow Warrior Healing on The Red Road* is to assist Tribal Nations in the Land Back movement to reclaim ancestral land and sacred sites. Her public speaking serves as a bridge for Ecological Activism and her poetic voice is a force to be reckoned with against all forms of Ecocide.

Lori earned a Bachelor of Fine Arts degree in Graphic Design from the Columbus College of Art & Design, which she draws on for both her photography and film projects. Her skills, with years of training and experience as a licensed massage therapist and an Akashic Record Reader, are blended into her private healing practice.

To book Lori for poetry readings, for public speaking at "Land Back" events, for service as a medicine wheel ceremonialist for groups or individuals, or to join the Serpentbird Rainbow Warrior Tribe, email **serpentbirdtribe@gmail.com** or visit **www.serpentbird.com**.

For Starseed soul healing in the Akashic Records, email
akashicsoulmystic@gmail.com
or visit **www.akashicsoulmystic.com**

Made in United States
Troutdale, OR
04/24/2025

30857743R00139